Holiday Stories All Year Round

Audience Participation Stories and More

Edited by Violet Teresa deBarba Miller

LIBRARIES
UNLIMITED
A Member of the Greenwood Publishing Group

Westport, Connecticut • London

Library of Congress Cataloging-in-Publication Data

Holiday stories all year round : audience participation stories and more / edited by Violet Teresa deBarba Miller.
  p. cm.
Includes bibliographical references and index.
ISBN 978-1-59158-675-3 (alk. paper)
1. Short stories, American. 2. Holidays—Fiction. 3. Storytelling. 4. Tales. 5. Holidays. 6. Activity programs in education. 7. Children's libraries—Activity programs. I. Miller, Teresa, 1922–
PS648.H54H65   2008
813'.6080334—dc22   2008021121

British Library Cataloguing in Publication Data is available.

Library of Congress Catalog Card Number: 2008021121
ISBN: 978-1-59158-675-3

First published in 2008

Libraries Unlimited, 88 Post Road West, Westport, CT 06881
A Member of the Greenwood Publishing Group, Inc.
www.lu.com

Printed in the United States of America

The paper used in this book complies with the Permanent Paper Standard issued by the National Information Standards Organization (Z39.48–1984).

10   9   8   7   6   5   4   3   2   1

Contents

FOREWORD

Photo by Kent Miles.

BY LAURA SIMMS

Whether a holiday is unique to a culture or country, religion or tribe, season or natural phenomenon, there is always a story to remind us what gives the date meaning. Teresa Miller's book is a gathering of such stories, chosen to provide significance and to offer a gift of happiness.

Every culture or religion throughout history has celebrated holidays. Many take place on the same days or seasons, but offer different reasons for their celebration. Knowing this is a source of great delight. It is wonderful for our children to know that the essence of history is change and diversity. And that sharing special times with others is wonderful. This book, as refreshing as cool water, reminds us of the diverse history of the peoples who make up the tapestry of America. It also signals that acceptance of variety is a cause of peace and richness, within each of us and in the world at large. We are particularly fortunate to be able to celebrate in so many ways.

For children, holidays are times to share gifts and memories, discover something new, or find out more about their family or culture's connection to history, nature, or ancestors. Having a book of stories that emphasizes the feeling of days of celebration helps to keep alive our inner capacities for humor, tolerance, and respect for self and others. There is always the promise within a holiday that we are part of a bigger story.

The best of holidays are those that bring joy and relaxation. As a child, I recall hours of play. It was a chance to experience a relationship to the changing seasons, the earth and sky. Going to the beach in the summer, on the Fourth of July for a picnic or waking up early to stand on the street in expectation of a parade was a thrilling summer memory. Our birthdays, as well as the birthdays of others and of important people who have made a difference in the world, give spice to our lives with a pause from the daily activities that carry us along. And when a story is told about the day, it increases the sense of meaning. Through imagination we recall the wonder and generosity of heroes and heroines from earlier or mythic times. Or we are given a time to feel deep sorrow for something lost. In that sharing is the possibility of compassion and a poignant knowing that regardless of our differences, our lives are fragile. The more we care for one another, the more peace is possible.

Storytelling itself is a mini-holiday. It draws us out of our ordinary preoccupations and engages us in meaning and adventure. The more generous the storyteller, or the reader, the more enriching the experience.

In the great rush of our lives, and the plethora of media that draws us into movies, news, and technologically produced stories, telling and hearing stories told in person is a vacation of renewal. The secret of this book lies in the way in which storytelling and story reading keeps our hearts open and reconnects us to our inner abilities to feel, imagine, and participate in the world with presence and compassion.

Teresa Miller, who has taken the time to create and compile this collection of celebratory tales, was herself deeply moved and motivated by stories told by storytellers over the past thirty years. Her first collection, with Anne Pellowski's assistance, for which I also had the pleasure of creating an introduction, was *JOINING IN: An Anthology of Audience Participation Stories and How To Tell Them.*

This collection expands her commitment to "joining in" by highlighting the many holidays that are celebrated by different cultures in the rich fabric of American society. With each holiday story, there is also a chance to explore the richness of this country, which is far greater and lasts longer than material wealth or ordinary gifts.

If there is a way to nurture the seeds of peace in our world, it is through opening this treasury of shared goodness and imagination. Each time we share a story with our children, we enhance our chances of becoming heirs to the whole history of the world, and the possibility of imagining peace in the future.

IN APPRECIATION

I am most appreciative of the assistance of the contributors and others who helped in the preparation of this collaborative book. I especially want to thank **Anne Pellowski** for her immeasurable help in launching this project, **Gail N. Herman** for her staunch support, and **Ruth Stotter** for her invaluable advice. And thanks to my brilliant Boston-attorney niece, **Joyce Perocchi.** If she did not herself have the answers to my legal questions, she knew which "Matlock" colleague to tap.

No amount of thanks could express my appreciation for **Margaret Read MacDonald,** who took a specialized bibliography of many sources to an infinitely better series of books for holiday telling. And **Laura Simms**—one of those people who bring energy and life into any room she enters. A huge salute for her wonderful foreword to this volume.

On the local level, while no "dreams" or "visions" have appeared before me, I have to believe that a God-driven Force works with me, to have put in my path and a slew of computer savvy, part-time college "secretaries," such as Tiffany Mann, Rachel Brinkman, Brett Hosler (graphics), Brittany Bayley, Meghan Malone, Sharon Bingle, Selena Barton, and Janet Johnson.

Also on the local front, Evansville, Indiana: Without **Ann Blandford**—my friend, chauffeur, and biblical scholar who helped substantially on the transcript of the Passover story—the following recommendations would have been difficult to obtain: **Rabbi Barry Friedman** from Temple Adath B'nai Israel who assisted in the "Passover" music; **Henry Miner, Ph.D.,** Associate Professor of German with the University of Evansville, who provided the German pronunciation of the lyrics for "Silent Night."

Then there is **Mike Boren** of the Guitar Lab in Evansville, Indiana, who was kind enough to provide music and guitar chords when needed. Last, but by no means least, thanks to retired dietician **Barbara Litschgi,** who keeps my body healthy enough to compete with a racing mind.

Everlasting thanks to **Barbara Ittner,** Senior Acquisitions Editor at Libraries Unlimited (LU). Her probing questions forced me originally to focus on important aspects that had not been previously addressed, and, more importantly, to follow endless suggestions that I believe resulted in a book of peerless perfection. (The questions posed by Elizabeth Budd of the copyediting division of LU completed the query.)

To local reference librarians, thanks. Ever since I learned how to read, libraries have been a second parent to me. Thanks especially to **Dee Dee Shoemaker,** Reference Services Department, Evansville Vanderburgh Public Library, and all other reference librarians at Central Library, and the personnel at the **McCollough Branch,** who were of inestimable aid.

Remember the character, Henry Higgins, in the screen version of *MY FAIR LADY*? Think of him singing "With a Little Bit of Luck." This has become my mantra. Once again, I thank all of the storytellers, friends, and scholars who have helped put this book together.

—Teresa Miller

INTRODUCTION

Photo by Mary Jo Huff.
Tellabration 2006

I happen to believe that the right story told to a person at the right time can help one find his or her destiny better than any lecture. Whether you are a storyteller, librarian-teller, teacher, parent, therapeutic professional, psychologist, or psychiatrist—yes, all of those—I hope you will *take risks* and try the stories in this book.

To laugh is *to risk* appearing the fool.

To weep is *to risk* appearing sentimental.

To reach out for another is *to risk* involvement.

To expose feelings is *to risk* exposing your true self.

To place you ideas, your dreams, before a crowd is *to risk* their loss.

To love is *to risk* not being loved in return.

To live is *to risk* dying.

To hope is *to risk* despair.

To try is *to risk* failure.

But risks must be taken, because the greatest hazard in life is *to risk nothing*.

The person, *who risks nothing, does nothing, has nothing, and is nothing.*

One may avoid suffering and sorrow, but he cannot learn, feel, change,

grow, love, live. Chained by his attitudes, he is a slave, he has forfeited his freedom.

Only a person *who risks is free*.

—*Author unknown*

"Taking risks" and I are no strangers to each other. I never thought in February 2006 that my voice would return sufficiently to be one of the storytellers in November 2006 at our area's "TELLEBRATION!"

Early that February, I was hit with a stroke, which rendered me unable to walk, unable even to talk. It seemed like an impossible dream that I would ever again tell stories anywhere. By the time I got enough confidence to learn a ten-minute story, I went to one of Margaret Read MacDonald's many books for instruction and inspiration (*SHAKE-IT-UP TALES! Stories to Sing, Dance, Drum and Act Out;* August House, 2000). The photograph at the opening of this Introduction shows me performing at the "Tellabration." I was thrilled to be able to tell again!

HOLIDAY STORIES ALL YEAR ROUND: Audience Participation Stories and More provides you with a collection from some of today's most talented storytellers and stories focused on holiday themes from around the world. The stories are meant to be used in libraries, classrooms, auditoriums, churches or other places where storytellers wish to share their own enthusiasm for a particular holiday.

In this book, you will find stories that spring from and celebrate a variety of cultures and traditions. You'll see stories for Martin Luther King Day and the Jewish Passover, from Buddha's Birthday to the Fourth of July, from Ramadan and International Peace Day——with plenty of "laugh tales" interspersed. This is a sampling of the best, so not all holidays are covered, but there should be enough to get you started.

Why audience-participation stories? Because they engage the listeners by involving everyone in actively telling the story. A kind of mutual ownership is instantly created. This gives listeners the message that "we're all in this together." It helps build community, and it forges a love of story, an important step in teaching literacy today.

Use these tales to liven up a holiday program or story time, to launch meetings, or to fill in the minutes before, between, and after any learning session.

The stories are presented in script form, with instructions for the teller and wording for the audience in the right-hand column of the scripts. This format helps you to deliver the story seamlessly—incorporating props, gestures, or audience responses into your telling.

Feel free to adapt each story to fit your audience, but I encourage you to "learn" the story first so you can perform it without reading directly from the script. This involves practice, but I think you'll find the results well worth your efforts. Your connection to the audience rather than to the page will be that much stronger if you train your eyes to their eyes.

The value of stories in *libraries, public classrooms, and other places*—especially the give and take of participation tales—is not only that they open the doorway to a discussion of *feelings,* but they also address a real need for trust among societies through dialogue and understanding.

It is my hope that one day *human behavior* will be taught in the lower grades as thoroughly as reading, writing, and arithmetic are taught today. I'm willing to bet that once this happens, you will see and notice an infinitely easier transition into adulthood.

I believe that the feelings exposed through this kind of participation story will greatly encourage discussions of all kinds.

My own understanding of *feelings* was enhanced by the steps undertaken in my efforts to become a professional storyteller. Looking back to my own childhood, which had absolutely zero guidance as to goals or purpose for living, I came to realize that a great deal of the "learning through living" depressions could have been avoided had I but known many of the values absorbed through stories that I heard at various festivals and workshops held for storytellers.

We really do need to communicate our hopes, fears, loves, dreams and so forth. If not in our growing years, then when? And to whom if nobody else is at hand? When do we reveal what we don't even know ourselves about which natural, inborn gifts (one or many) could be explored and even exploited for worldly gains?

MY STORY

Let me tell you how I became enamored with storytelling. STORYTELLING? A complete blank to me in 1980. Or was it 1979? Outside of a 9-to-5 job as a well-paid executive secretary in an advertising agency, I was engrossed in yoga and healthy food for effective living.

You may remember a World War II song called "Pennsylvania 6-5000." That was the telephone number of a hotel where traveling musicians lived while performing in the New York City area. By the time I came to know it, the hotel had changed ownership. Now it was known as The Statler Hotel. I was there frequently for many lunch or tea stops before commuting to my home in the suburbs. Events were publicized at their registration desk, and heavy publicity was given in all of NYC's media about a weekend hosted by the World Health Organization.

Many of the attractions at the convention had nothing to do with organic food—for example, DIANE WOLKSTEIN, PROFESSIONAL STORYTELLER. *STORYTELLER?!!!!* It was like waving a marvelous script and a surefire contract in front of a starving thespian who had never really lost an urge to find her way to the Broadway stage.

Diane's performance space was in the penthouse ballroom. A plush red rug covered what was not an obvious dance floor. I was there early and noticed that more and more chairs were brought in to hold what turned out to be an overflowing crowd. There must have been more than a thousand people waiting. A couple of musicians started to play some mood music. The room was hushed even before Diane uttered one word. It remained that way until the very end of her story.

After substantial applause, a number of people approached her with whatever words they had to say. Thanks? Congratulations? I simply waited in my seat until everyone else had left, then went to her with one question in my mind: "How do you become a professional storyteller?" She said she'd be holding a beginner's class in the fall at a location two hours from my office. That was a risk in itself. I had to resign from my job to attend her 6–8 P.M. classes. It was worth it.

Diane told our class about the storytelling festival to be held in a picturesque seacoast town of Camden, Maine, featuring Donald Davis, a storyteller renowned throughout the East Coast. I can hardly describe how his dry humor, punctuated with a ministerial stance, kept my laughter going on and on. Incidentally, some years later, I attended his workshop—probably in Jonesborough, Tennessee—in which he deplored the tendency of storytellers to pull out a noted personality from the past rather than tell "their own story." Note, dear Donald Davis, that at least one of your audience of some five hundred people heard your words. This is "my own story" of the steps it took for me to satisfy myself that I finally made the grade as a Certified (professional) Storyteller.

Diane's instructions preceded my attendances at many other storytelling workshops, seminars, festivals, and conferences, including the annual NAPPS (National Association for the Preservation and Perpetuation of Storytelling). Festivals are held each October in Jonesborough. (Today this organization is known as The National Storytelling Network.)

In New York City, I joined a burgeoning group of storytellers who met monthly for more than thirteen years to exchange stories and ideas. Preceding each "story swap" were workshops conducted by such nationally known storytellers as Joseph Bruchac, Michael Parent, Peninnah Schram, Nancy Schimmel, and Natalie Babbitt.

One summer, I attended the annual conference of the American Library Association. Diane had arranged for a group of storytellers to have our own room, with an aisle in the center to make it easier for people to get around. One day she surprised us all by introducing her new book, which Dutton had just published. She began by inviting some members of the audience to the stage to help her tell it. You will find her script for the "The Magic Wings" in the book I compiled with Anne Pellowski, edited by Norma Livo: *JOINING IN: An Anthology of Audience Participation Stories and How To Tell Them.* The book is available in many public libraries.

The audience was completely eager to participate in Diane's story, and utterly delighted with the result. One of the women in the aisle next to me had a copy of the book in her hands. "But," wailed she at its conclusion (believe me, it was a disappointed *wail*), "none of that is in this book!" That paved the way to creating *JOINING IN.*

Through the years, I have been fortunate to hear and study with numerous luminaries in the storytelling world—Anne Pellowski, Laura Simms, Heather Forest, Carol Birch, and countless others.

If Diane was Mentor No. 1, then assuredly Laura Simms was Mentor No. 2. As often as I could, I kept returning to hear more of her stories in museums and other venues, told in an inimitable fashion. I attended her Annual Storytelling Residency, a week-long program held at the Eugene O'Neil Theatre Center in Connecticut. Said she, "A story is alive textually, ephemeral, and delicious. It is more than facts and information." Then she demonstrated how this was so within her daily workshops. Oh, but her "extras!" The evening before our last day, Laura introduced us to a Cambodian family that had arrived only recently in the United States. The entire family, dressed in native costumes, entertained us with music and dance. Such grace! From fingertips, to hands, to wonderful body movements. And what a story they had to bring us of their Cambodian experience!

But the biggest breakthrough for me as a teller was my rapt attendance at a nine-month Certificate program held at Teachers College, Columbia University, called PAIS (Performing Artists in the School). This was designed for accomplished performing artists who seek opportunities to practice their craft with schoolchildren. The program not only focused on the art form of performance but also provided an understanding and background in identifying funding sources to support artists-in-school (local, state, national), as well as an understanding of the "whys" and "hows" of showcasing. That's when it became apparent to me that only private and privileged schools generally have good access to guest artists. What about underprivileged schools, which includes public schools or schools for the minorities? Unfortunately, too often these schools do not have sufficient funding to offer the arts as part of their education. Too often, the arts are completely overlooked amid other aspects of teaching.

The magic of stories must not be underrated. Storytellers have changed my life, and they have the power to change the world. Author Gary Zukav calls such visionary people "an emerging force, the next step in our evolutionary journey." I hope you will embrace the telling of stories and impart your wisdom and playfulness through storytelling. To close, one more story:

"Tell me the weight of a snowflake," a coal mouse asked a wild dove.

"Nothing more than nothing," was the answer.

"The coal mouse replied, "I sat on the branch of a fir, close to its trunk, when it began to snow. Not heavily, not in raging blizzard.

"No, just like in a dream, without a word and without any violence. Since I did not have anything better to do, I counted the snowflakes settling on the twigs and needles of my branch. Their number was exactly 3,741,952. When the next snowflake fell onto the branch—that was the 3,741,953rd.

"Nothing more than nothing, as you say. Yet the branch broke off."

Having said that, the coal mouse flew away.

The dove, since Noah's time, an authority on the matter, thought about the story for awhile, and finally said to herself, "Perhaps there is only one person's voice lacking—for peace to come to the world."

I humbly assert that by sharing the stories from our hearts, we can become the one voice needed. Read, enjoy, tell!

January

## ARLEAN HALE LAMBERT

New Year's Eve and New Year's Day are celebrated on December 31 and January 1,
respectively, in many countries, including the United States.

Horace the Horrible

INTRODUCTION

The story of "Horace" came to me in a moment of desperation when I was unsuccessful in finding a story about New Year's resolutions for children. I had recently heard a short children's sermon told in church about a boy named Horace whose horrible attitude had been changed when he read a ten-word sentence. With the name and the sentence, I wove it into this New Year's story.

NOTE: If no blackboard is available, you will need a poster board or flip chart with the words "Be a Better Boy" written on it, with ten empty lines drawn underneath.

STORY SCRIPT

Sometimes Horace was simply called Horace, but most of the time he was called Horace the Horrible because he behaved in horrible ways. At home, he wouldn't allow his younger sister to play with his toys. His room always looked like a tornado had just passed through, and he refused to clean it up. Mealtimes were unpleasant because he always complained about the food, no matter how delicious it was. Had it not been for bad manners, Horace would have no manners at all.

Horace behaved no better at school. He never did the work his teacher, Mrs. Tremble, assigned. He talked out of turn, and frequently, he was the cause of his classmates' losing special privileges. I can't tell you how many days Horace spent time in the principal's office because of his horrible behavior. Mrs. Tremble tried to think of ways to make Horace behave, but she had no more luck than his parents.

Right before winter vacation, Mrs. Tremble gave everyone in her class a paper leaf. She explained how a resolution was a resolve to improve something about yourself in the New Year. Then she gave them a holiday assignment: "Write on one side of the leaf your New Year's resolution, and on the other side how you plan to carry out your resolution."

Horace crammed the leaf into his pocket. He had every intention of throwing it away as soon as he left the building, but as he was leaving the front door, someone bumped into him. He began pushing and shoving and ended up in a fight. The leaf stayed in his pocket, completely forgotten.

Winter vacation was anything but pleasant for Horace's family. When Horace did not receive the gifts he had demanded for Christmas, he threw a tantrum. Almost every day, he teased his sister to tears. To give his mother a rest, his father agreed to take him to his office the day before Horace was due back in school. This was something Horace had always begged to do, but his father had always shuddered at the thought.

While going up in the elevator of his father's office building, Horace put his hand into his coat pocket—the same coat he had worn to school just before vacation. His fingers touched the paper leaf Mrs. Tremble had given him, and he pulled it out.

"What's that?" asked his father. Before realizing what he was doing, Horace explained the assignment about the New Year's resolution.

"Great idea!" exclaimed his father. "You can do it while I'm at a meeting this morning."

Horace did not have a chance to argue with his father because, as soon as they stepped off the elevator, he began to meet all of his father's friends. Everyone shook his hand, telling him how pleased they were he had come to work with his dad, and what a fine young man he was. Horace had never heard so many nice things before. Usually people were telling him how horrible he was.

Horace felt very important at his father's desk with a computer, and even a fax machine at his fingertips!

As soon as his father left for the meeting, Horace decided he *would* write a New Year's resolution. He didn't have to think very long because he wrote on one side of his leaf, **BE A BETTER BOY.**

That part was easy. How could he carry out this resolution? What should he write on the other side? That was going to be harder!

As Horace read the sentence over and over, thinking, he noticed a poster on his father's wall. Horace was not a good reader, but he could read this poster perfectly because it had only ten words. Each word had only two letters. It occurred to him that this was the ideal way to tell how he was going to become a better boy. Quickly, he turned his leaf over and copied down the ten-word sentence. That was the simple part.

At lunch with his father, Horace tried to put his resolution into practice. He did not talk with his mouth full. He did not refuse to eat his vegetables. He even used his napkin, instead of wiping his sleeve across his mouth.

When Horace arrived home that evening, he actually gave his sister permission to play with his toys. His mother could not believe her ears, especially when there were no complaints about his not having pizza for dinner but an actual compliment: He *liked* the meal she had prepared! Horace even went to bed without the usual begging to watch one more TV show.

Next morning, he even tried to straighten up his room a bit. At school, that first day of the new year, he was also different. Even before Mrs. Tremble suggested to her class that they should begin the year with clean desks, Horace was pulling out and throwing away the old papers he had crammed in there last fall.

Horace remained different throughout that whole day. He waited his turn before speaking. He did not push in line. He didn't even start a fight on the playground when he didn't get his way. Mrs. Tremble and his classmates noticed quickly that Horace was not his usual horrible self.

By the end of the third day, Mrs. Tremble announced that everybody should be ready to tell about their New Year's resolution the following day. Horace was excited because this was the first time he had an assignment actually completed.

Next morning, when Mrs. Tremble asked for volunteers to talk about their resolutions, Horace's hand shot right up. His classmates were happy to let him go first because they were eager to find out what had happened to make Horace change so much.

Horace went to the blackboard and wrote out his resolution—**BE A BETTER BOY.**

> Note to storyteller: If no blackboard is available, use a poster board on which you have written **BE A BETTER BOY,** with ten empty lines drawn underneath.

Horace explained about going to his father's office where he had seen the poster with only ten words on it and each word had only two letters.

"Now," said Horace, "see if you can figure out what that sentence said. You won't get the whole sentence right away. I will write in each two-letter word I hear—where it fits—OK? Think of some two-letter words you know. Go ahead—just say out loud any two letter word you can think of."

> Ask the audience to help Horace think of two-letter words. As the audience utters each word, put it where it occurs on the blackboard or on the poster board. Eventually you will arrive at this sentence:
> **IF**
> **IT**
> **IS**
> **TO**
> **BE,**
> **IT**
> **IS**
> **UP**
> **TO**
> **ME**

Well, I want to tell you that hands began popping up right away! "WOW!" exclaimed his classmates, when the sentence was completed. "That's a great sentence!" Mrs. Tremble was very excited as she congratulated Horace—not only about his resolution, but about his good behavior.

All of his classmates copied down the ten-word sentence. They wanted to see if their parents could figure it out when they got home.

There were times when Horace slipped back into his old ways, because habits sometimes die slowly. It always helped when he reminded himself of his own ten-word sentence.

Happily, his classmates stopped calling him "Horace the Horrible." Now, they simply call him Horace.

ABOUT THE STORY

The origin of the ten-word sentence in the story's conclusion is uncertain. A man who told the story in church said he had always heard the phrase used in scouting groups. Later, I had a chat with a man from Alabama who said his father passed that bit of wisdom on to him as a child. Regardless of its origin, it is a concept worth preserving in a story.

RELATED STORIES

1. "The Gossipy Child." This story shows how gossip has a life of its own. "The Farmer and the Spider Weaver" shows how one good turn deserves another. Both of these excellent participation stories can be found in *EASY-TO-TELL STORIES FOR YOUNG CHILDREN* by Annette Harrison (National Storytelling Association, 1992).

2. "Going to Cervieres." This folktale from France is about Grey Goose waking up with a headache after heavy indulgence of sweets on New Year's Eve. It can be found in *CELEBRATE THE WORLD* by Margaret Read MacDonald (The H.W. Wilson Co., 1994).

3. "New Year's Hats for the Statues" by Yoshiko Uchido. A kind old man is richly rewarded when he gives his hats to snow-covered statues. This story can be found in several sources. See Caroline Feller Bauer's book *SNOWY DAY* (Lippincott, 1986).

4. "The Magic Mortor" by Jay O'Callahan is a "pourquoi" Japanese story explaining why the sea is salty. See *READY-TO-TELL TALES* by David Holt and Bill Mooney (August House, 1994).

ACTIVITIES: FAMILY, GROUP, OR SCHOOL

I. Discuss superstitions or beliefs connected with this holiday. Do you believe them? Can you name others besides these:

1. On New Year's Eve, use noisemakers to chase evil spirits away.

2. Open the window a few minutes before midnight to let the bad luck out and the good luck in.

3. On New Year's Day, nothing should be taken *out* of one's house. This prevents bad luck from flowing into the house throughout the year.

4. Wipe the slate clean by paying off old debts, returning all borrowed items, let past offenses committed by or to you be forgotten—and all before midnight of the old year.

II. Discuss resolutions in families or groups:

1. What did each member present resolve to do last year? Did he or she do it?

2. Pass out paper and pencils. Ask each person to write down three resolutions for the coming year. Next, tell them to fold up the paper, bring it home, and attach it to the calendar in the month of December. Set a date for "Resolution Discussions" for the following year.

III. If possible, hold your own "Open House" for two hours on the afternoon of New Year's Day. Prepare one ethnic dish to honor good friends from another land or one of your family's treasured recipes. In America, for example, believing it brings good luck, many Southerners serve and eat black-eyed peas with greens and cornbread.

IV. Creative groups may wish to work up a story with any of the following facts about January:

1. *Name:* January was named after Janus, a Roman god. Janus had two faces that looked in opposite directions—one into the past, the other into the future. Janus comes from the Latin word *janua,* which means gate.

2. *Birthstone:* Traditionally, a birthstone brings good luck to one born in a given month. This concept stems from the biblical story of Aaron, who was the first high priest of the Israelites. Aaron's breastplate was covered with twelve precious stones all linked to the 12 months of the year, as well as the 12 signs of the zodiac. Garnet is the birthstone for January.

3. *Zodiac Signs: January 1 to January 19—Capricorn* (Sign of the Goat). Capricorns are serious people continually seeking to improve themselves. They are good organizers and planners. Three descriptive words: cautious, ambitious, and practical.

    January 20 to January 31—Aquarius (Sign of the Water Bearer). Aquarians are sometimes opinionated and liberal at the same time. They believe in democracy and the divine rights of humans. They pride themselves on being independent thinkers, and tend to gravitate socially toward people with like interests.

4. *Flower:* The snowdrop and the carnation are January flowers.

5. *Presidents born in January:*

    Millard Fillmore: Born January 7, 1800. 13th president (1850–1853)

    William McKinley: Born January 29, 1843. 25th president (1897–1901)

    Franklin D. Roosevelt: Born January 30, 1882. 32nd president (1933–1945)

    Richard Nixon: Born January 9, 1913. 37th president (1969–1974)

NOTE: New Year's was once a special holiday for women: In the 1800s, metal pins to hold jewelry in place were scarce. British law formerly permitted shopkeepers to sell metal pins only on January 1 and 2. Husbands would give their wives money to purchase pins on those days. This is where the phrase "pin money" originated.

HOLIDAY BACKGROUND INFORMATION

Margaret Read MacDonald, *THE FOLKLORE OF WORLD HOLIDAYS* (Gale Research, 1922), lists eighteen celebrations for New Year's Day, from Austria through Yugoslavia. From other sources, the following data was accumulated:

In 45 B.C., Julius Caesar set January 1 as the date to celebrate the new year, but for hundreds of years Christians observed it on March 25. Only when the Gregorian calendar was introduced in the 1500s did January 1 become the accepted date among Christians. Not until 1752 did the date became accepted by Protestant England and the American colonies.

The Jewish New Year is celebrated in late September at the time of the autumnal equinox. Chinese people follow the lunar calendar; traditionally, their new year commences on the day of the second New Moon following the winter solstice or sometime between January 21 and February 19. In other countries, the date depends in large part on the practice of different religious groups.

The American custom of making resolutions at the beginning of each new year seems to have originated in England, where it was believed that good luck would come to those who cleaned their chimneys on New Year's Day. We still use the phrase "cleaning the slate," which evolved from "cleaning the chimney" and has come to mean making resolutions to "clean up our act" or begin the new year on a positive note by resolving to correct bad habits or behaviors.

Noisemaking—driving out the old year noisily before welcoming in the new year—originated in Babylon and India. Chinese use firecrackers to scare off evil spirits. Siamese fired off guns to frighten away demons, and some people still do the same in America, mostly in the South.

"Open House Afternoons" on New Year's Day originated in ancient China. In more recent centuries, subordinates living in France and Germany made formal calls of respect to the homes of superiors. The young were made to visit elderly relatives and old family friends.

For more information, use the Internet. For example, www.holidaysmart.com/1newyearsday.htm.

BIOGRAPHY

Arlean Lambert is a storytelling librarian. As a media specialist, she has been happily telling stories (to four through eight year olds) for the past twenty-four years at Marshall School, South Orange, New Jersey. The New Year's story, created out of desperation when she was unable to find a story to explain "resolutions" to her young charges, has become a legend. "If it is to be, it is up to me," is now the Marshall School motto. This quote appears over the stage in the school auditorium in two-foot felt letters created by Marshall students in art classes.

CONTACT

Arlean Lambert
7 Crowell Place
Maplewood, NJ 07040
E-mail: donarlean@verizon.net

Hogmanay, a new year celebration in Scotland, begins on December 31 and lasts for two days.

A Different Kind of New Year's Celebration—Hogmanay

INTRODUCTION

Most New Year customs are embedded in pagan, rural traditions in which the New Year is a new beginning and should emphasize renewed beginnings and the start of new growing seasons.

STORY SCRIPT

Dougal and Morag McKissick were all excited. This year, instead of visiting their gruff grandfather in Scotland in the rainy, windy summer, they were going to be there for the winter holidays. Dougal always thought that his grandfather was gruff because of the "mmphm" sounds he often made, such as when he greeted them on their arrival.

Grandpa McKissick lived on the Outer Islands where the winds blew continuously and rains were familiar. In fact, one summer when they were visiting the small village, Morag started laughing. Dougal poked her in her ribs and snorted, "What's so funny?"

"Look at the sign in that store window!"

Her twin brother looked and started laughing himself. The sign read, "Small plants that will grow in windy places." This wasn't like their home back in Pennsylvania. Anything grew there with no problems—in fact, now that they noticed it, the island didn't have trees. With Dougal's attention turned to the windiness, he followed up this knowledge with an experiment. As he and Morag played on the beach, he got his harmonica out of his pocket and held it up into the wind. Yep! It was windy. Windy enough for his harmonica to make wind music!

Show me different ways you can think of that a strong wind is blowing. Maybe your hands in the air can go wild, maybe your mouth expresses strong whistles.

Come on now, show me!

⇨ Participants demonstrate how many different ways they can show that a strong wind is blowing.

Winter on the island was windy and wet and cold. Christmas was coming soon, and one evening as the thirteen-year-old twins sat around the fire chatting with their grandfather and grandmother, they got to talking about holiday customs there. Grandpa was rocking in his favorite chair that was the same green as the color of his eyes. His hair was gray, but the twins never knew him when it wasn't gray. Mother used to joke, "You should have known your grandpa when his hair was flaming red."

The twins shared their Christmas customs from back home. Then the conversation turned to New Year's celebration. New Year's, or Hogmanay in Scotland, was something special.

How many different ways do you and your family celebrate New Year's Day? Show me some hands!

At a show of hands, allow the audience to respond to the following questions: How many of you stay up late on New Year's Eve? How many eat something special on New Year's Day?

The twins were usually in bed at midnight on New Year's Eve, but when they became older, they stayed up with their parents and hugged each other, got in a circle, held hands, and sang "Auld Lang Syne" with everyone there. Mom had made sure the twins knew that the song was written by Scotland's revered poet, Robbie Burns.

Mom and Dad had told them only that New Year's in Scotland was DIFFERENT.

"Now, in Scotland," Grandfather said, "the first part of the ritual was with cleaning." Each year at this time, Grandmother McKissick began an orgy of housecleaning. Their home was neat enough, but Grandmother said, "We must do more than redd up at Hogmanay." Morag asked her, "Why is that so important?" Her reply was, "If we want a new year of good luck, it must start out right. You must start out clean!" It was very important to make sure the fireplaces in the house were thoroughly cleaned so a fire could be laid to start the new year. Small juniper fires were burned throughout the house while cleaning it to ensure that any evil spirits which might have moved in during the year were also cleaned out.

What customs or habits get you ready for the new year? Let's talk about them.

Hands go up to discuss their customs or habits. For example, do any of you take down Christmas decorations before New Year's day? Do you follow other customs or habits?

Morag then asked, "What is this Hogmanay I keep hearing about?"

"Oh my child, Hogmanay is the celebration that welcomes the new year. It is a time of hope and looking forward to a better year," said Grandmother McKissick as she put a dust cloth in Morag's hand and motioned for her to clean the windows.

"Hogmanay, when I was a child on our farm," started Grandfather McKissick, "meant that the men cleared the barn and raked the floor clean for the dancing. Our music was provided by people regardless of whether they played a scratchy fiddle, or squealed on a flute. That was all accompanied by the heartbeat thump on the bodhran." (The bodhran is a Celtic drum held in one hand by crossbars built into the frame on its back. It is played with a two-headed stick with either leather or rubber tips on both ends.)

"If we were lucky, someone played the bagpipes, too. Altogether, it was a time of happiness and celebration for everyone, all ages included, to enjoy. I remember times when the young'uns fell asleep, they were wrapped up in their blankets and placed on hay to sleep while the party went on."

"Right," chuckled Grandmother. "I also remember how sometimes rascals would change the blankets on the youngsters. At the end of the dance, in the wee hours of the morning, sometimes people were too tired to notice that they were taking someone else's baby home instead of their own."

"Hogmanay was a two-day celebration, though," Grandfather added. "When the bells rang out at midnight, first footing began. It is believed that the loud sounds of the bells scared away evil spirits. A tall, dark, and hopefully handsome fellow would be recognized as the first footer to visit the homes in our village. You would welcome the first visitor to cross the threshold after midnight on New Year's Eve as the "first footer." He brought not only good fortune to the house for the coming year, but gifts as well.

> Teller starts a chant and motions everyone to join in saying, "Who is at my door?" Repeat the chant three times: "Who is at my door?"

The first footer carried a canvas bag that held gifts such as an egg, a lump of coal, a stick of wood, a bit of salt and other small things to bring good fortune to the house for the coming year.

"That is true," remembered Grandmother. "The lump of coal or the stick of wood would be placed in the fireplace to symbolize warmth, the salt was thought to bring wealth and flavor, maybe a cake or biscuit to ensure that the householders would never go hungry and sometimes a coin for good luck. After all, it was also considered good luck to make sure all your debts were cleared before the new year."

"Mmphm, one time when I was the first footer, I remembered to give a toast to the family and I used *'Here' tae us. Wha's like us, damn few, and they're a' deid!'* Folks there liked the humor of it," smiled Grandfather.

Who can create a toast to the "first footer"? Let me see some hands.

> Listen to several toast suggestions. Teller selects one of the toasts. The participant whose toast has been selected places an arm out pretending to hold a glass on high and presents the toast.

"We must offer food and drink to the first footer," said Grandmother, reminded of her duty as lady of the house.

"Is there anything else that would be special about the first footer?" asked Dougal.

"Oh yes, lad," replied Grandfather. "If he is a doctor, minister, or grave digger, bad luck will follow. Also, it is crucial that the first footer's eyebrows don't meet in the middle."

Grandmother smiled. "Auld lang syne is the name of an old Scottish tune and means 'old long ago,' or quite simply, 'the good old days.' " She had the look of someone who had seen many 'good old days.'

> Storyteller sings alone first, a cappella. Teller motions with hands for audience to join in the chorus. Audience joins in chorus.
> "For auld lang syne, my jo,
> For auld lang syne,
> We'll tak' a cup o' kindness yet,
> For auld lang syne."

And so, preparations for this two-day celebration continued. In Scotland, January first and second are both considered holidays. Sure enough, a tall, dark, and handsome young man knocked on their door just at the stroke of midnight. Gifts were exchanged, and then he went on to his appointed rounds to other houses in the neighborhood. Dougal and Morag remembered that special first footing night for the rest of their days. It certainly was something that they took back to Pennsylvania with them, and they passed on this grand custom to others.

As Dougal and Morag were getting ready to return to Pennsylvania, gruff Grandfather hugged them one more time. "Mmphm, you know young'uns, maybe you can come visit us for another New Year's celebration and we will show you some more things to remember.

How would you develop a tender "mmphm" sound?

➯ Several participants share their tender "mmphm" sound.

"In olden times, people dressed up in the hides of cattle and ran around the village, being hit by sticks. These old times also included the lighting of bonfires, rolling blazing tar barrels down the hill, and tossing blazing torches. These helped ward off evil spirits.

"But the most fantastic event that can still be seen today is the spectacular fire ceremonies. Giant fireballs weighing up to 20 pounds are lit and swung around on five feet long metal poles. Sixty men carry them as they march up and down the street swinging these large flaming balls over their heads. When they are finished marching, they make sure they end up near a loch or run that they can throw the fireballs into and listen to the sizzle as the water puts the fire out. Yes, there are still some special sights you haven't seen yet!"

They hugged everyone all around and thought about the holiday surprises yet to come. "Goodbye, Grandmother and Grandfather. We love you and thank you for everything you have shared with us. We'll remember especially grandfather's 'mmphm.' " Dougal said, "We just figured it out, if our dog could purr, it would probably sound like grandfather's 'mmphm,' sort of growly but really an expression of love."

Then the two of them, Dougal and Morag in unison, imitating grandfather's growl, uttered "mmphm!"

They marched out to the car to go to the airport, and the last thing their grandparents heard were them singing, "Auld Lang Syne."

How many of you know who Robert Burns is? Would you care to share your information?

➯ Teller encourages audience members to raise their hands and share what they know.
By show of hands, audience shares information about Robert Burns.
Just so you never forget again, here is the traditional music to Robert Burns's "Auld Lang Syne."
Teller passes out music.

AULD LANG SYNE

Words by
ROBERT BURNS

TRADITIONAL

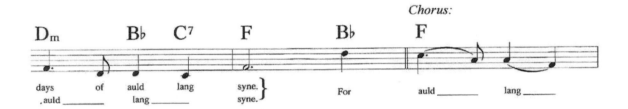

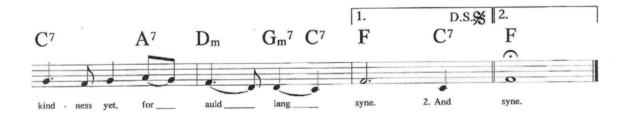

All Rights Reserved

0003b6bf-cff7-0001-5f52-4d53534f4c52

Words by ROBERT BURNS. Music: Traditional Scottish Melody. © 1990 BEAM ME UP MUSIC c/o CPP/BELWIN, INC. All Rights Controlled and Administered by Alfred Publishing Co., Inc. All Rights Reserved. Used by permission of Alfred Publishing Co., Inc.

HOLIDAY BACKGROUND INFORMATION

For information about this holiday, Norma suggests the book *FOLK LORE SUPERSTITIOUS BELIEFS IN THE WEST OF SCOTLAND WITHIN THIS CENTURY* by James Napier (Project Gutenberg, 2005). Also consult the Internet: http://en.wikipedia.org/wiki/Hogmanay.

As explained in the Story Script, this holiday is currently celebrated in Scotland and in pockets throughout the world where the Scots' influence is strong. For instance, the area of western Pennsylvania in which the author grew up contains a heavy population of Scot and Irish. People still practice these traditions and variations of them today. This is most prevalent in rural communities.

Other New Year Customs Throughout the World

- Celebrations of the New Year are the oldest of all holidays. It was first observed in ancient Babylon about four thousand years ago. It developed into the New Year beginning with the first New Moon after the vernal equinox.

- In ancient times, people in Scotland would dress up in the hides of cattle and run around the village being hit by sticks. The festivities would also include lighting bonfires, rolling blazing tar barrels down a hill, and tossing torches. Animal hide was also wrapped around sticks and ignited, which produced a smoke that was believed to be very effective to ward off evil spirits.

- Traditionally, people make New Year's resolutions to guarantee good luck and changes for the better in the New Year. In every festival, each person is expected to wear new clothes to show that the New Year will be a good, rich one.

- Loony douk is held in South Queensferry, outside of Edinburgh on New Year's Day every year. A few brave lunatics, take a short douk (Scots for "dip") in the freezing cold waters of the Firth of Forth.

- The Romans observed the New Year in late March. However, because their calendar was continually changed by various emperors, it soon became out of synchronization with the sun. Julius Caesar established the Julian Calendar, which established January 1 as the new year.

- It was in Greece that the tradition of using a baby signified the New Year. This image was brought to early America by the Germans.

- Many cultures believe that anything in the shape of a ring is good luck.

- Chinese families gather together for dinner with traditional foods such as dumplings, chicken and fish signifying good luck. Nine days for the holidays are common.

- It is believed in Korea that you should not sleep on New Year's Eve because your eyebrows will turn white. At midnight, a bell is struck thirty-three times to remember the thirty-three fighters who died to restore the nation of Korea.

- Many people in Mexico gather with their family and friends on New Year's. When a bell rings twelve times, they eat one grape and make a wish. There is a lot of hugging and giving of best wishes. When a woman wears red underwear, it expresses the hope that she will find love in the next year.

- The Hmong of Southeast Asia hold a New Year's Festival. This is the high point of village life and is anticipated all year. In each village, the heads of clans, who are always the eldest men, meet to arrange the event. Each village plans its festival to take place at a different time so that villages can invite one another to their activities.

    The New Year's festival is often the beginning of intense courtships in which young people select and woo their mates. Wearing their finest embroidered clothes and silver jewelry, young men and women pair off and toss soft balls made of cloth back and forth to each other. Anyone who drops the ball must forfeit a gift (to be returned later) or sing a folksong. Later, the young man might visit the girl's house. He might whisper to her through the woven bamboo wall and play music on a small mouth harp. These activities begin a process of courtship that culminates with a raft of marriages following the New Year's celebration. (Refer to *Folk Stories of the Hmong* by Norma J. Livo and Dia Cha, published by Libraries Unlimited, 1991, and *Teaching with Folk Stories of the Hmong* by Dia Cha and Norma J. Livo, published by Libraries Unlimited, 2000.)

• For Finnish New Year's customs, refer to *The Enchanted Wood and Other Tales from Finland* by Norma J. Livo and George O. Livo. Libraries Unlimited, 1999.

BIOGRAPHY

Norma J. Livo, Professor Emerita, University of Colorado at Denver, is the author and coauthor of numerous books, many of them award-winners, including *Storytelling: Process and Practice* (1986*), Folk Stories of the Hmong* (1991), *Troubadour's Storybag* (1996), *The Enchanted Wood and Other Tales from Finland* (1999), and *Bringing Out Their Best* (2003). She served on the board of the National Storytelling Association and is Founder of the Rocky Mountain Storytelling Conference. She received NSN's 2002 ORACLE Award for Lifetime Achievement in Storytelling.

CONTACT

Norma J. Livo
11960 West 22nd Place
Lakewood, Colorado 80215
E-mail: Njlivo@aol.com

LINDA GOSS
with Activities by Gretchen Shannon

Martin Luther King, Jr. Day, a federal holiday, is observed on the third Monday in January in the United States.

The Caterpillar's Blues

INTRODUCTION

"The Caterpillar's Blues" story can be a song or recited as a poem. The story gives the audience an opportunity to show a range of emotions from sadness to joyfulness. The pacing of the story varies from slow and bluesy in the beginning, gradually building to an uplifting upbeat rhythm. The storyteller can create his or her tune and rhythm with the audience joining in. The setting is an African tropical forest.

STORY SCRIPT

Remember this refrain: Do doop, do doop. Doop, doop, doop, doop. Do doop, do doop, day aye.

> Set the tone of the story by chanting in a slow, sad rhythm. Make a sad face and invite the audience to make a sad expression.

> The audience makes a sad face.

Do doop, do doop. Doop, doop, doop, doop. Do doop, do doop, day aye. Can you repeat after me? Help me out now! One line at a time.

Do doop, do doop. Doop, doop, doop, doop.

> Audience responds: Do doop, do doop. Doop, doop, doop, doop.

Do doop, do doop, day aye.

> audience responds: Do doop, do doop, day aye.

Do doop, do doop. Doop, doop, doop, doop.

> Audience responds: Do doop, do doop. Doop, doop, doop, doop.

Do doop, do doop, day aye.

> Audience responds: Do doop, do doop, day aye.

17

Come gather 'round, my people. I have a story to tell. About this little friend of mine, who isn't very well.

There once was a caterpillar. Who was sad as he could be. He felt that he didn't belong. He didn't fit in the community.

He moped around the neighborhood. Singing his same old song. Mama Elephant heard his cry. And she said, "My child, what's wrong?"

"I wonder as I wander," he said. "Feeling blue, oh me oh my. I look at all the animals. And I ask, oh, why can't I? Why can't I be like the bumblebee? Why can't I be like the ant? I want to run as fast as a cheetah. But I can't. Oh Lawdy, I can't.

I'm looking at that tall giraffe. I want a long neck too. Mama Elephant, you're big and strong. I want to be like you. I want to go over the mountain. I want to see across the sea. But all I do is crawl on the ground. Hoping no one will step on me.

Chant the refrain with me now! Do doop, do doop. Doop, doop, doop, doop. Do doop, do doop, day aye. Do doop, do doop. Doop, doop, doop, doop. Do doop, do doop, day aye. Say it with me!

> **Audience responds:** Do doop, do doop. Doop, doop, doop, doop. Do doop, do doop, day aye.
> Do doop, do doop. Doop, doop, doop, doop. Do doop, do doop, day aye.

Ooh, I'm feeling blue—ooh. I don't know what to do. Ooh, I'm feeling blue—ooh. I don't know what to do—ooh.

All of a sudden, Mama Elephant made a trumpet-like sound. "CHEEEEEER UP!"

Can I hear the elephant sound?

> **Audience responds:** CHEEEEEER UP!

Oh, little caterpillar, you shouldn't feel that way. A change is going to come one day. Please listen to what I say.

> Here we go now! All of us will say, YOU ARE A STORY. YOU ARE A POEM. YOU ARE A SHINING STAR. YOU ARE UNIQUE. YOU ARE ONE OF A KIND. BE PROUD OF WHO YOU ARE.

Help me out now!

> **Audience responds:** YOU ARE A STORY. YOU ARE A POEM. YOU ARE A SHINING STAR. YOU ARE UNIQUE. YOU ARE ONE OF A KIND. BE PROUD OF WHO YOU ARE.

Mama Elephant continued, "Life is not always pleasant. Many things will make you cry. But you've got to hold on because within your soul lives a BUTTERFLY!

"You will soar over the mountain. You will fly across the sea too. So get to work. Jump right in. See what life has in store for you."

> **Audience responds:** YOU ARE A STORY. YOU ARE A POEM. YOU ARE A SHINING STAR. YOU ARE UNIQUE. YOU ARE ONE OF A KIND. BE PROUD OF WHO YOU ARE!

> Say help me out again with our chant!

One more time now!

> **Audience responds:** YOU ARE A STORY. YOU ARE A POEM.

YOU ARE A SHINING STAR.

YOU ARE UNIQUE. YOU ARE ONE OF A KIND.

BE PROUD OF WHO YOU ARE!

Now the little caterpillar listened to what Mama said. He dried his eyes. He began to smile. And he lifted up his head. "Thank you, Mama Elephant. I know what you're talking about. I'm going to stop complaining and start my training. So my own little BUTTERFLY can come out."

Let's say it together again:

> I AM A STORY. I AM A POEM! I AM A SHINING STAR! I AM UNIQUE. I AM ONE OF A KIND. I KNOW I CAN GO FAR!

Let me hear it again!

> I AM A STORY. I AM A POEM! I AM A SHINING STAR! I AM UNIQUE. I AM ONE OF A KIND. I KNOW I CAN GO FAR!

You see, all of us are caterpillars. All of us have a BUTTERFLY inside.

Remember Dr. King and Rosa Parks? Let your conscience be your guide.

The moral of this story, I hope is very clear. Believe in yourself. Follow your dreams. Enjoy every day of the year.

> The storyteller instructs the audience to sing, dance, flap their wings like butterflies and fly.

DO DOOP, DO DOOP. DOOP, DOOP, DOOP. DOOP! FLY, BUTTERFLY, FLY! DO DOOP, DO DOOP. DOOP, DOOP, DOOP, DOOP! FLY, BUTTERFLY, FLY! Come on, all of us!

> COME ON AND FLY, BUTTERFLY, FLY! COME ON AND FLY, BUTTERFLY, FLY! FLY, BUTTERFLY, FLY! FLY, BUTTERFLY, FLY!

ABOUT THIS STORY

I wrote this story to encourage the schoolchildren of Philadelphia, Pennsylvania. This story represents the spirit of Martin Luther King, Jr. He had to overcome many obstacles in his quest to let freedom ring for all. As a caterpillar transforms into a butterfly, the message of Martin Luther King, Jr. transformed a nation.

RECOMMENDED BOOKS

1. *THE DREAM KEEPER AND OTHER POEMS* by Langston Hughes (Knopf Books for Young Readers, 1996).

2. *HONEY, I LOVE AND OTHER LOVE POEMS* (Reading Rainbow Series) by Eloise Greenfield (Harper Trophy, 1986).

3. *I CAN MAKE A DIFFERENCE: A Treasury to Inspire Our Children* by Marian Wright Edelman (Amistad, 2005).

4. *PEACE TALES* by Margaret Read MacDonald (August House, 2005).

5. *TALK THAT TALK: An Anthology of African American Storytelling* by Linda Goss and Marian Barnes (Simon & Schuster, 1989).

A RECOMMENDED SONG FROM KATHY CULMER

LIFT EVERY VOICE AND SING by James Weldon Johnson; Music, J. Rosamond Johnson. Referred to as the "Negro National Hymn" (Edward B. Marks Music Corporation, 1949).

In 1900, Johnson, a school principal in Jacksonville, Florida, was asked to speak at an Abraham Lincoln Birthday celebration. He decided to write a poem and to ask his brother, music teacher J. Rosamond Johnson, to turn his poem into a song. Together, they turned out over two hundred songs and a novel: *AUTOBIOGRAPHY OF AN EX-COLORED MAN.*

The NACCP adopted *"LIFT EVERY VOICE AND SING"* as its official song.

ACTIVITIES DESIGNED BY GRETCHEN SHANNON

These activities were created to wake up the imagination.

Caterpillar Dream Book

Each child starts by cutting two pieces of paper. Construction paper may be used. One measures 2½ x 16 inches, and the other measures 2 x 15½ inches. Glue the two pieces together by centering the smaller piece on top of the larger piece. While it is drying, cut out the butterfly and caterpillar-head shapes.

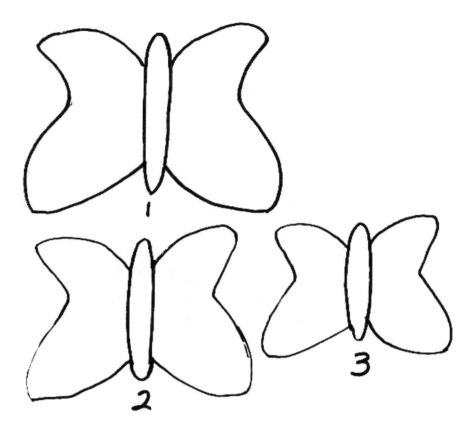

These butterfly shapes can be cut out. The spine will be used to glue together the different-sized butterflies.

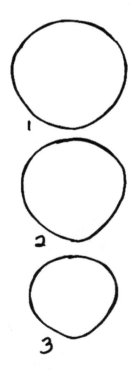

These Caterpillar heads can be cut out.

1. Color and decorate your butterfly shapes and caterpillar shapes.

2. Glue butterfly shape two (2) to butterfly shape one (1) placing the glue only on the spine of the butterflies and not on the wings.

3. Glue butterfly shape three (3) to butterfly shape two (2) in the same manner. You want to be able to fold the wings upward. See below.

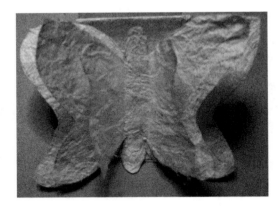

1. Decorate your caterpillar faces and glue face two to face one (1) and face three (3) to face two (2).

2. Mark 1¾ inches from each end of your long strip and then mark 1¼ inches intervals between the two ends.

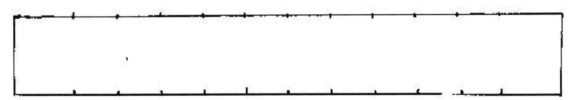

Pretend you are a caterpillar. What would you dream? Write a story, poem, song, or vision about your dreams on the strip of paper or use a separate sheet for your story, poem, song, or vision. You can also decorate your strip with pictures, designs, or patterns.

1. Glue your caterpillar head to the left end of your strip on the first section.

2. Glue the butterfly to the right end of your strip on the last section.

3. When dry, begin to fold your strip accordion style using the measurement marks you made as a guide. See below.

Butterfly Fly Book

Cut out the four butterfly shapes. Use construction paper if you wish.

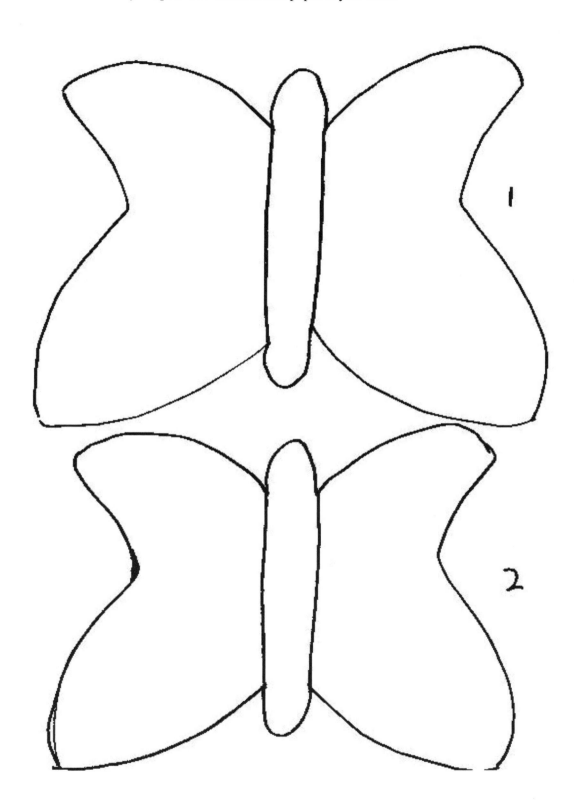

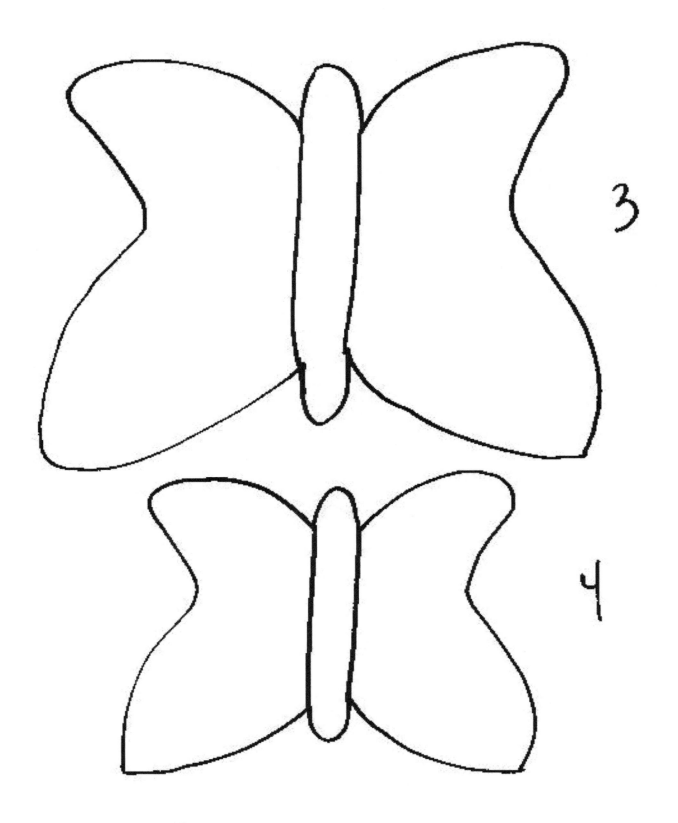

3

4

1. Pretend you are a butterfly. Where would you fly?

2. Write a story, poem, or song about where you would go if you were as free as a butterfly.

3. Write only on the wings and leave the spine of the butterfly blank.

4. Glue butterfly two (2) to one (1) and three (3) to two (2) and four (4) to three (3).

5. Let dry and fold the wings up at the spine.

HOLIDAY BACKGROUND INFORMATION BY KATHY CULMER

See the King Center—Official Web site of Martin Luther King, Jr. Center in Atlanta, Georgia: www.thekingcenter.org.

Although it does not follow the official format for background information used in this text, Kathy Culmer sent us a story about Martin Luther King that points out his human reaction to everyday situations.

KATHY CULMER'S STORY

Once upon a time, right here in America, there lived a real KING. He did not wear rich, royal robes or a crown. No. He wore regular clothes like the rest of us. His parents' clothes were poor, and his grandparents wore what you might call rags. You see, his grandparents were slaves.

On January 15, 1929, Martin Luther King, Jr. was born in Atlanta, Georgia, USA. It did not take long for the boy to learn that his brown skin caused him and many others like him a great deal of suffering. For example, one day young King went to visit a friend. They had played together often. One day, his playmate told him they could not be friends anymore. He wouldn't even say why not. That hurt bad—real bad.

He went to his mama. She understood. She happened to be a bright woman and told him right off it was not his fault—not his fault at all. As gently as she could, she talked about how his grandfather was among hundreds who had been kidnapped in Africa and brought to America and other countries to become slaves—which means they worked in other people's houses and fields for no pay, no thank-yous, nothing but abuse and even beatings when they tried to escape.

Then she said something he would always remember. "Seems the only way some people can feel good about themselves is by makin' other folks feel bad about themselves. It's called prejudice." So that was why the parents of his little white friend had stopped them from playing together!

Lucky for young King, his intelligent mom went on talking. "Remember this, son—no matter what happens, you're just as good as anyone else."

"Just as good as anyone else." He repeated the words to himself many times.

As he grew older, he realized more and more how much injustice existed. All the unfair treatment he was ate into his very soul. He became determined to do all he could to get rid of this evil thing—this *prejudice*—poisoning the minds and hearts of people everywhere.

He was just fourteen when a truly terrible thing happened. His teacher had brought him by bus to a different city. She saw great promise in this lad and had entered him in a contest. He won second place for his delivery of his own composition, "The Negro and the Constitution." He really could talk about the Negro and his rights in America. And did, every chance he got!

He and his teacher, Mrs. Bradley, had just settled back in their seats for the long ride home to Atlanta. They had risen at dawn to get to the speech competition on time, had dashed around all day to locate the hall, arriving just in time to make the presentation. They were exhausted. When they sat down for the return trip home, all of a sudden in a real nasty tone of voice, the bus driver yelled at them to get out of their seats, to give them to the white passengers who had just boarded the bus. Then, the bus driver began to curse them for being so slow to get up—like the were something less human. For ninety miles, they stood—holding on to the straphanger, swaying in the dark.

Outraged, the young King's blood boiled. What right had the bus driver to do such a thing? What right had anyone to treat another human being in that manner?!

His mind churned around words he had spoken that very day in his speech: "We hold these truths to be self-evident—that all men are created equal." Words from the Constitution that had given him and countless others real hope. What a joke! Then he recalled the time he was in their car with his father. A policeman pulled his daddy over to the side of the road. "Let me see your license, Boy," said the officer. The driver kept his dignity, and said, "Sir, this is a boy (indicating Martin Luther, Jr.). I am a man."

Remembering his father's quiet ways calmed his mind. After a while, he could even let the anger go and believe again, in his heart, that important changes could be made, that the unfair treatment would disappear, not immediately, but yes, definitely, sooner or later.

Martin Luther King, Jr. became a mighty leader. He led people first in one battle, then another—and another—and another. First small battles, then bigger and bigger ones. He and his people fought not with guns or knives or swords, but with speeches and songs, with prayers, with word protests. They fought by standing up for their rights, sitting in, marching, boycotting. Their enemies were not people but attitudes: segregation, injustice, hatred, prejudice, poverty.

Like his idol, Abraham Lincoln, Martin Luther King, Jr.'s life was cut short by an assassin. It happened on April 4, 1968, but, like Lincoln's Emancipation Proclamation, his "I Have a Dream" speech is as alive now as when the words were first uttered.

Dignity, fundamental human rights, decency—all would follow.

BIOGRAPHIES

Linda Goss is cofounder of the National Association of Black Storytellers and the author of six books. For further information about Linda, consult www.lindagoss.com and http://www.folkloreproject.org/folkarts/artists/goss_l/index.cfm.

Gretchen Shannon is a multidisciplinary artist and textile designer.

Linda and Gretchen have been collaborating since 1998. For further information about Gretchen, consult www.gretchenshannon.com.

CONTACTS

Linda Goss
6653 Sprague Street
Philadelphia, PA 19119
E-mail: lindagoss84@hotmail.com

Gretchen Shannon
P.O. Box 126
Elverson, PA 19520
E-mail: gretchen.shannon@gmail.com

Kathy Culmer
E-mail: khculmer@aol.com

February

LARRY JOHNSON
ELAINE WYNNE

Groundhog Day occurs in North America on February 2.

The Great Groundhog-Day Get Together

INTRODUCTION

Celebration on February 2 is ancient, marking the time halfway between the winter solstice and the spring equinox as "The Return of the Light," a festival of rebirth and renewal. We wrote the story for our grandchildren.

STORY SCRIPT

Phil, Julie, and Suzie lived near a beautiful park, filled with trees and flowers in the summer, and snow and ice in the winter. They loved the snow and ice for sledding, skating, and snowballing. They even loved the cold, but not when it went on and on.

One day, while sliding in the park, they decided the cold had been too much. "I hate this long, cold winter," said Phil.

"Me, too!" said Suzie. "I wish we could get rid of it."

"We should go ask Aunt Tina how to make winter go away," said Julie. "Aunt Tina knows a lot of stuff."

They all agreed and began to pull their sleds toward Aunt Tina's home. Aunt Tina was a writer and the owner of a small business. She lived near the park and was home much of the time, thinking, organizing, and writing. When she saw the children coming, she put the hot chocolate on the stove.

As the children burst in, kicking off their boots and hanging jackets, mittens, and scarves near the heat register, Aunt Tina asked, "Would you like some hot chocolate?"

Since hot chocolate was one of the best parts of winter, the children all shouted, "Yeah!"

What did they say?

☞ **Audience responds:** YEAH!

While guzzling down the hot chocolate, Suzie demanded, "We want to get rid of winter!"

"Yeah, we're sick of winter!" Julie chimed in. "Aunt Tina, do you know a way to get rid of it?"

31

Running a finger down the side of her cheek as she thought, Aunt Tina replied, "No, there's no way I know to get rid of winter. Winter is just something we have here in Minnesota. You just learn to put up with it."

"But, Aunt Tina," Phil insisted, "Albert gets rid of winter!"

"Yes," Aunt Tina answered, "but Cousin Albert's family can afford to go to Florida during winter. It's very warm there. He doesn't get rid of winter. He just leaves the cold behind for a while."

"OH, NO!" the three kids groaned in unison. Aunt Tina groaned along with them.

What did the kids say?

> **Audience responds:** OH, NO!

"Well," Aunt Tina said, "there is one thing I remember. It's old Brother G, the groundhog. He lives in a hole the other side of the hill in Wirth Park. Some call him a woodchuck. Do you remember a teasing chant that goes, **"HOW MUCH WOOD COULD A WOODCHUCK CHUCK IF A WOODCHUCK COULD CHUCK WOOD?**

Come on, chant with me!

> **Audience responds:** HOW MUCH WOOD COULD A WOODCHUCK CHUCK IF A WOODCHUCK COULD CHUCK WOOD?

"Anyway," continued Aunt Tina. "They say that if the woodchuck comes out from hibernating on February 2—why, that's today!—and doesn't see his shadow, winter will be much shorter."

"We're out of here!" shouted Phil, as the children thanked Aunt Tina and headed out into the cold.

"Just remember," Aunt Tina called out, "Most of them have a big G on their door outside the cave! Remember, that if he sees his shadow, winter will be longer."

The children were so excited, they made it around the hill in no time, and there they found themselves looking for the round, wooden door with the big G.

Phil jumped up, shouting, "Whee! This is it!" Then, looking at the sun, and shadows all around him, he muttered, "Wait, there are shadows everywhere. If he comes out, he'll see his shadow for sure. What're we gonna do?"

"I know," said Julie. "We gotta use science. You two go stand out there. I'm gonna stand here, like I'm the groundhog coming out. I'm gonna find a place for you to stand where my shadow is behind me when I look at you."

Remember, we've got to chant to wake up the sleeping groundhog. Chant, now!

> **Audience responds:** HOW MUCH WOOD COULD A WOODCHUCK CHUCK IF A WOODCHUCK COULD CHUCK WOOD?

Julie moved her friends all over the field, till they were in a spot where she was looking at them with her shadow behind her. "That's it!" she screamed excitedly.

"Stay right there. It's time now to sing the song I taught you.

Think of "Twinkle, Twinkle, Little Star." Sing, now!

As they finished singing, the children stood amazed, watching the groundhog as he lumbered out of his hole, mumbling loudly, "Whoa, who's doing that beautiful singing?"

> **Audience sings to the tune of "Twinkle, Twinkle, Little Star":**
> Wake up, wake up, Brother G
> Sunshine's what you want to see.
> It will make you feel real good,
> Even if you can't chuck wood.
> Wake up, wake up, Brother G
> Sunshine's what you want to see.

Phil and Suzie and Julie looked at the groundhog, and then at each other in delight.

"He didn't see his shadow!" They all screamed together. "He didn't see his shadow! Let's tell everyone about it!" They went all over the town, telling everyone:

> **Audience responds:** He didn't see his shadow! Tell someone about it.

It turns out there were people all over the town who couldn't wait for winter to be shorter. When they heard what was going on, it did not take long before they were all down at the field for *The Great Groundhog-Day Get Together*. I can't tell you everything they did, but I can teach you how to sing and dance from that party.

> Storyteller demonstrates, singing once again to the tune of "Twinkle, Twinkle, Little Star." This time, the teller turns halfway around at the point that begins "when you turn yourself around" and when he or she sings the next line, "hide your shadow on the ground," the teller comes back to his or original position. Then the teller directs the audience to dance along with him or her.

> **Audience sings along with teller:**
> Wake up, wake up, Brother G
> Sunshine's what you want to see.
> It will make you feel real good,
> Even if you can't chuck wood.
> Wake up, wake up, Brother G
> Sunshine's what you want to see.

And that's the way it was at *The Great Groundhog-Day Get Together*.

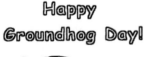

HOLIDAY BACKGROUND INFORMATION

A trip to the library will yield any number of children's books adapting the general theme of a groundhog emerging on February 2 and seeing or not seeing its shadow. However, if you really want to know groundhogs and Groundhog Day, we recommend going to www.dougelliott.com. Doug Elliott is a true naturalist and storyteller and a world-renowned authority on "Groundhogology." Doug knows groundhogs inside and out and often walks the earth with one on his shoulder. If you want to celebrate this deeply spiritual day in its most recent incarnation, you should be going for depth. Doug Elliott has it when he tells stories and when he writes about the groundhog.

Larry and Elaine (well, especially Larry) have celebrated February 2 long before the Bill Murray movie *Groundhog Day,* made it famous (especially the annual celebration in Punxsutawney, Pennsylvania). They told the story once in Scandinavia, and the audience loved it, particularly the "imagination" and the dance. It was a great adventure with them trying to figure out what a groundhog really was.

When Christianity began converting ancient pagan celebrations such as Christmas (originally the birth of the Sun god) or Easter (a tribute to fertility goddesses such as Ishtar or Eostre), February 2 came along as Candlemas to celebrate "the light shining into darkness" or the coming of the "light of the world" referred to frequently in the book of John in the New Testament.

It never became popular until the early European settlers to North America revived an old, related myth about hibernating animals coming out into the light.

Somehow the groundhog caught on over bears and others, and Groundhog Day was born and celebrated, particularly in North America.

BIOGRAPHIES

Larry Johnson and Elaine Wynne, as "Key of See Storytellers," have spent their entire working lives teaching people of all ages to use story in their work in the world. They have done that throughout the United States, as well as in Scandinavia, Germany, Great Britain, South America, and Asia. Larry is trained professionally as a storyteller/educator; Elaine as a storyteller/psychologist. In 1986, they won the grand prize in the Tokyo Video Festival for helping children on either side of the Atlantic share their deepest stories via video, and in 1996, they represented storytelling at the Founding Convention of the Cultural Environment Movement, a predecessor to current media reform efforts. They offer a workshop called "Storytelling for Parents, Grandparents, and Other Activists, Trainers, and Leaders."

In addition to periodical get-togethers, they regularly gather their thirteen grandchildren for "Cousin Camp." These are the kind of grandkids who would use science to help the groundhog not to see its shadow.

CONTACT

Key of See Storytellers
Box 27314
Golden Valley, MN 55427
E-mail: topstory7@comcast.net

CATHY SPAGNOLI

Setsubon, held on February 3 near the Japanese lunar New Year, marks the end of winter. This holiday is a centuries old ritual to chase away evil spirits and to welcome spring with good fortune.

Oni Wa Soto

INTRODUCTION

I use limited audience participation. I invite the children to repeat the growing refrain of things swallowed, and they quickly jump in to join me. They like to repeat the sound-words, which I wrote out phonetically in the story. I simplify the woman's repeated trips to the priest, saying the same words each time, having the audience repeat them with me as well.

To add more participation, you might ask for gestures to help you "search and find" some of the characters: the bug, the frog, the snake, and so on.

STORY SCRIPT

Mu-kah-shee, mu-kah-shee . . .

Long, long ago in Japan, an old couple lived in peace. But the old man had a big problem: He ate too many beans. Bean paste, bean curd, bean soup, and more . . .

One day, he suddenly cried, "*EETIE, EETIE*, I MAY DIE! My stomach hurts! Oh, how it hurts!"

"Maaaa! What can I do?" wondered his wife. "Ah, I'll go ask the priest." So she ran to the temple, *choh-koh choh-koh.*

Can you say *choh-koh choh-koh?*

> **Audience responds:** *Choh-koh choh-koh.*

At the temple, the wife called out to the priest, "*Doh-ka, ta-su-keh-teh koo-dah-sie,* which means: Sir, please help me. My husband's stomach hurts from too many beans."

What did she say?

> **Audience repeats:** Sir, please help me. My husband's stomach hurts from too many beans.

"What can we do?" asked the priest. "I know—a bug! Feed him a bug to eat the beans."

What did she do? She caught a bug and hurried home. At home she said, "OPEN WIDE for some medicine!" What did she say?

☞ **Audience responded:** OPEN WIDE for some medicine!

Then he swallowed the bug that nibbled the beans. He smiled. AHHHH . . .

But all of a sudden, he went, "*Pah-koo pah-koo*" while crawling like a bug.

"Maaa!" cried the wife in dismay, and back she ran to the priest. "*Dohka, tasukete kudasai,*" she cried. (Which means, Sir, please help me. My husband's stomach hurts from too many bugs.)

Repeat after me, what did she say?

☞ **Audience responds:** *Dohka, tasukete kudasai.*

The priest tried to think, then said, "I KNOW! Feed him a frog to eat the bug."

The kind wife searched here and there, *ah-chee ko-chee*, to find the perfect frog. At last, she caught one and ran to her husband. "Open wide," she cried as he swallowed the frog that bit the bug that nibbled the beans. And he smiled. "Ahhhhh!"

What did her husband say?

☞ **Audience responds:** Ahhhhh!

But all of a sudden, he went, *pe-yown pe-yown*, jumping just like a frog. Back in the temple she begged for help. "Now he hops like a frog, what can I do?"

The priest scratched his head then said, "I know . . . a snake. Feed him a snake to eat the frog."

So the wife chased a snake and brought it home. In went the snake that swallowed the frog that bit the bug that nibbled the beans.

The husband smiled, then suddenly slithered, *sue-rue sue-rue,* just like a snake.

"Maaa," sighed the poor woman and returned to the temple.

What did she say?

☞ **Audience responds:** Maaa.

"Well," said the priest, "how about a bird?" Soon, she fed a bird to her husband. The bird ate the snake that swallowed the frog that bit the bug that nibbled the beans.

BUT, all too soon, her husband flapped his arms, *bah-sa bah-sa*, flying like a bird.

Back to the temple she ran, to find another plan. The priest shook his head, then said, "Find a hunter to hit the bird!" So she did. And she pushed him inside her husband. With a gulp, he swallowed the hunter

that hit the bird

that ate the snake

that swallowed the frog

that bit the bug

that nibbled the beans.

Her husband grinned in relief. But then . . . *BAHN BAHN*! He started to march just like a hunter.

Back at the temple, the wife begged for help. The priest sighed, then tried for one more idea.

At last, he said, "AN ONI! Find a big oni to scare the hunter." (An *oni* is a popular character in Japanese folk lore, usually translated as "ogre." He is often red in color, but blue and green *oni* are also found, and is usually fierce, with his big teeth and eyes.)

But where could she find an *oni*? She looked here and there, *achi kochi*, and at last saw a huge red *oni* in a cave, holding his big stick. She quickly pulled him to her house and somehow stuffed him into her husband, big stick and all. And the *oni* scared the hunter

that hit the bird

that ate the snake

that swallowed the frog

that bit the bug

that nibbled the beans.

BUT suddenly the husband choked on the stick that stuck out of his mouth. At once the woman raced to tell the priest.

"I don't believe it," said the priest. "Well, how about beans?

To make the *oni* go, throw these beans and call out, *ONI WA SOTO! ONI WA SOTO!*"

which means "*Oni,* go out! *Oni,* go out!" Back home she hurried, happily holding the beans from the priest.

"Oni wa soto! Oni wa soto!" she called out as beans flew through the air.

What did she say?

Audience responds: Oni wa soto! Oni wa soto!

Suddenly, with a great shout, the *oni* rushed out, taking the hunter, the bird, the snake, the frog, the bug, and the beans with him.

"Ahhhhh," said the husband happily. He patted his empty stomach and smiled.

His wife smiled, too.

But all of a sudden he said, "How strange . . . I'm feeling a little hungry right now. . . ."

What did he say?

➥ **Audience responds:** How strange . . . I'm feeling a little hungry right now. . . .

So he reached for the bean cake, bean paste, and bean soup, too. And what happened next, you really don't want to know. Oh-wah-ree. That is all.

ABOUT THE STORY

I heard it first from a marvelous teller in Fukushima in northern Japan. Yokoyama Sachiko is a good friend, too, who tells with great humor and animation. When she told it to a folktale group one day, she introduced it as a legend about the origin of the *Setsubon* holiday practice of throwing beans. But she smiled as she said that, for the origins of the festival are deeper indeed.

This story is fun to tell with its repetition and humor and for the great Japanese sounding-words it shares.

RELATED BOOKS

1. *BEST-LOVED CHILDREN'S SONGS FROM JAPAN* by Yoko Imoto (Heian International, 1997). Lovely collection of songs if you'd like to share a song after telling the tale.

2. *THE YANAGITA KUNIO GUIDE TO THE JAPANESE FOLK TALE* by Fanny Hagin Mayer, editor (Indiana University Press, 1986). A fine sourcebook, in English, of Japanese folktales collected last century, with notes on tale types and regional variants.

3. *AN ILLUSTRATED DICTIONARY OF JAPANESE ONOMATOPEIC EXPRESSION* by Taro Gomi (Japan Times, 1989). Great fun and useful learning are bundled together in this clever dictionary.

4. *JAPANESE CHILDREN'S FAVORITE STORIES* by Florence Sakade, editor. (Tuttle Publishing, 2003). The latest edition of this classic, with a useful collection of stories.

5. *HOW MY PARENTS LEARNED TO EAT* by Ina Friedman (Houghton Mifflin, 1984). A Japanese woman marries an American sailor. Both want to eat in the same way they always have. Eventually, compromise is reached.

ACTIVITIES

The favorite activity for the holiday is to throw beans and *oni* masks. For a lovely model of an *oni* mask, visit: http://www.canon.co.uk/paperart/celebrations/MaskOgre.asp.

Each child can make a mask, with colored paper and markers, to take home later. Or you can make one large mask and hang it on the wall. Then distribute dry or roasted beans to the children and have them all throw the beans at the mask, while calling out, "*Oni* wa soto, fuku wa uchi" (Onee wah soh toh, Foo koo wah oo chee). "*Oni* out, happiness in."

HOLIDAY BACKGROUND INFORMATION

Today the most common activity for *Setsubon* is to throw roasted beans in homes, temples, and shrines while calling out, "*Oni wa soto, fuku wa uchi.*"

Many temples and shrines have elaborate *Setsubon* ceremonies, with people gathering as the priests toss beans over the crowds of the faithful. In homes, one man scatters the beans at the entrance of each room, while repeating the words to chase out the bad and bring in the good. Afterward, everyone eats as many beans as his age that day, for the best of fortune. Some children also wear *oni* masks and happily shower beans on each other.

BIOGRAPHY

Since 1986, storyteller Cathy Spagnoli has given storytelling programs and workshops to thousands of listeners throughout Asia and the United States. Cathy has researched Asian storytelling traditions for three decades, with support from the Japan Foundation, the Korea Foundation, the Indian Ministry of Culture, and others. Funding from the U.S. State Department, the United States Information Agency and varied Asian organizations supports her numerous storytelling workshops in South, Southeast, and East Asia. Cathy has written sixteen books on Asian tales and storytelling techniques; many of them are translated into various Asian languages. Her stories are also on several cassette tapes, on a new bilingual storytelling tape with Japanese teller Honda Kazu, in more than forty articles in journals and anthologies, and in the *Encyclopedia of Modern Asia*. At present, Cathy is also teaching storytelling at Hannam University in South Korea. She and her husband, sculptor Paramasivam, built their own home on Vashon Island near Seattle. They also spend time in their second home, Cholamandal Artists' Village, South India.

CONTACT

Cathy Spagnoli
27225 97th Avenue SW
Vashon, WA 98070
E-mail: cathy.spagnoli@gmail.com
www.cathyspagnoli.com

DIANE WOLKSTEIN

Saint Valentine's Day or Valentine's Day is celebrated on February 14 in the United States, Europe, some Middle Eastern countries, Africa, Brazil, Colombia, Japan and South Korea.

White Wave

INTRODUCTION

White Wave is a Taoist story of love and caring in the human, animal, plant, mineral, and spirit realms. A boy is drawn to a stone, which turns out to be a snail. He feeds and cares for the snail and in return the spirit of the snail (the Moon Goddess, White Wave) cares for him, offering him tasty food and lovely flowers. By telling the story and by listening to the story, we participate in life's transitory nature—stones crumble, people die—as well as its eternal aspects—love, memory, and story.

STORY SCRIPT

In the hills of southern China, there once stood a shrine. It was made of stones—beautiful white, pink, and gray stones—and was built as a house for a goddess.

What colors are the stones? Do you recall?

> Wait for reply. Audience responds with names of colors.

Now the stones lie scattered on the hillside. If you, who are listening, should happen to find one, remember this story . . . of the stones, the shrine, and the Goddess, White Wave. (Long pause.)

Long ago, in the time of mysteries, a young man was walking home in the evening. He walked slowly, for he was not eager to return to his house. His parents had died two years before. He was too poor to marry and too shy to speak with a girl.

As he passed a small forest, he saw a stone gleaming in the moonlight, a beautiful white stone.

> Bend over and mime the picking up and the holding of the stone. Turn the stone this way and that, considering.

It wasn't white. It was every color in the rainbow. And when he held it in his hands, he saw it wasn't a stone at all, but a shell, a moon shell. And what was the most wonderful good fortune—there was a snail in it and the snail was alive!

He carried the moon shell gently home and placed it in an earthenware jar. Then, before fixing his own dinner, he gathered fresh leaves for the snail.

The next morning the first thing he did was to look in the jar. The leaves were gone. The snail had eaten them. He picked four more leaves and went off to the fields to work.

When he came home that evening, he found his dinner waiting for him on the table—a bowl of cooked rice, steamed vegetables, and a cup of hot tea.

He looked around the room. No one was there. He went to the door and looked out into the night. No one. Still he left the door open, hoping that whoever had prepared his dinner might join him.

The next evening his dinner was again waiting for him—and this time there was a branch of wild peach set in a vase on the table.

The young man asked in the village if strangers had arrived. No one knew of any.

Every morning he left leaves for his snail. Every evening his dinner was waiting, and always there was a wild flower in the vase.

> Look from side to side, puzzled; then speak to audience in a whisper.
> Say: "Who can it be? Who is giving me this gift? Who cares for me? Who could it be? Can you guess?"
> If answers come, respond in a way that keeps the story in suspense.

Could it be a friend I don't remember?

One morning he woke up earlier than usual and started off as if he were going to the fields. Instead he circled back to the house and stood outside the window, listening. It was quiet. Then, as the first light of the day touched the earth, he heard a sound. He looked inside the window.

> Remember where you placed the window in your imagination and look at that place.

When he looked inside, he saw rising from the jar, a tiny white hand. It rose higher and higher as a girl's head began to appear. Then a second hand came up and touched her heart. Then both hands covered her face and rose slowly above her head.

As she moved, her hands, which were still above her head, moved slowly from side to side. She was pure light. Her dress was made of silk. At every movement, her dress rippled, changing from silver to white to gold. Wherever she stepped in the room, the room shone.

He knew, though no one had told him, that she was a moon goddess. And he knew, though no one had told him, that he must never try to touch her.

> On the words "he knew," he let both hands go to his heart. He remained motionless.

The next morning before he went to work, he watched her—and the next morning and the next.

From the time she came to live with him, his loneliness disappeared. He skipped to the fields in the morning and walked quickly home in the evening. His dinner was always waiting. The house was shining. The air was sweet. And his heart was full.

Many days passed. Then one morning, as he watched her sweep the floor, and as he watched her long black hair fall across her face, a great longing came upon him. He wanted to touch her hair. His desire burst upon him so strongly and quickly that he forgot what he knew. He opened the door and rushed into the room.

↳ Standing still, move your torso forward from your hips and then stop abruptly.

"Do not move," she said. "Who are you?" he asked. "I am White Wave, the moon goddess. But now I must leave you, for you have forgotten what you knew."

"No! No!" he cried.

"Good farmer," said she, "if you can hold yourself still and count for me, I will leave you a gift. Let me hear you count. Count to five."

"One," he whispered.

↳ Invite audience, by nodding your head and mouthing the number, to repeat the word.
Audience responds: One.

She crossed in front of him and walked toward the open door. "I leave you my shell," she said. "Two," said he softly.

↳ Invite audience, by nodding your head and mouthing the number, to repeat the word.
Audience responds: Two.

"Three," he said more strongly.

↳ Invite audience, by nodding your head and mouthing the number, to repeat the word.
Audience responds: Three.

"If you are ever in need, call me by my name, White Wave, and I will come to you." "Four," said he.

↳ Invite audience, by nodding your head and mouthing the number, to repeat the word.
Audience responds: Four.

There was a streak of lightening and a great roll of thunder. He shouted above it . . . . "Five!"

↳ Invite audience, by nodding your head and mouthing the number, to repeat the word.
Audience responds: Five!

A huge wave came and swept the goddess into the air. He ran outside. The rain poured down so fast, he could not see her. He stood in the rain a long time, then he went back into the house. The snail shell was there. No living creature was inside.

He went to the fields, but he did not think of his work. He thought only of White Wave and how to bring her back. As he was wandering across the fields, his foot hit a stone. He bent over to look at the stone.

↳ Bend over and mime the picking up and the holding of the stone. Turn the stone this way and that way, considering.

As he held the shell, he knew what he would do. He would build a shrine for White Wave—a beautiful house in which she might live peacefully. He spent more time choosing the stones for her—beautiful white, pink and gray stones—than working in the fields.

What colors were the stones he chose?

> 👉 Audience names the colors. Remember they were white, pink and gray.

When the harvest came, it was very small. He ate the little there was. He ate the supplies he had stored, and after that, he lived on berries and wild grass.

The evening that the shrine was complete, he was so weak with hunger, he could barely walk. He stumbled into his house and tripped over the earthenware jar. The shell fell out. Quickly he picked it up, and as he held it, he remembered the words of the goddess.

> 👉 Whisper to audience: "Do you remember her words? Do you remember what she said? 'If you are ever in great need, call me by my name, White Wave . . . .' "

He held the shell in front of him. Then he raised it in the air. With his last strength he cried out: *White Wave, I need you.*

> 👉 Hold your hands in front of you and above you head as if you are holding a shell.

Slowly he turned the shell toward him, and a wave of rice, gleaming white rice, cascaded out of the shell and onto the floor.

> 👉 With the word, "cascaded," let your hands slowly open and slowly descend—in a triangular form—to your side.

The rice was solid and firm. It was enough to last him until the next harvest.

He never again called her name, for he was never again in great need. With the flowing of the rice, a new strength came to him. He worked hard in the fields. The rice grew. The vegetables flourished. He married and had children. But he did not forget White Wave.

He told his wife about her, and when his children were old enough, he told them the story of White Wave. The children liked to hold the shell in their hands as they listened to the story.

The shrine stood on a hill above their house. The children often went there in the early morning and evening, hoping to see White Wave. They never did.

When the old man died, the shell was lost. In time, the shrine, too, disappeared. All that remained was the story.

But that is how it is with all of us. When we die, all that remains is the story. And especially with lovers, when they are gone, what remains is the story, the story of their love.

ABOUT THE STORY

This version is adapted from the books, *WHITE WAVE: A Chinese Tale*, © Diane Wolkstein, Illustrated by Ed Young (Thomas Y. Crowell, 1979), and *WHITE WAVE: A Chinese Tale* (Harcourt, 1996) © Diane Wolkstein.

HOLIDAY BACKGROUND INFORMATION

From http://en.wikipedia.org/wiki/Valentine'sDay:

Saint Valentine's Day or Valentine's Day (February 14), is the traditional day on which lovers express their love for each other by sending Valentine's cards or candy. It is very common to present flowers on Valentine's Day. The holiday is named after two men, both Christian martyrs among the numerous Early Christian martyrs named Valentine. The day became associated with romantic love in the circle of Geoffrey Chaucer in the High Middle Ages, when the tradition of courtly love flourished.

The day is most closely associated with the mutual exchange of love notes in the form of "valentines." Modern Valentine symbols included the heart-shaped outline and the figure of the winged Cupid. Since the nineteenth century, handwritten notes have largely given way to mass-produced greeting cards. The mid-nineteenth century Valentine's Day trade was a harbinger of further commercialized holidays in the United States to follow. The U.S. Greeting Card Association estimates that approximately one billion valentines are sent each year worldwide, making the day the second largest card-sending holiday of the year behind Christmas. The association estimates that women purchase approximately 85 percent of all valentines.

BIOGRAPHY

Known as a "Storyteller's Storyteller," Diane gives worldwide performances at festivals, museums, and universities. Her recordings and twenty-three award-winning books have helped create and sustain the modern storytelling movement. Two of her most popular books for storytellers are *The Magic Orange Tree and Other Haitian Folktales* and *Inanna, Queen of Heaven and Earth*. Her latest book, *Treasures of the Heart: Holiday Stories that Reveal the Soul of Judaism,* is detailed in our "Bibliography of Holiday Books."

Diane teaches storytelling and gives workshops throughout the world on diversity and tolerance. Her most recent DVD is *A Storyteller's Story*, documenting Diane's forty years of storytelling. For further information about Diane: http://dianewolkstein.com.

CONTACT

Diane Wolkstein
10 Patchin Place
New York, NY 10011
www.dianewolkstein.com

Retold by

TERESA MILLER

Presidents' Day is observed in the United States on the third Monday in February.

The Little Loyalist

INTRODUCTION

The story that follows is a brief biography of Abraham Lincoln. If you can gauge approximately how many people will attend your performance, have this copied for distribution as indicated in the story. If time is an issue, you may wish to start from "The Story Begins Here."

STORY SCRIPT

Enter into my imagination. I'm looking at a time machine. What do you suppose we need to get it going? What's the first thing we do?

> Get suggestions from audience.

Here's a hint: What's the first thing you do when you get into *any* machine?

Sure, we get into it! Sit at the controls, right? What is the next step?

> No matter what you hear, say "that's possible" or "that might work." Never discourage replies by disdain for any answer.

So, you're now inside the machine. Well, I see dials and a lever and a CLOCK, which I imagine will take us to the time we would like to be in. Since this story concerns Abraham Lincoln, what year would you suggest we set the clock *for*?

> Some audience members will toss out dates. Look for anything between 1846 and 1865.

What do you think was the most famous event in Lincoln's time? Here's a hint: remember, he was the sixteenth president of the United States.

> If nobody says, "Maybe the Civil War?" toss out hints. Does the word "war" mean anything?

THE CIVIL WAR, yes! The story takes place during the Civil War. Set your dials, pull the lever of your time machine—Let's GO!

> If nobody moves, say, "You're not coming along? Come on, we'll miss you if you don't!"

⮡ Raise your right hand, pull down the lever, and watch the chronograph spin backwards in time.

⮡ Encourage the audience to join in the countdown from 1867 to 1862.

I'll start—1950, 1900, 1875, 1867: Count down with me starting from 1866: 1866, 1865, 1864, 1863. Oh look, it stops on 1862.

⮡ The Story Begins Here.

We are in the state of Maryland, near Washington, D.C. We are in the living room of a farmhouse. You see a fireplace holding down a roaring fire, making the room warm and comfy.

An army man, Major Butler, grins down at his young daughter, who is pirouetting in her first hooped skirt. He begins to sing. (Sings a cappella.)

> *Now crinoline is all the rage*
>
> *with ladies of whatever age*
>
> *a petticoat made like a cage*
>
> *Such a ridiculous fashion!*
>
> *'Tis formed of hoops and bars of steel*
>
> *and worn by girls to be genteel,*
>
> *or if they've figures to conceal.*
>
> *Such a ridiculous fashion!*

Would you like to sing it with me? It's fun—Want to try it? Let's sing it together.

⮡ See music at the end of the story.

⮡ **Audience responds:**
Now crinoline is all the rage
with ladies of whatever age
a petticoat made like a cage
Such a ridiculous fashion!
'Tis formed of hoops and bars of steel
and worn by girls to be genteel,
or if they've figures to conceal.
Such a ridiculous fashion!

The major's twelve year-old daughter laughed. "It's a wonderful birthday present. Thank you! Father, isn't it beautiful? I'm so happy! A dress with real hoops!"

Smiling, her father said, "Well, it does make you look like a pretty little barrel. And I think you'll be even happier when you come with me to Washington today."

"Father!" She said excitedly, "Are you to see the president again?" She was not sure whether to be glad or sad when he said "yes." It might mean another farewell. When he first joined the Union Army, he had returned wounded and had not fully recovered.

They set out right after breakfast with horse and buggy. The Executive Mansion was a good half-day's drive from their farm. Further down the road, her father frowned as they passed a larger farm. Not all

Maryland men joined the Union. Sons of their neighbors, the Kimballs—good friends once—had chosen to join the Confederate Army. Suddenly, their friends had become enemies.

When they reached the White House, Jessica, as always, was astonished at how quickly they were summoned to the president's office as soon as her father's name was uttered. She had only a glimpse of a tall, tall man with a tired face who came to the door, shook her father's hand, and drew him right inside his private office. Jessica waited outside for her father's return.

No sooner had they settled back in the buggy to ride home than Major Butler announced, "I must leave very early in the morning. If anyone comes to inquire about my health, say I'm well again and back in service. It will be true. I shall return home in a month or two."

Early next morning, Jessica was surprised to find her father already up and dressed—not in his handsome uniform, but in old work clothes. He hugged her, embraced his wife, and left with a wicker basket on his arm that contained some jars from Mrs. Butler's pantry. Then, joking about having gone into the business of knocking on doors to sell the jams and jellies, he left.

All that day, Mrs. Butler was fearful. She well knew her husband's real mission. He was a spy. She knew spying was much more dangerous than soldiering. She also knew that her husband would do anything for President Lincoln.

Three months went by. Then four, then five. Wife and daughter never spoke of their fears but began to wonder if Major Butler would ever return. Was he lying dead somewhere? However, they spoke only comforting words to each other.

One morning, Mrs. Butler went to bring eggs to a neighbor. Jessica was in the kitchen beginning to fix breakfast. She heard the door open, turned to see her father stumble as he entered. "Quick! Hide these! They're for the president." He handed her some papers. Speaking with a gasp, he fell into the nearest chair.

She tossed the papers onto the table and cried out, "Father! You're hurt!" He shook his head from left to right, caught his breath enough to utter, "Water!" Then he gulped some water down before speaking, much faster than usual.

"On my way back North, I ran across Rob Kimball, who recognized me. He's on my trail. "Quickly, hide those papers, they're maps."

"Surely, Rob would not come into our house. It's enemy territory!"

"Hurry, child. They would go anywhere to get those charts! Besides, he's in disguise, and I am without a pistol."

Jessica disappeared into her bedroom, returning a few minutes later wearing her birthday dress with its hoops flaring. She grabbed a shawl, tied bonnet ribbons under her chin, and said firmly, "Father, I'm taking the papers to the president myself." Major Butler raised his hand in protest, but Jessica merely laughed. "Don't worry, they're well hidden."

As she led her horse out to the road, she met Rob Kimball with another soldier. Rob shouted, "Search that child! She's the daughter of the man we're after!"

Jessica blazed out, "You ought to be ashamed of yourself, Rob Kimball. Don't you dare!" She remembered when they went wading together, only a few years back.

Embarrassed, his face red, Rob finally came up with, "I'll take you home and have mom search you." Turning to his companion, he said "You go up and search Butler's house."

Mrs. Kimball's face reflected such joy at seeing her son again that Jessica was glad for her, although it hurt that the woman with whom her mother had shared pies and cakes actually did search her.

Mrs. Kimball emptied the contents of Jessica's drawstring purse. She examined the sleeves of her dress. She felt inside the bodice and even shook the crinoline skirts.

It's hard to say which of them was more relieved when she discovered nothing.

Rob apologized as he helped Jessica back into the buggy. "Jessica, I'm sorry we had to do this, and I still like you, even if you are on the wrong side."

"It's you who is on the wrong side!" said Jessica sharply, as she rode away.

She sang aloud as she continued along, the same song used by men who answered the president's call for volunteers.

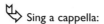 Sing a cappella:

We are coming, we are coming,
Our Union to restore.
We are coming, Father Abr'am,
with three hundred thousand more.
We are coming, Father Abr'am,
with three hundred thousand more.

It helped to sing the hearty words out loud as she rode along. She pretended lots of people were singing with her. Want to sing this with me?

 Audience responds:
We are coming, we are coming,
Our Union to restore.
We are coming, Father Abr'am,
with three hundred thousand more.
We are coming, Father Abr'am,
with three hundred thousand more.

Finally—Washington, D.C.

Once the doorman heard she had something from Major Butler for the president, he lost no time taking her to Mr. Lincoln. Long legs approached. Deep-set expressive eyes with dark circles around them smiled down on her. "Now what can I do for you, pretty lady?"

Inside his office, Jessica stammered, "If you don't mind, sir, will you please look the other way for a minute?" His smile deepened as he obliged. She finally called, "Ready!" and placed in his hands several papers, needle-pricked around the edges, otherwise undamaged.

"They're from my father, from Major Butler." Mr. Lincoln's smile broadened before turning to his desk with the papers. When he looked up again, he said, "I don't suppose you remember what day this is."

"Why, yes, it's February twelfth."

"It's my birthday, and you have given me the nicest, the best birthday present I could have asked for. These charts you brought me will be of great help to our generals and may even shorten this terrible war. But tell me, how does it happen they were delivered by you?"

Jessica was surprised to find herself completely at ease talking to this great man. It was like talking with her father. She explained the situation.

He asked, "One thing you haven't told me. How did you manage to conceal the papers when you were searched?" Jessica blushed, hesitated, then said, "I sewed the papers with long loose stitches to the strips of crinoline between the steel bands of my hoops, that's all. The rustle of the crinoline concealed the rustle of the papers."

A very happy Loyalist rode home as fast as she could, where she learned that her father had been captured earlier and held prisoner, but he eventually escaped to complete his mission. That was why he was so late getting back home.

With a few hours' rest, Major Butler became his old teasing self again. "For once, I'll admit," he said, "your little barrel came in handy." He began to sing again:

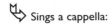 Sings a cappella:

Now crinoline is all the rage
With ladies of whatever age.
'Tis formed of hoops and bars of steel.

Jessica shushed him by saying, "Now you can't make fun of those hoops after what they've done!"

"Can't promise that!" His laughing voice was tender as he pulled his daughter close for a long hug and a few kisses. "I'm sure of one thing, however, I'm real proud of the little Loyalist inside them!"

 Optional ending:

That's the end of the story. Now—on your own, let's see you set the dials on your time machine to get home.

The Crinoline Song

Transcibed Courtesy of The Guitar Lab, Evansville IN 47715

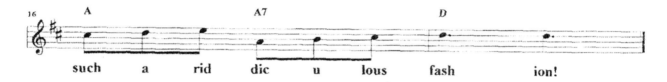

Words by James Sloan Gibbons; Music by L. O. Emerson

52

We Are Coming, Father Abr'am

Transcribed Courtesy of The Guitar Lab. Evansville IN 47715

Words by Lionel Monckton; Music: Unknown

ABOUT THE STORY

The original title was "A Patriot in Hoops." Written by Frances Cavanah, it appeared in a book entitled *HOLIDAY ROUNDUP*, selections by Lucile Pannell and Frances Cavanah. Published in 1950, Philadelphia, Macrae Smith Co.

The original story was given to me in 1997 by Dr. Daniel Bassuk, then president of the "Association of Lincoln Presenters." Dr. Dan Bassuk was the epitome of Lincoln storytellers for schoolchildren everywhere, usually bearded and dressed in a black frock coat and stovepipe hat. I was so sorry to hear of his death in 2005. See tribute to Dan Bassuk (1939–2005) at http://www.lincolnpresenters.org/DBTribute.htm.

RELATED STORIES

1. *ABE LINCOLN'S HAT* by Martha Brenner, illustrated by Donald Cook (Random House, 1994). For grades 1–3.

2. *ABE LINCOLN AND THE MUDDY PIG* by Stephen Krensky, illustrated Gershom Griffith (Simon & Schuster Children's Publishing Division, 2002). Also juvenile.

3. *A BOOK FOR ABE* by Virginia Frances Voight, illustrated by Jacqueline Tomes (Prentice-Hall International, 1963).

4. *TRUE STORIES ABOUT ABRAHAM LINCOLN* by Ruth Belov Gross, illustrated by Jill Kastner (Lothrop, Lee & Shepard Books, 1973).

BOOKS ON LINCOLN

NOTE: *Thousands* of Lincoln books exist that cover all aspects of this remarkable man's life, including biographies, discussions, his own writings, books about specific episodes, books of pictures. Check your library's computer or use the Internet. Here are six books recommended by Dr. Bassuk:

1. *ABRAHAM LINCOLN* by Ingri and Edgar Pasin D'Aulaire (Doubleday, 1957, republished by Dell, 1979). Flowing text and distinguished color lithographs portray a very human man from the day he toddled after his father's plow, to the boy walking through the woods to a distant sound. Grades 2–6.

2. *THE STORY OF THE GETTYSBURG ADDRESS* by Kenneth Richards, illustrated by Tom Dunnigham (Children's Press, 1969). Grades 4–7.

3. *AMERICA'S ABRAHAM LINCOLN* by May McNeer, illustrated by Lynd Ward (Houghton Mifflin, 1957). This discerning biography tells of Lincoln's growth in spiritual strength and wisdom throughout his entire life.

4. *LINCOLN: A PHOTOBIOGRAPHY* by Russel Freedman (Clarion Books, Ticknor & Fields, Houghton Mifflin, 1987). Dozens of carefully chosen photographs and prints highlight research. The text tells how Lincoln stood out in a crowd for his height. Describes his wit and rollicking humor. Grades 4 and up.

5. *HONEST ABE*. An oversized picture book with paintings by Malcah Zeldis, words by Edith Kunhardt (Greenwillow Books, 1993). Unusual paintings and simple words weave the major events in Lincoln's life.

6. *ABE LINCOLN GROWS UP* by Carl Sandburg. This text consists of the first twenty-seven chapters of his original two-volume biography, *ABRAHAM LINCOLN: THE PRAIRIE YEARS* (Harcourt, Brace & World, 1928). Brings alive the time of Lincoln's grandfather, for whom he was named, through his birth, various homes, and final departure from his family to begin life in New Salem, Illinois.

ACTIVITIES FOR FAMILY, SCHOOL, OR GROUP

1. Ask your group such questions as:

    • If you grew up with Abraham Lincoln, what would you remember most?

    • Where would you have lived?

    • Where would people get their food?

    • What would you have done for fun?

    • What were the biggest dangers on the frontier?

    • What was Springfield, Illinois, like?

2. Check local schools and libraries to find out if special events open to the public are available for Presidents' Day.

3. There are 150 living "Lincolns" who tour the nation, giving presentations that educate, entertain, and inspire. Consult, http://www.lincolnpresenters.org/ for more information.

4. If possible, visit any of the following locations (each visit is an education in itself).

In Kentucky

The Kentucky Heritage Council
300 Washington Street, Frankfort, KY 40601
Tel: (501) 564-7004

Abraham Lincoln's Birthplace National Historic Site
2995 Lincoln Farm Road, Hodgenville, KY 42748
Tel: (270) 358-3137

Lincoln's Boyhood Home
7 miles NE of Hodgenville, Kentucky, on U.S. 31 E in Knob Creek
Tel: (270) 358-3137

NOTE: The Lincoln Heritage Trail Auto Tour connects the sites commemorating Lincoln in Kentucky, Indiana, and Illinois. See http://en.wikipedia.org/wiki/Lincoln_Heritage_Trail.

The National Park Foundation
1101 17th Street, N.W., Suite 1102
Washington, DC 20036
Tel: (202) 354- 6460

In Indiana

Superintendent
Lincoln Boyhood National Memorial and Lincoln State Park
P.O. Box 1816, Lincoln City, IN 47522
Tel: (812) 937-4541

The Lincoln Museum
Curator
200 East Berry, P.O. Box 7838
Fort Wayne, IN 46801-7638
Tel: (219) 455-3864

NOTE: Mail-order catalogue with full-color photos of historic events may be ordered from James Townsend & Sons, based in Pierceton, Indiana. See www.jastown.com.

In Illinois

Lincoln's New Salem State Historic Site
15588 History Lane
Petersburg, IL 62675
(217) 632-4000

Lincoln Home National Historic Site
413 South Eighth Street
Springfield, IL 62701-1905
Tel: (217) 492-4241

Lincoln-Herndon Law Offices (The Old State Capitol Building restored)
Sixth and Adam Streets
Springfield, IL 62347
Tel: (217) 782-2717

Lincoln's Tomb State Historic Site
Superintendent, Oak Ridge Cemetery
Springfield, IL 61548
Tel: (217) 782-2717

In Pennsylvania

Superintendant
Gettysburg National Military Park
97 Taneytown Road
Gettysburg, PA 17325
Tel: (717) 334-1124

In Washington, D.C.

Ford's Theatre National Historic Site
Ford's Theatre
511 10th Street, N.W.
Washington, DC 20004
Tel: (202) 426-6841

BACKGROUND INFORMATION

Until 1971, both February 12 and February 22 were observed as federal public holidays to honor the birthdays of Abraham Lincoln (February 12) and George Washington (February 22). In 1971, President Richard Nixon proclaimed one single federal public holiday, Presidents' Day, to be observed on the third Monday of February, honoring all past presidents of the United States of America. For more information about Presidents Washington and Lincoln, consult: http://homepages.rootsweb.com/~maggieoh/Pd/prindex.html.

For a list of all the presidents of the United States, consult http://en.wikipedia.org/wiki/List_of_U.S._Presidents. Choose the president who appeals most to you. What do you remember most about him? For example, if you are talking about President George Washington (served 1789–1797), do you think it is myth or true that he actually told a lie when asked if he cut down the cherry tree? Or you might discuss housing at that time—What was the furniture like, what kind of clothes did people wear, and so forth.

No matter which president you would like to learn about, living or dead, any visit to a museum or library in his honor is an education in itself.

Now let's talk about Lincoln:

At six feet four inches, always wearing a tall stovepipe hat (his favorite "file" for papers), Abraham Lincoln stood out physically wherever he went. Named after his pioneering grandfather, our sixteenth president was born on February 12, 1809, in a log cabin reconstructed in Hodgenville, Kentucky.

As a young man, Lincoln's incredible physique allowed him to fell mighty trees, clear land for farming, help build log cabins, become a powerful wrestler, build flatboats, navigate rivers, and beat any fighter when necessary.

Because both parents were illiterate, he and his sister learned only their numbers from one to ten and a smattering of reading, spelling, and writing during their early childhood in Kentucky. They later attended what was called "a blab school" because, in one room, pupils of all ages uttered their lessons aloud in unison. But Lincoln continued to study on his own, in every spare moment. He learned public speaking from a book and the rudiments of grammar from another. He also studied mathematics and geometry, two subjects he enjoyed.

At age twenty-two, he went to New Salem because he had been promised a job there. In his own words, he was "friendless, uneducated, penniless." But he had such a gift for telling stories and jokes that he made friends easily. The schoolmaster, Mentor Graham, liked him so much that he taught him correct English grammar and loaned him books, which Lincoln devoured omniverously. Lincoln also taught himself surveying, later using the knowledge as the assistant surveyor for the county.

The nickname "Honest Abe" came about early because, as a clerk in New Salem, he walked three miles to repay a woman who had given him six and a quarter cents too much in change. His well-known honesty received a severe test later on, which he passed with flying colors. When a partner died, leaving bills totaling $1,100 (a fortune Lincoln called "the National Debt"), he worked all sorts of odd jobs to clear himself. It took fifteen years, but he paid off every cent.

It was in Springfield, Illinois, that Lincoln began his law practice, married Ann Todd, was elected to the U.S. House of Representatives, and then was nominated for the presidency by the Republican Party. After he was elected, he moved to Washington, D.C., to live in the White House. Sadly, he was returned to Springfield in a casket after his assassination forty days into his second term. His wife and children are also buried in Springfield.

The Civil War began while Lincoln was in his first term. Lincoln signed the Emancipation Proclamation, which freed America's slaves. He has long been admired by those who knew of his rare character, his integrity, his sense of humor, and his never-failing empathy for the underdog. He established in 1864 "the last Thursday of November . . . as a day of Thanksgiving and praise to Almighty God, the beneficent Creator and Ruler of the Universe."

NOTE: Numerous organizations exist to keep our nation's history alive. Two related to Lincoln and the Civil war are the following: The Civil War Preservation Trust (www.civilwar.org), 1331 H Street, NW, Suite 1001, Washington, D.C. 20005; the Gettysburg Foundation, Post Office Box 3997, Gettysburg, PA 17325.

BIOGRAPHY

Teresa Miller, long-time storytelling activist and performer, has been writing "forever." With the assistance of Anne Pellowski, she edited *JOINING IN: An Anthology of Audience Participation Stories and How to Tell Them.* Available in many public libraries.

CONTACT

Teresa Miller
E-mail: mamat@insightbb.com

March

St. Patrick's Day celebrates Saint Patrick (circa 385–461), one of the patron saints of Ireland. It takes place internationally on March 17, the date on which Patrick is said to have died.

Saint Patrick and the Musical Leprechaun

INTRODUCTION

St. Patrick's Day is often celebrated in many countries by Irish and non-Irish people alike. These celebrations include parades, wearing shamrocks and green clothes, and eating green foods. In schools, stories about leprechauns are told around St. Patrick's Day because leprechauns are associated with Ireland. In Ireland, St. Patrick's Day is considered a Holy Day and a national holiday. However, for many people, it is a secular one; it is a time to have fun.

Before beginning the narration, I introduce myself and the story. I will often tell the title (unless it is a surprise at the end) and the author. I hold up the book (or mention the source) to show where I found the story. Sometimes I tell the group why I like this story so much.

NOTE: To prepare to tell this story, review story notes, tips for telling the story, and section on instruments at the end of the story.

STORY SCRIPT

Far across the sea in Ireland, where the fields of grass are as green as emeralds, there lived a group of little wee people. They were the leprechauns, the leather workers who lived under the tree roots and made shoes, belts, and aprons. But one leprechaun, Lonnae, was different. He heard sounds and rhythms everywhere; he heard rhythms in his hammering, in his breathing, and in the chatter of the animals, birds, and insects.

None of Lonnae's wee folk neighbors ever listened to the sounds of the world. They were too busy working, so they never knew the joys that sounds and rhythms could bring to a body while he worked. Sometimes Lonnae made up his own rhythms. Here is one of his rhythm-chants:

> Work, work
>
> Work, work
>
> Work is what we like to do.
>
> Work, work
>
> Work, work
>
> Work upon our little shoes.

Try it with me.

 The first time I say the word "work," I say it in a higher tone than the second "work." I do the same with the third word. I say the third "work" in a higher tone than the fourth word. Also show the audience how to keep the beat by pretending to hammer.
Work, work
Work, work
Work is what we like to do.
Work, work
Work, work
Work upon our little shoes.

One day, while working on his leather shoes in his underground workshop, Lonnae heard a new sound.

 Play a percussion instrument such as a temple block, a tone block or a wood block. Use a mallet to beat like the pecking of a woodpecker. Strike the block in four rapid strikes and repeat this three times. See section on "Instruments Used" at the end of the story for details.

Lonnae thought to himself, "Oooh, I wonder what's making that sound?" Then he stopped working and climbed up to see what it was.

 Mime climbing up a ladder and peeking up out of the underground workshop.

But when he reached the top and looked around, he saw nothing. Lonnae thought to himself, "Oh, I love that sound. I wonder what made it. Wait a minute! I'm a creative leprechaun. I design interesting shoes and belts. So I'll just picture what is making that sound."

And so Lonnae closed his eyes and began to picture what might have made that rhythm. What do you think Lonnae pictured in his mind?

 Ask the listeners to picture something that could make that sound. Then ask them to raise their hands to show they have an image in mind. Call on a listener to share an idea. Point to him or her.

 Listen and then repeat what the listener said, as if you are picturing it yourself. Then say: "You're right! Why, that is exactly the first thing he thought of!"

But then another picture popped into his mind's eye.

Play the instrument again and vary the rhythm. I use a horse hoof beat or another rhythm. Call on two or three listeners for ideas and each time reply: "You're right! That is the next thing Lonnae pictured in his mind!"

When the sound stopped, Lonnae went back to work, underground, way down under the roots of the big tree in his little workshop. He continued to make his own rhythms as he worked.

> Work, work
> Work, work
> Work is what we like to do.
> Work, work
> Work, work
> Work upon our little shoes.

Try it with me.

Audience responds with teller:
Work, work
Work, work
Work is what we like to do.
Work, work
Work, work
Work upon our little shoes.

All of a sudden he heard a different sound.

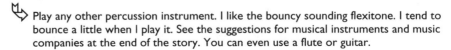

Play any other percussion instrument. I like the bouncy sounding flexitone. I tend to bounce a little when I play it. See the suggestions for musical instruments and music companies at the end of the story. You can even use a flute or guitar.

Lonnae said, "Oooooh! What could be making *that* sound?" He stopped working and climbed up to see what it was.

With your hands, mime climbing up a ladder and peeking up out of the underground workshop. Some listeners usually mime the hand movements with me, even without invitation. If not, invite them to mime with you.

But when Lonnae reached the top it was too dark to see what was making that bouncy sound. So he decided to use his imagination again. "I'll just picture what is making that sound."

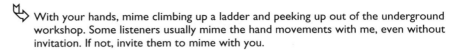

Ask listeners to picture something that could make that sound. Then ask them to raise their hands to show they have an image in mind. Images might include bouncing on a trampoline, or a jumping grasshopper. Call on one listener. Say: "What do you think Lonnae saw in his mind's eye?"

Listen to the audience member's idea and then repeat whatever was said, as if picturing it yourself.

Suggestions come forth.

Why, that is exactly what he thought of! But then another picture popped into his mind's eye.

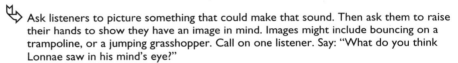

Call on two or three people for ideas and say: "That is exactly the next thing Lonnae pictured to be making that sound."

Then Lonnae got an idea. He ran over to his neighbor leprechauns' workshop and climbed down and said, "Come! Listen to the wonderful sounds, my friends."

His neighbors looked at him and frowned. They said, "Leave us alone, Lonnae, we're working! We have much too much work to do on the leather strips we're cutting and sewing and hammering!"

Lonnae was too excited to go back to work. So he went around inviting other leprechauns to come and listen to the wonderful sound. He went from workshop to workshop under big roots of the trees.

None of the other leprechauns wanted to be bothered with silly sounds. "Go away, Lonnae, we're working!" they all said.

Actually, the working leprechauns were quite annoyed at being bothered with all of Lonnae's interruptions. So Lonnae turned around to go back to his workbench underground. But as he was going back he heard a thumping rhythm.

> Play a drum with a ONE-two walking rhythm. Stress the first beat. Do this pattern several times.

Lonnae said, "Oooooh! I think I know what's making *that* sound. Probably, a person walking with a wooden staff or a *shillelagh* [pronounced "shi-lay-lee" with emphasis on "lay"].

Lonnae peeked around a tree and saw one of the large folk, a man walking along the very ground where Lonnae was standing. On his first footstep, the man's staff hit the ground hard. On the second footstep, it made an even louder sound. Lonnae liked this simple, clear rhythm.

> Play the drum again with the walking rhythm.

A cricket and a frog nearby were making soft rhythms that fit right into the man's rhythm.

> Snap fingers and slap thighs.

Lonnae was always afraid of large folk. He was afraid of being captured and having to give away his pot of gold. But he couldn't help himself. He started to tap his feet and nod his head to the rhythm. This man was none other than Saint Patrick himself, who had just finished ridding all of Ireland of the snakes! He heard the tapping of Lonnae's feet and saw the little man.

St. Patrick said to Lonnae, "Well, my little man, you seem to want to play along with us. Now, why don't you get your instrument and join our little band?" Lonnae heard the kindness in the big man's voice and wasn't afraid any longer. He looked sadly at St. Patrick and explained, "Oh, no sir. You see sir, I have no fine staff or sound makers like you and your friends here." He pointed to cricket and frog.

Saint Patrick said, "As my name is Patrick, for sure we can make some fine sound makers for you, my lad."

Well, sure as the sky is blue, Patrick kept his word. They set to work and made many instruments from the twigs, seeds, and pods which they found in the forest.

They had such fun making instruments that they made many more, more than what Lonnae had needed to play in the band with frog, cricket, and St. Patrick. Here, in fact, are the ones they made.

> Place in front of you any percussion instruments you can find and give their names. I use two real mimosa seedpods, a cabasa, an African drum, a rainstick, a rattle made with seeds, a maraca, etc.

Lonnae thanked St. Patrick for such wonderful instruments but said there were too many for him to play by himself.

At that point, cricket and frog called on their other friends to help.

Who would like to help Lonnae play the instruments?

> Look for people who can raise their hands quietly. Point to as many listeners as you have instruments.

64

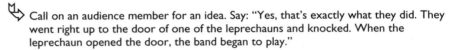
Each participant stands (or sits) in a row behind their instrument, facing the audience with the storyteller at one end.

Then St. Patrick began to lead the band. Everyone joined.

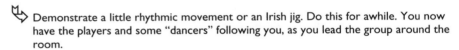
Play a strong rhythm on an Irish drum, or any drum. Invite the volunteers to join in, first the instruments with mallets and then the shakers.

Lonnae said to St. Patrick, "How can we have the other leprechaun workers hear our great sounds and rhythms?"

Ask listeners to give you an idea. Storyteller validates the idea by using it. For example, an idea might be to knock on the door of the leprechauns, or to go down and play with them.

What do you think frog and cricket decided?

Call on an audience member for an idea. Say: "Yes, that's exactly what they did. They went right up to the door of one of the leprechauns and knocked. When the leprechaun opened the door, the band began to play."

Well, wouldn't you know it? Their neighbor leprechauns began to get the rhythm in their heads, in their hands and in their feet. The band went from door to door.

Finally, lots of leprechauns were dancing to the rhythms of Lonnae, the frog, the cricket, and their friends.

Demonstrate a little rhythmic movement or an Irish jig. Do this for awhile. You now have the players and some "dancers" following you, as you lead the group around the room.

The leprechauns and the band played and played until they were exhausted!

Saint Patrick said, "Well, now, that was a flight of fancy for a wee bit of time but I must be getting back to my prayers before dark."

He left, with the band cheering him on. And that my friends, is how the leprechauns came to love music and dancing.

ABOUT THE STORY

In "St. Patrick and the Leprechaun," Lonnae is so taken by St. Patrick and his simple rhythms that he does not stay hidden. Perhaps he knew that St. Patrick never took a bribe from a noble person or any king, as did the Druid priests. Perhaps Lonnae felt safe with St. Patrick and knew he wouldn't try to steal his pot of gold.

The Druid priests had used the shamrock (a three leaf clover) for non-Christian purposes, but St. Patrick made the shamrock a symbol of Christian teaching. Many sources explain that St. Patrick utilized the shamrock to teach about the Holy Trinity: the Father, the Son, and the Holy Spirit.

TIPS FOR TELLING THIS STORY EFFECTIVELY

Storytellers often do not memorize exact word-for-word renditions of stories. I use memory aides, such as a picture map of the story. The picture map can be the whole story on one page, similar to a map but showing people as well as places, or a storyboard in the form of cartoon-like boxes with pictures and some words to help you remember events.

After retelling the story from the pictures, I often make a list outline of the story parts (or chunks) as another aide. Here is a bit of an example:

I do memorize the first sentence I decide to use. This might be the first sentence in the written story or one I make up. It can change with different audiences.

"Far across the sea in Ireland, where the fields of grass are as green as emeralds, there lived a little leprechaun." Next, I include words and phrases to help me remember items I want to retell, such as:

> —(Name) Lonnae
>
> —He was one of the wee little folk, looked somewhat like an elf
>
> —Leather worker, made shoes, belts, aprons
>
> —(Place) Underground, under the roots of big trees
>
> —(Action) He was different (heard sounds, hammering, breathing, animals above)
>
> —None of the other leprechauns heard the sounds
>
> —Lonnae made up rhythms about work

- After your list, memorize "work" chant

- Play a tone block, temple block, or claves

> —Lonnae was curious about what made that sound
>
> —He climbed up and up to see (mime climbing a ladder)
>
> —He looked out but couldn't see anyone making that sound

- Continue making your outline of points you want to remember to share. Be sure to use lots of paper so you can see "the chunks." When you have repeated events, you can number them. For example, Lonnae hears sounds three times (three big chunks). Within these, Lonnae repeats the actions of listening, climbing, looking, and imagining.

- Finally, after you make the picture map and outlines, retell your story to yourself and friends. See the pictures and the story structure, hear the voices and sounds, and feel the movements and feelings of the characters. By now, you know the story by heart. You do not have to tell it with the exact words; you can improvise. You might want to use some phrases several times, but if you forget them, you will have many others to use and you will not spoil the flow of the story. You might pause for a second or two and then see, hear, or feel what is happening and where you need to go next in your telling.

INSTRUMENTS USED

In this story, the teller uses several percussion instruments. Your local music store has Percussion Catalogs, which have pictures and descriptions, for example:

Temple block or tone block or claves: These instruments have a sharp sound, which can create many rhythms such as the rhythm of horses hooves, woodpeckers pecking, and water dripping.

Flexatone: A bouncy sounding instrument made of metal, which can be associated with jumping on a trampoline and animals that jump.

Kokiriko: Originated in Japan. I understand that the Japanese people brought it to Brazil where it became very popular. It is made of small wooden slates intricately strung together with string and creates a clicking sound like a rattlesnake, cricket, or duck sound.

Other instruments you might like to include:

- —*A log drum:* Usually a box with slits of different lengths in the top. Played with a mallet.
- —*A stir drum (or stir xylophone):* Consists of a circle on the bottom with wooden slats of different heights around it. Played with a mallet.
- —*A dried, hollow, gourd* with beads or shells or seedpods strung on the outside.
- —*A cabasa:* This is similar in concept to the gourd but made of metal with metal beads/ball bearings on the outside.
- —*A real mimosa seed pod* from a mimosa tree. When dried, the seeds inside rattle.
- —*A maraca,* a rain stick, or other container of seeds, pebbles, shells, etc.
- —*Any type of hand drum*
- —*A vibration,* gong, bell, chimes, or triangle. These are all metal and are capable of sustained tones.

You can find world percussion instruments as well as novelty (sound-effect) percussion instruments on the Internet. One Web site is http://www.westmusic.com, which has pictures of them.

RELATED BOOKS AND STORIES

1. *SHAMROCKS, HARPS, AND SHILLELAGHS* by Edna Barth (Houghton Mifflin, 2001). Gives information about the symbols of the St. Patrick's Day holiday.

2. *IRISH FOLK TALES* by Henry Glassie, editor (Pantheon, 1985). This is one of the most respected collections of Irish stories. Three stories include St. Patrick's work as a priest in Ireland and several others are about the wee folk called leprechaun, cluricaune, and other fairy folk. The larger human folk are no match for the wee folk. Tricks of word and deed make the humans blink or turn their heads. Thus, they allow the leprechauns to escape and the gold to remain in place.

3. *THE LAST SNAKE IN IRELAND: A Story about St. Patrick* by Sheila McGill-Callahan (Holiday House, 2004). A tall tale using St. Patrick's legend and the Loch Ness.

4. *FAIRY & FOLK TALES OF IRELAND* W. B. Yeats, editor (Macmillan, 1973). In the Appendix, Yeats describes leprechauns as clever little misers who wear red coats with buttons counting seven in two rows. They also wear hats with the brim turned up in two or three places. You can usually see them making shoes under a row of low-growing trees or bushes. They will avoid humans because humans try to capture leprechauns' pots of gold. They like to joke and play tricks. According to Yeats, leprechauns are said to be children of an ashamed fairy.

HOLIDAY BACKGROUND INFORMATION

St. Patrick was a priest who lived in the fourth century A.D. and into the fifth century. He was not Irish by birth but felt a calling to work in Ireland to convert people to his religion.

Druids were the non-Christian priests of the time. As prophets and sorcerers, they took money from the kings, and therefore they had the protection of various kings from any enemies. St. Patrick chose to not affiliate with any king but to convert children and townspeople to Christianity.

St. Patrick carried a staff with him while walking about converting people to his religion. Legend has it that one day he delivered a sermon standing on a hill with his staff by his side. This was the sermon that drove all the snakes out of Ireland. Evidently, St. Patrick made the snakes believe that Ireland was deleterious to their health and well-being. However, many people believe that Ireland never had snakes at that time, and so the story may have been a metaphor for St. Patrick driving out the "devils" and replacing them with Christianity. Almost all of Ireland was converted to Christianity, in large part because of St. Patrick's work.

Another legend claims that one of the serpents (snakes) would not leave Ireland. St. Patrick thought and thought about what to do. All of a sudden, he had an idea. St. Patrick made a box for the snake, but the gift was not well received because that snake thought it was just too tiny for the grand likes of him. St. Patrick insisted it was perfect and very well made at that, I might add. The snake decided to put an end to this foolish argument. He slithered inside the box to show how lacking in gracious space it was. St. Patrick was ready. He calmly reached out and gently closed the lid right over the box and proceeded down to the sea, where he threw it far and away, past the setting sun. That was the very last of the snakes to call Ireland their home!

For more information, consult:

History of St. Patrick's Day: www.festivefever.com/patrick/history.htm

History of St. Patrick's Day: www.wilstar.com/holidays/patrick.htm

From the History Channel: www.history.com/minisites/stpatricksday/

Crafts for after-school or in-school fun: www.enchantedlearning.com/crafts/stpatricks

BIOGRAPHY

Gail N. Herman, Ph.D., is a professional storyteller, a college teacher, author, and an educational consultant in the visual and performing arts as well as in the field of talent development. She teaches Cultural History through Storytelling for Lesley University; educational courses for Garrett College; and Storytelling, Mime & Movement, and Primary Enrichment for the University of Connecticut's CONFRATUTE, a summer conference/institute on enrichment learning. Gail also travels extensively, most recently to Estonia, Latvia, and Lithuania, where she performed and collected stories. She directs the Tall Tale Liars' Festival in Oakland, Maryland, and was the director of Coal Talk, an oral history project archived at Garrett College. For more information about Gail's activities: www.gcnet.net/storyteller, www.storynet.org, and www.alleganyarts.org.

CONTACT

Dr. Gail N. Herman
166 Lodge Circle
Swanton, MD 21561
E-mail: gnherman@gcnetmail.net

April

The Thai New Year is celebrated April 13–15 annually.

The Legend of Songkran, the Thai New Year

INTRODUCTION

The cosmology of Thailand includes many beings. *Thevada* [tewädä] can refer to animistic spirits living in trees or to heavenly beings. *Phra In* [Prä In] is the Hindu god Indra. In the Hindu heaven, there are sixteen heavens, each ruled by a different *prom,* or ruler. Thao Kabinlaphrom [Käbinläprom] is Brahma, who rules the highest heaven. The *rasi* [räsee] in the story is a concept describing a person's inner glow.

STORY SCRIPT

In this story, there is a riddle based on a concept for which there is no English word.

The riddle deals with the Thai word *rasi*. This is best described as a person's inner glow . . . his sense of beauty or well-being.

There was once a rich a man who longed for a son. One Songkran Day, the rich man decided to pray to the *thevada* (or spirit) which resided in a huge *sai* tree. The *thevada* felt pity on the man, who had riches but no son. So the *thevada* flew to heaven and approached Phra In (the Hindu god Indra). "Please, Phra In, this man deserves a son. He has prayed many times for this. Could you not send a son down to him?" So Phra In ordered one of the heavenly consorts, Thammaban, to go down and be born as a son to the rich man.

The rich man showered good things on his son. A house seven stories tall was built near the *sai* tree for Thammaban Kuman (Thammaban's son). There Thammaban grew and became wise. Listening to the birds singing in the branches of the *sai* tree, Thammaban Kuman soon learned the language of the birds. By the time he was seven years old, Thammaban Kuman was wise enough that people began to come to listen to his teachings.

Now in those days, most villagers worshiped Thao Kabinlaphrom. This was the god to whom they went for guidance. But now, more and more people were going instead to sit at the feet of young Thammaban Kuman. Thao Kabinlaphrom was angry at this imposter. He came down from heaven and challenged Thammaban Kuman to a contest.

"If you answer my three questions, I, Thao Kabinlaphrom, will cut off my own head. If you cannot solve the questions, then I will behead you, Thammaban Kuman."

Without waiting for an answer, Thao Kabinlaphrom posed his questions. "Thammaban Kuman, you know that a man's *rasi* is his inner glow.

In the morning, where is a man's *rasi*?

At noon, where is a man's *rasi*?

In the evening, where is a man's *rasi*?"

"Let me see if I understand the question," responded Thammaban Kuman.

In the morning, where is a man's *rasi?* Is that the question? [To audience:] "Tell me, is that the question?"

Audience responds: Yes.

At noon, where is a man's rasi? Is that the question?

Audience responds: Yes.

In the evening, where is a man's *rasi*? Is that the question?

Audience responds: Yes.

"Those are questions," said Thao Kabinlaphrom. "What is your answer?"

Thammaban Kuman spoke carefully. "Give me seven days to consider these questions. If I cannot answer by the seventh day, then, as you say, you may cut off my head."

For six days, Thammaban Kuman pondered these questions. But no answer came to him. On the seventh day, he sat down under the *sai* tree in despair. While he sat there, he suddenly became aware of a conversation going on up in the tree between two birds. It was a pair of eagles.

The eagle wife asked, "Husband, where will we go tomorrow to find food?"

Her husband answered, "No problem, tomorrow we can eat right here. Our food will be Thammaban Kuman."

The wife said, "Is Thammaban Kuman to die tomorrow?"

"Definitely," said her husband. "Thao Kabinlaphrom gave him three questions. He will never learn the answers."

"What are the questions he must answer?" asked the female eagle.

"These are the questions," said her husband.

"In the morning, where is a man's *rasi*? Is that the question? Tell me, is that the question?"

Audience responds: Yes.

"At noon, where is a man's *rasi*? Is that the question?"

Audience responds: Yes.

72

"In the evening, where is a man's *rasi*?" Is that the question?"

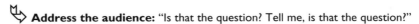

Audience responds: Yes.

The female eagle thought for a while. "Husband, what can be the answers to these questions?"

The husband replied, "The answers are these, my dear:

"In the morning, a man's *rasi* is on his face. That is why men wash their faces when they rise in the morning.

"At noon, a man's *rasi* is on his chest. That is why men sprinkle fragrant water on their chests.

"In the evening, a man's *rasi* is on his feet. That is why men wash their feet before going to bed."

Thammaban Kuman, who was listening, heard every word that the eagle couple spoke. He leapt to his feet and hurried back to the palace.

The next day, Thao Kabinlaphrom arrived. "Well, let's hear your guess to my questions. Then I will get into the business of beheading you, Thammaban Kuman. We will see to whom the people should be paying their respects in the future."

"First question: In the morning, where is a man's *rasi*?"

Address the audience: "Is that the question? Tell me, is that the question?"

Audience responds: Yes.

"That is easy," said Thammaban Kuman.

"In the morning, a man's *rasi* is on his face. That is why men wash their faces when they rise in the morning."

Thao Kabinlaphrom was stunned. How could Thammaban Kuman have known this?

"Well, the second question is "At noon . . . where is a man's *rasi*? Is that the question?"

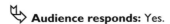

Audience responds: Yes.

"That is simple," replied Thammaban Kuman.

"At noon, a man's *rasi* is on his chest. That is why men sprinkle fragrant water on their chests."

Thao Kabinlaphrom began to worry now.

"The last question: In the evening . . . where is a man's *rasi*? Is that the question?"

Audience responds: Yes.

"This answer I know as well!" exclaimed Thammaban Kuman.

"In the evening, a man's *rasi* is on his feet. That is why men wash their feet before going to bed."

"Your answers are correct, Thammaban Kuman! I will not break my promise!" Drawing his sword, Thao Kabinlaphrom prepared to behead himself.

But the head of Thao Kabinlaphrom was no ordinary head. He could not let it just fall casually to the ground. Instead, he called his seven daughters to him.

"Daughters, as you know, my head is the center of all heat in the universe. If my head falls to the ground, fire will spread all over the world. If my head is thrown into the air, the weather will become so dry that no rain ever falls again. If my head falls into the sea, the sea will dry up. So you, my dear daughters, must carry my head carefully throughout the 365 days of each year. You must never let it fall."

So saying, Thao Kabinlaphrom sliced off his head. His eldest daughter caught the head, placed it on a tray, and flew off with it. For sixty days she flew, circling Mount Sumeru, holding the tray. Then she placed the tray in a cave on Mount Kraita and paid homage to her father's severed head, putting flowers and incense around it. Vetsukam, God of the Builders, came to build a crystal building to house this head.

And now, every 365 days, another of Thao Kabinlaphrom's seven daughters take over guardianship of their father's head. When the head passes on to the next daughter, a full Thai year is said to have passed.

The seven daughters of Thao Kabinlaphrom are honored on Songkran Day. If Songkran falls on a Sunday, Thungsa is honored. If on a Monday, Korak is honored. If Songkran falls on a Tuesday, Raksot is the honored daughter. And if it falls on Wednesday, Mantha. On Thursday, Kirini is the honored one. On Friday, it is Kimitha. And if on a Saturday, it is the turn of Mahothon. Thus, through the hands of the seven daughters, the fiery head of Thao Kabinlaphrom is guarded from year to year.

ABOUT THE STORY

A more lengthy version of this story is found in *THAI TALES: Folktales of Thailand* by Supaporn Vathanaprida, Margaret Read MacDonald, editor (Libraries Unlimited, 1994, pp. 109–114).

RELATED BOOKS (ON THAILAND)

1. *LAO TALES* by Wajuppa Tossa and Kongdeuane Nettavong; Margaret Read MacDonald, editor (Libraries Unlimited, 2008).

2. *THE GIRL WHO WORE TOO MUCH: A Pu-Thai Folktale* retold by Margaret Read MacDonald; Thai text, Supaporn Vathanaprida; Illustrated by Yvonne LeBrun Davis (August House, 1998). A girl wears too many dresses to the dance.

3. *EVEN A LITTLE IS SOMETHING* by Tom Glass (Linnet Books, 1997). Delightful short stories recount events in the life of a girl in northeastern Thailand.

4. *THAI TALES: Folktales of Thailand* by Supaporn Vathanaprida; Margaret Read MacDonald, editor (Libraries Unlimited, 1994).

HOLIDAY BACKGROUND INFORMATION

Songkran Festival is celebrated April 13–15, the traditional Thai New Year. This is the time for Thais to pay homage to Buddha images, clean their houses, and visit and pay respects to elders, including family members, friends, and neighbors. The term *Songkran* comes from Sanskrit *Sankranta* and means "a move or change"—in this case the move of the sun from Pisces into the Aries zodiac.

April 13 marks the end of the old year and is also known as *Wan Payawan*. This is the first official day of the New Year. On this day, people cleanse the Buddha images in their homes as well as in the temples with scented water. Time is spent cleaning houses and performing personal cleansing before performing some merit-making rituals such as offering food to the Buddhist monks or giving a bath to the Buddha images.

April 14 is a day of preparation, *Wan Nao*. Family members gather to prepare more offerings for the monks and to exchange gifts with friends and neighbors. Thai people try to have a happy face and avoid using bad words. As a way to show respect and goodwill, they pour festive water over friends, family, and even strangers. In the evening, they bring sand to the *wats* (temples), for the building of sand *stupas*. Then they decorate them with colorful flags and flowers.

April 15, *Wan Thaloeng Sok,* marks the beginning of the New Year. Thais spend the day performing charitable acts such as presenting offerings to the monks, listening to sermons, sprinkling holy water on Buddha images and monks, propping up the sacred *Bo* tree in the temple grounds, and calling on elders to receive their blessings.

The most obvious celebration of Songkran, also known as the Water Festival, is the throwing of water. People roam the streets with containers of water or water guns, or post themselves at the side of roads with a garden hose and drench each other and passersby. Among young people, the holiday evolved to include dousing strangers with water to relieve the heat. Water is symbolic of the cleaning process and signifies purity, but splashing water during *Songkran* has another benefit: Water helps cool your body temperature in the hottest month of the year, April, when temperatures can rise to over 100°F (or 40°C) on some days.

Apart from marking a new beginning, Songkran is also a time for thanksgiving. It is an important time for individuals to reflect upon the many acts of kindness and thoughtfulness each has personally experienced and to remember how such acts of generosity and compassion bring peace, happiness, and well-being. Songkran is also the time for reunions and family ties are renewed.

The underlying significance of Songkran is the process of cleansing and purification—the purging of all ills, misfortune, and evil as well as starting the New Year afresh with all that is good and pure. Water is symbolic of the cleaning process and signifies purity.

BIOGRAPHIES

Margaret Read MacDonald is author of *CELEBRATE THE WORLD: Twenty Tellable Folktales for Multicultural Festivals* (H.W. Wilson, 1994), *TEN TRADITIONAL TELLERS* (University of Illinois, 2006), which includes a chapter on Phra Inta Kaweewong, and many other folktale collections. She was a Fulbright Scholar in Northeastern Thailand in 1995–1996 and continues to offer storytelling workshops in Southeast Asia. See www.margaretreadmacdonald.com.

Supaporn Vathanaprida is author of *THAI TALES: Folktales of Thailand* (Libraries Unlimited, 1994) and coauthor of *THE GIRL WHO WORE TOO MUCH* (August House, 1998). Su is a librarian for the King County Library System, Seattle, Washington, offering storytelling and cultural programs throughout Western Washington.

CONTACT

Dr. Margaret Read MacDonald
11507 NE 104th Street
Kirkland, WA 98033
E-mail: mrm@margaretreadmacdonald.com
Website: www.margaretreadmacdonald.com

Supaporn Vathanaprida
13016 14th Place, NE
Seattle, WA 98125-4018
E-mail: suvathan@kcls.org

Retold by

PENINNAH SCHRAM

Passover occurs in accordance with the Jewish calendar, usually in April.

A Blessing in Disguise

INTRODUCTION

Jews everywhere celebrate Passover more than any other holiday because it is home-based with an emphasis on family. It is their Thanksgiving feast. Elijah the Prophet (the Master of Miracles) plays a central role in the Passover Seder (pronounced SAY-der—in other words, the first "e" is a long "a" as in the word "say"), highlighting the story's theme of "hospitality rewarded." This folktale also utilizes a play on words, a favorite device in Jewish folklore.

STORY SCRIPT

🖐 Begin with opening quote from the Haggadah.[1]

Let anyone who is in need—in need of food,
in need of companionship, in need of
experiencing the glory of the Jewish tradition—come and spend Passover with us.

Many years ago, there was a good couple who lived in Casablanca. The husband studied the Torah, the Hebrew Bible. He performed many good deeds, giving charity to the poor and helping wherever he could. His wife, too, was a good woman, distributing charity and offering hospitality to anyone who knocked on their door. They had one son, David. The parents taught him the ways of God and how to follow His Commandments faithfully, just as they themselves did.

When David grew old enough to marry, his parents arranged a marriage—as was the custom in those days—with the parents of a beautiful and learned daughter named Sarah. Everyone they knew, rich and poor alike, was invited to the wedding celebration.

Let's all wish them "Mazel Tov." In Hebrew, that is the way to say "Congratulations!"

and "Good Luck!"

🖐 Encourage the audience to repeat "Mazel Tov" three times.

🖐 **Audience repeats:** "Mazel Tov! Mazel Tov! Mazel Tov!"

1. The Haggadah is a traditional Jewish Book recounting the story of the Exodus from Egypt, read at the Passover Seder.

You may also wish to say "L'chaim"—or "to life." The Hebrew word is "L'chaim." Encourage the audience to hold out their arms as though holding a glass of wine to toast the bride and groom and call out "L'chaim"! The "ch" sound is a back-of-the-throat guttural sound like the end sound of "yech."

To audience: Let's do it three times.

Audience responds: "L'chaim! L'chaim! L'chaim!"

As you might imagine, to have a baby is considered by most young newlyweds to be the greatest blessing of all. Alas, David and Sarah were not so blessed. Several years went by. No child. It grew harder and harder for them to see friends enjoying their babies. Sometimes they wept bitter tears. Soon, they began to imagine looks of pity from other people.

So they socialized less and less. They went to the marketplace or synagogue only when it was absolutely necessary.

Springtime came to the land and Passover, a most important Jewish holiday, was approaching. Passover is the commemoration of the Jews' Exodus from slavery in Egypt and the celebration of their freedom as a people.

On the first night, the young couple prepared everything according to Jewish tradition. The ceremony, along with a feast, is called a "Seder." [See introduction for pronunciation.]

While she was listening to her husband reciting the sacred words of the Haggadah, Sarah began to cry. When her husband saw her tears, he understood immediately why she was weeping. He said, "My wife, do not worry. God will not forget us. We will have a child. Come, cheer up, sing with me."

Pass out music for the song, which you will find at the end of this story.

David began to sing a song in Ladino, "Esta Noche Es Alavada," in honor of Elijah the Prophet. The English translation of this Sephardic Passover song, which I have just given to you, means: *This night is praised. Lights in our houses are kindled. The child is safe with the prophet Elijah.* Let's hear it with all your heart!

Refer to music you have just received and let's sing it together with all our hearts!

As David and his wife were singing, they heard a tapping at the door. When David opened it, he saw a weary traveler. Without hesitation, the couple invited this old man to enter, to join them for the Seder.

They all sat and recited the holy words together. Then they ate together, having a lively discussion about the meaning of this holiday and exchanging stories.

After the Seder was completed, the old man rose from his place to leave, declining the couple's invitation to stay the night. He did not thank the couple, as might be expected after sharing a meal. What did he say? Instead, he spoke these words: "I asked God that I may be able to visit you next year at this time. I asked, too, that your table will be filled with ee-seder, disorder, at that time!" And the old man disappeared. Simply vanished! The couple understood that the traveler had been Elijah the Prophet.

What strange words! What an ungracious "thank you"! The couple was astonished. However, they did not wish to offend him, since he was their guest. After all, they had offered him hospitality with their whole hearts, without a thought for any reward or even a thank you. So the husband and wife smiled and wished their guest a safe journey.

Not long after the holiday, Sarah knew that she was expecting a child. Three months before the next Passover, a beautiful baby was born to Sarah and David, and they knew great joy.

When the holiday arrived, the couple again sat down at their seder to read the Haggadah. What a difference from the year before! This time there was much happiness, because they held a baby on their laps.

The child behaved like all babies. He wiggled and laughed; he reached for the glass of wine, pulling at the tablecloth to get it. He squealed merrily when plates fell down on the floor. And what did the parents do?

They behaved like all new parents everywhere. They laughed with joy. They watched with laughter and spoke with delight about their child's behavior. And they were not at all concerned that their seder was in disorder, rather than order.

Suddenly, there was a knock at the door. And when they opened it, the couple saw the same traveler who had come the year before. Again, they invited him in. All of a sudden, as they looked at their guest, they recalled his parting words. Do you?

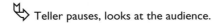 Teller pauses, looks at the audience.

Do you remember that he had wished not only to visit them again at the next seder, but "that your table will be filled with disorder at that time"?

Now they understood, for the first time, that these words had really been a blessing—a blessing in disguise!

Sarah and David began to talk at the same time, thanking the man for his blessing, which had come true! Then they asked for his forgiveness because they had completely misunderstood his words the previous year.

The old man smiled—he had the sweetest, most beautiful smile! He said, "There is no need to ask my forgiveness. How could you possibly have understood my words at that time?"

 And he gave them a traditional Jewish blessing: "May you be worthy to bring your child to study Torah and do good deeds; may you bring your child to the *Chuppah,*" the Jewish wedding canopy. [The "ch" is like the "ch" at the end of "yech." It's a guttural sound. It's the same sound as for the "ch" in "L'chaim."]

And the old man disappeared. Simply vanished! Then the couple understood that the traveler had been Elijah the Prophet.

To remember his name always, will you sing with me, again, the melody about Elijah the Prophet.

Let me sing it first. Then let us sing it out loud twice.

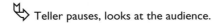 Teller sings song and directs the audience in two more rounds.

ESTA NOCHE ES ALAVADA
(THIS NIGHT IS PRAISED)

Esta noche es alavada
de encender luzes de maziadas
la criatura sea guadrada
con Eliyahu hanavi

This night is praised
lights in our houses are kindled
the child is safe
with the prophet Elijah

("Esta Noche Es Alavada" is a Sephardic folk melody in Ladino Judeo-Spanish language of the Sephardic Jews). See *THE GERARD EDERY SEPHARDIC SONG BOOK,* reprinted with permission of the publisher, Sefarad Publishing, New York, 2003.

ABOUT THE STORY

Another version of the story by Peninnah Schram appears in her book, *TALES OF ELIJAH THE PROPHET* (Jason Aronson Inc., an imprint of Rowman & Littlefield, Lanham, MD, 1991). Its source is found in the oral tradition as transcribed in the Israel Folktale Archives where the variants are classified as from Morocco and Iraq.

The story includes the recurrent motif, especially important in the Middle East, of hospitality offered with an open heart, and such hospitality is always rewarded.

As a folklore hero, Elijah the Prophet is a master of miracles. He helps those in need, especially the poor and the pious. He brings hope and reconciliation. He tests and heals. He sees who is unselfish, who offers hospitality, who gives charity, who deserves help. He often appears in disguise as an old man, a magician, a merchant, a handsome horseman, and so on. He is most often associated with Passover but is also present at births, weddings, and other life events. Usually, an empty chair is placed in the room to represent Elijah's chair.

The kernel of this story revolves around the play on the word "seder," which can mean the sequence of the ritual Passover dinner, as well as a harmonious arrangement. Thus, the mysterious guest wishes the couple disorder (ee-seder), as opposed to order (seder).

There are fifteen steps within the "seder," a "talk-fest in four acts." The four acts are outlined in detail in Ron Wolfson's *THE ACT OF JEWISH LIVING: The Passover Seder* (Los Angeles, CA: The Federation of Jewish Men's Clubs and the University of Judaism, 1988, p. 55).

OTHER STORIES (AMONG MANY) FOR PASSOVER

1. "The Magician," in *THE SEVEN GOOD YEARS AND OTHER STORIES OF I. L. PERETZ* by Esther Hautzig (Jewish Publication Society, Philadelphia, 1984).

2. *THE UNINVITED GUEST AND OTHER JEWISH HOLIDAY TALES* by Nina Jaffe, Illustrated by Elivia Savadier (Scholastic, 2004).

3. *WONDERS AND MIRACLES*: *A Passover Companion,* Eric A. Kimmel, editor (Scholastic, 2004).

4. *THE KIDS' CATALOG OF PASSOVER: A Worldwide Celebration* by Barbara Rush and Cherio Karo Schwartz (Jewish Publication Society, 2000).

5. "A Passover Tale" and "The Passover Elf Helps Great-Grandmother" in *YIDDISH FOLKTALES* by Beatrice Silverman Weinreich (Pantheon Books, 1988).

ACTIVITIES FOR FAMILY, GROUP, OR SCHOOL

1. Ask the children if they know what their parents wish for them. Ask the children what they would wish for their parents.

2. What blessings do you know from your culture or religion?

3. Ask the children if a "stranger" has ever helped them when they had fallen, when they lost something, or in some other way. Could it have been Elijah the Prophet in the guise of a friend?

4. Discuss the word "slave." Does it mean only physical restraints? Can you be a "slave" to your fears? Your desires? Try to have stories shared about some forms of slavery—for example, when you are not free to express certain thoughts or opinions.

5. Discuss the word "freedom." Does it mean to be free to do anything you want to do? Can a person be free even though in a "prison" (not just in an actual prison)? How does a person achieve "freedom"? Share stories.

NOTE: You may wish to limit the sharing of stories to a specified time limit (perhaps two or three minutes) to allow for more people to share.

INFORMATION ABOUT DIFFERENT JEWISH TRADITIONS

The Jews are a pluralistic people. Thus, there are many customs and traditions practiced by one group of Jews and not by others. This is the result of living experiences in many different countries and borrowing customs from the majority culture. Different customs arise among Jews when they are separated from other groups of Jews over long periods of time. Each group has its own melodies for the chanting of liturgy and other songs, although there may be a common text. Mainly, what unifies the Jews is their faith in one God, the common experience of biblical history, the holidays, and the Hebrew language.

There are primarily two groups of Jews: Ashkenazi Jews (called Ashkenazim), whose families had come from Eastern Europe, and Sephardic Jews (called Sephardim), whose ancestors came from Spain but now live in various other countries. However, "Sephardic" has become an umbrella term referring to all Jews who are not Ashkenazi. There are non-Ashkenazi Jews who are not strictly Sephardim, but rather Oriental (from Yemen, Libya, Egypt, etc.) and Babylonian (Iraq and Iran). The new term used for all the non-Ashkenazi Jews is Edot HaMizrach, Jews of the East.

Thus, we see that certain Passover traditions associated with Jews who come from Eastern Europe are not necessarily practiced among the Sephardim. Indeed, there are also some different traditions between the Eastern Sephardic Jews (those Sephardim who live in the Middle East) and the Western Sephardic Jews (those who live in Western Europe and North America).

For example, certain traditions associated with Elijah are usually practiced by Ashkenazi Jews, who originally stem from Eastern European countries. But there is also a crossover between groups. Thus, a seder may be a combination of traditions.

SELECTED BIBLIOGRAPHY OF BOOKS ON JEWISH TRADITIONS

Cardin, Rabbi Nina Beth, *THE TAPESTRY OF JEWISH TIME: A Spiritual Guide to Holidays and Life-Cycle Events* (Behrman House, 2000).

Frankel, Ellen, and Betsy Platkin Teutsch. *THE ENCYCLOPEDIA OF JEWISH SYMBOLS.* (Jason Aronson, 1992). Includes glossary of traditional symbolic foods on the seder plate and other Jewish references.

Telushkin, Rabbi Joseph. *JEWISH LITERACY: The Most Important Things to Know about the Jewish Religion, Its People and Its History* (William Morrow, 1999).

Wolfson, Ron. *THE ART OF JEWISH LIVING: The Passover Seder* (The Federation of Jewish Men's Clubs and The University of Judaism, 1988).

Wolkstein, Diane. *TREASURES OF THE HEART: Holiday Stories that Reveal the Soul of Judaism* (Schocken Books, 2003). Through the sacred narratives that have been read aloud in synagogues for centuries, the book highlights the Jewish yearly cycle, beginning with Passover.

HOLIDAY BACKGROUND INFORMATION

The Jews had been enslaved in Egypt. Finally, the Jewish leader, Moses, asked Pharaoh to let the Jews go free. When he refused, God sent down the awe-full Ten Plagues to persuade the Pharaoh to liberate the Jews from bondage. The Tenth Plague, the killing of the Egyptian firstborn males, convinced Pharaoh to finally let the people go.

According to the Torah, the first seder took place on the eve of the Exodus from Egypt. The Jews, still enslaved, ate the paschal lamb, and used its blood to mark the two doorposts of the house so that the Angel of Death would pass over the Jewish homes, visiting only the Egyptian homes and killing their firstborn males. The period of bondage was 75 years, approximately from 1300 to 1225 B.C.E. The Exodus took place approximately 1225 B.C.E. (These dates come from *THE ISRAELITES,* from the series THE EMERGENCE OF MAN (Time Life Books, 1975.)

Passover, a home-centered holiday, celebrates the Jews becoming a people, a nation, as a result of being freed from slavery by an Almighty God. Passover is a time to commemorate the Jews' Exodus from Egypt to the Promised Land. This holiday celebrates the birth of the Jewish people. For more than three thousand years, Jews have been retelling this story. The celebration has evolved over the years. Because the rabbis in the Gaonic period (sixth through eleventh centuries) reworked the seder, it has evolved even further.

Beginning on the fifteenth day of the Hebrew month of Nisan, Passover comes at the start of springtime when all of nature renews itself. Thus, it is a time for renewal and redemption.

Enlarging on the history, Passover has taken on allegorical meanings. Ron Wolfson explains: "Redemption, an old theme, took on new meaning. Beneath all the recollections there came a new understanding and a new hope: That which God had done, God could again do. This God makes and keeps promises. Having been redeemed from one Egypt, we could be assured that we would be redeemed from the next. The story of our ascent from slavery became more than the public pageant of a national celebration of independence; it grew into an affirmation of the possible, the wellspring of hope" (from *THE ART OF JEWISH LIVING: The Passover Seder* by Ron Wolfson, cited in the preceding Specialized Bibliography).

Families observe the holiday for eight days, but on the first two days is held a seder, a ceremonial dinner which includes the retelling of the story of the Exodus. (In Israel, there is one seder on the first night only.) Because the seder takes place in the home, this is the most popular family holiday in the Jewish calendar. Matza replaces bread, and there are many special Passover dishes served at the seder, along with ritual foods, that commemorate the Exodus from Egypt and the celebration of the freedom of the Jewish people. For more information, consult http://www.jewishvirtuallibrary.org/jsource/Judaism/holidaya.html and other Web sites.

BIOGRAPHY

Peninnah Schram, Associate Professor of Speech and Drama at Stern College of Yeshiva University, is featured at many conferences and festivals, including the National Storytelling Festival. She is the author of ten books of Jewish folktales including *Jewish Stories One Generation Tells Another* (Lanham, MD: Jason Aronson, an imprint of Rowman & Littlefield, 1987) and *The Hungry Clothes and Other Jewish Folktales* (New York: Sterling Publishing, 2008). She has recorded a CD, *The Minstrel and the Storyteller* with singer/guitarist Gerard Edery. Peninnah is a recipient of the prestigious Covenant Award for Outstanding Jewish Educator (1995), awarded by the Covenant Foundation of New York, NY. In 1999, she received the Circle of Excellence Award from the National Storytelling Network (NSN). She was also awarded NSN's 2003 Lifetime Achievement Award. For more about Peninnah, consult http://www.92y.org/content/peninnah_schram.asp and other Web sites.

CONTACT

Peninnah Schram
525 West End Avenue, 8C
New York, NY 10024
E-mail: Peninnah1@aol.com

Earth Day is celebrated on April 22 in the United States and in 175 countries around the world.

The Earth Dreamers

INTRODUCTION

The Earth Dreamers is the story of everything on Earth, and how we humans must wake up and participate in the preservation of our planet. Please respond to the questions asked.

STORY SCRIPT

In the center of the Central Mountain of the World, there live an Old Man and an Old Woman. It is their job each night to dream the World into Being. They dream all the sights, smells, and sounds of the Earth for us. They are the Earth Dreamers.

The World they dream for us is beautiful: red-rocked mountains, black and orange butterflies, emerald beetles. They dream the tumbling waterfalls, the meandering rivers, the foam-flecked seas. They dream the pungent smell of sweet basil, the clear essence of pine, the shriek of the eagle, the laughter of sea otters. All of the colors, textures, sights, smells and sounds of the World is in their Dream and all that is in their Dream is in the World. What are some other sounds, smells, and sights that they might be dreaming?

    Ask audience: "Did you see anything beautiful or unusual from the natural world on your way here today?"

    Encourage remarks from the audience about what they saw.

I'm sure that all of that is in their dreams.

If something is not remembered in their dream, it begins to disappear. Without the Earth Dreamers, the World would gradually fade until the Earth was just a barren pile of rocks; until even the rocks disappeared.

The Earth Dreamers have always been helped by the people of the Earth. Our songs, our stories, even our thoughts about the wonders and mysteries of life reach them and remind them to remember everything in their dreams. Sadly, there came a time when the people started to forget to remember.

Humans got so busy just being humans, only paying attention to the people part of life, they began to forget about other life forms.

👌 Ask audience: "What are some of the things that distract us so that we don't notice and appreciate nature?"

👌 Encourage remarks from the audience.

It happened that one by one, certain birds, certain plants, certain minds of the people had faded from the Dreamers' Dreams.

Some people who lived in the forest moved to the city. Someone else came in and cut down all the trees. The forest that once housed oak, maple, chestnut, beech, poplar, and sassafras was cut and emptied. Gone were the birds that sang in the beech trees. Gone were the squirrels that lived on the acorns of the oaks. In some places, streams were dammed, rivers ceased flowing, lakes dried up, and the green Earth turned brown. More and more parts of the Dream disappeared.

👌 To audience: "Are there any other things that have changed since you were little? Is there something here you would hate to have disappear?"

👌 Teller keeps sympathy brief.

There was a village near the Central Mountain. *Aqua Clara* they called it, which means "Clear Water." In the middle of this town, there was a fountain. The tumbling water had been the sweet center of life in Aqua Clara forever. The fountain had been built over a deep spring. Its clear water had given the village its name.

The people of Aqua Clara had kept the memories alive long after others had forgotten. They rejoiced at the sun's daily arrival, which made sparkling rainbows in the fountain. They sang to the corn planting in spring and danced for its harvesting in autumn. They told wondrous stories of butterflies and bears, crystals and caves.

But even in Aqua Clara, the memories began to fade. Mothers and fathers had no time to sing the World's songs to their children, which meant the children did not learn them and remember them for their children. The vibrancy of life paled, and the town became dry and dusty.

The water of the fountain no longer sparkled and splashed. There was no joy to the ear and very little relief to the parched throats of the people from its waters. The spring was receding, pulling back deeper and deeper into the Earth. As the water began to disappear, so did life in the little town. It began to fade.

Two children, a girl and a boy, watched their world turn sad and dusty. Their parents spoke in whispers about certain birds that were no longer to be seen, certain herbs that could no longer be gathered. They hinted about whole forests that had withered, whole countries turned to desert. And in other parts of the world, the seas were rising.

The children went to their grandmother, hoping for help. She was wise. She had kept the ways of the Old Ones long after most of the townspeople had stopped singing the old songs.

"Grandmother, what is wrong? Why is our village fading? Where has the water gone?"

The old woman looked at them. Then she closed her eyes and began to hum a tune, one that the children remembered from the lullabies she had sung them when they were tiny. She opened her eyes and said, "My grandfather, your great-great-grandfather, told me a story once about an old couple who live in the heart of the Central Mountain. He taught me a song about them. Do you remember? I used to sing it to you.

☞ Teller hums the tune, then sings the song. See music at end of story.

The old woman began to sing:
In the Mountains
They are Dreaming.
They are Dreaming
Of the Mountains.
All of Life
In their Dream.
We must help them Dream.

Then the old woman began to sing again. This time the audience participated in the singing.

☞ **Audience sings with teller:**
In the Mountains
They are Dreaming.
They are Dreaming
Of the Mountains.
All of Life
In their Dream.
We must help them Dream.

The old woman continued, "They are called the Earth Dreamers. My grandfather told me to go to them if our world began to disappear."

She looked at the children. "You must go to them now. I am too old to make the journey into the Mountain, but you can find them. Go and ask them what we must do to keep our World from disappearing."

Early the next morning, as the sun turned the world pink and yellow, the children left their village. They walked along a road that narrowed to a trail and then became a rocky path as it climbed. Higher and deeper they journeyed into the heart of the mountain. They sang as they climbed. (See music at end of story.)

We are searching
For the Dreamers.
We are seeking,
We are singing.
You who dream
Help us please
Keep our World alive.

The path disappeared and there in front of them, sitting by a great reaching tree, were two beautiful old people. "Yes!" the Old Ones called out, "We've been waiting for you. Come and sit down. We are so glad you are here." They gave the children nut cakes and fruit to eat, sweet pure water to drink.

When the children were rested and fed, they reached out to the woman and man and asked, "Grandmother, Grandfather, our world is fading into dust. No water flows. No birds sing. How can we help the people to bring it back to life?"

The old couple sat quietly for a moment. The man spoke first. "Tell the people that to save the World, they must love the World; and to love the World, they must simply pay attention to it, to look and listen to what is around them. Then they must celebrate it: sing, dance, tell stories, paint pictures, give thanks in prayer. Tell the people that this is their business on Earth: To love Life and to celebrate it every day. Every, every day."

"You see," said the Old Woman," there are four Worlds here on Earth, each important, each an equal part of the whole. Each of these Worlds has its special place in the design.

> Teller ticks them off with a hand or a finger.

We have *Mineral World*—rocks, quartz, mica, granite, and so forth.

We have *Plant World*—pine trees, roses, bamboo, apples, and so forth.

We have *Animal World*—earth worms, elephants, etc.

And oh yes, there are *Human Beings*.

> As the Four Worlds are introduced, the audience can be asked to name other examples from each. If there are lots of ideas, as with the animals, teller says: "Everyone think of an animal. When I count to three, shout out the name." Audience responds to teller.

Let's talk about the Mineral World: sand, rocks, crystals. The Old Ones taught us that the Mineral World holds and keeps this Earth and its ancient story.

Think about stone circles such as Stonehenge. Think about crystals, or rocks.

> To audience: "What are some things that the mineral world holds?"

> Teller responds to each suggestion.

Then we have the Plant World—grasses, flowers, trees—which gives us so much. Food, shelter, clothing. Can you name a few?

> Teller names each member of the plant world as it is announced by audience.

Right. Now we have the Animals, which enliven and share our world with us. They give us food, shelter, clothing, and companionship.

> To audience: "Can you name a few?"

> Teller responds to each suggestion: "Right!" (or if wrong, correction needs to be made).

Then there are Human Beings: Humans have a special place in the design, for while we are part of the design and must live in harmony and balance with the others, we have something none of the others has. Humans have a mind that can see itself seeing itself!

Although we understand much of what we see, obviously we don't see clearly enough. In many ways, humans determine what happens to our planet and all other life forms upon it. That is a big responsibility. What are some of the ways we can determine what happens here on earth? How do we change things . . . positively as well as negatively?

☞ Teller reacts to each response, using common sense.

The Old Man spoke up again, "Part of your responsibility is to remember. When you remember and celebrate life, we remember it and dream the world into being. When a child delights in the taste of a ripe sweet peach, we share her delight and dream of the peach tree. When a man cries over a fallen oak, hit and split by lightening, we hear his sorrow and remember the oak tree.

"So when you get dressed in the morning, thank the sheep for the wool of your sweater. When you eat a piece of bread, remember the wheat, remember the wood that made the fire to bake it. The more you remember, the more we can dream; the better our dreaming, the better the World. Everyone on earth can help keep this world alive."

The children sat quietly for a while, breathing in this simple Truth. Then they thanked the Earth Dreamers and began their journey home. They noticed many things on their way back that they had not noticed on their way to the old couple. They felt the strong support of the rocks beneath their feet. They breathed the pine-scented air. They noticed the fleck of yellow in a flicker's wings and heard each other's laughter at seeing the beauty all around them.

When they entered Aqua Clara, it was a hazy afternoon. The people were sitting around the town square, their eyes clouded, their mouths dusty with sadness. Something had disappeared, but the people could not remember what.

The children sat down in front of an old woman, took her hands and asked, "Grandmother, please tell me your favorite memory of the Fountain."

"The Fountain?" said the old woman. "The Fountain? Oh . . . the Fountain. The water used to splash so high, it caught the light of sun. There were rainbows shooting into the air. Oh yes, the light in the water is what I remember, the light in the water and the rainbows."

As the boy and girl ran from person to person, asking them about their memories, slowly, slowly the stories began to be told. One man drummed the heartbeat of the wolf cub. A woman showed her belt, woven with the pattern of lightening. Children joined together in a circle and danced the Planting of the Corn.

As more and more people added their memories, the faded World became brighter, stronger. The people once again were telling their stories and celebrating Life. Once again the Earth Dreamers could Dream the richness of the World. And once again, the fountain splashed cool, clear water filled with rainbows.

The Earth Dreamers

Lyrics & Music by Regina Ross

ABOUT THE STORY

The ideas and images in this story have their roots in the simple concept that everything on earth is interconnected, an idea held by many cultures around the world. If we humans forget, or worse, deny our connection to the earth and all upon it, we disconnect ourselves from life and run the risk of disconnecting life as we know it.

The Earth Dreamers is not based on any particular cultural or religious teaching but simply offers a description of deep ecological awareness, a metaphor for our needed participation in "keeping our world alive."

RELATED STORIES AND BOOKS

Earth Day may be a relatively new holiday, but the idea that all life on earth must be honored and taken care of is as old as human culture.

1. "Gluscabi and the Wind Eagle" from *KEEPERS OF THE EARTH: Native American Stories and Environmental Activities for Children* by Michael J. Caduto and Joseph Bruchac (Fulcrum, 1988). A wonderful story that speaks of the destruction of the air and water quality because of selfishness and greed. Global warming, anyone?

2. *THE LORAX* by Dr. Seuss (Random House, 1971). A classic tale of the spirit who "speaks for the trees."

3. "Papa God's Well" from *EARTH CARE: World Folktales to Talk About* by Margaret Read MacDonald (August House, 2005). A delightful Haitian story that speaks of water and our need to share it and take care of it.

4. "The Sea of Gold" from *THE SEA OF GOLD and Other Tales from Japan* by Yushiko Uchida (Charles Scribner's Sons, 1965). A Japanese folktale about a cook on a fishing boat who is the only one who thanks the fish for giving up their lives so that the humans can feed their families. The fish return the thanks and change his life.

5. *SUN MOTHER WAKES THE WORLD: An Australian Creation Story,* adapted by Diane Wolkstein, illustrated by Bronwyn Bancroft (Harper Collins, 2004). Sun Mother tells the first humans to " look after your birthplace . . . and to walk the land to keep it alive."

RECOMMENDED BOOKS

1. *KEEPERS OF THE EARTH: Native American Stories and Environmental Activities for Children* by Michael J. Caduto and Joseph Bruchac (Fulcrum, 1988). One of a series of books by Bruchac and Caduto with great stories and follow-up activities.

2. *THINKING LIKE A MOUNTAIN: Towards a Council of All Beings* by John Seed, Joanna Macy, Pat Fleming, and Arne Naess (New Society Publishers, 1988). This book includes essays by some of the leaders in the "deep ecology" movement. It describes a group process, the "Council of All Beings," in which participants take on various life forms and talk from these perspectives. I've led this process with both children and adults. It is fun and leads to awareness and connection with life on earth.

3. *CELEBRATING THE EARTH: Stories, Experiences, and Activities* by Norma J. Livo (Teacher Ideas Press, 2000). A wonderful collection of stories with follow-up activities.

4. *EARTH IN BALANCE: Ecology and the Human Spirit* by Al Gore (Houghton Mifflin, 1992). Also *AN INCONVIENENT TRUTH: The Planetary Emergency of Global Warming and What We Can Do About It* by Al Gore (Rodale, 2006).

ACTIVITIES AND DISCUSSION TOPICS

1. Local or familiar details can be added or substituted. For example, if you are telling the story in New York City, the rivers, ocean, and granite under the skyscrapers can be mentioned. Search the Internet for details about your own area.

2. An excellent song to sing at the end of this story is "My Two Hands Hold The Earth" by New England singer/songwriter Sarah Pirtle (www.sarahpirtle.com).

3. The Earth Dreamers say they need to hear the sounds of the animals. What are some animal sounds we can make?

4. For Earth Day activities in the school or community, go to www.earthday.net.

HOLIDAY BACKGROUND INFORMATION

In 1969, U.S. Senator Gaylord Nelson created a plan to bring environmental issues into national focus. Based on the antiwar and civil rights "teach-ins" at colleges during the 1960s, the senator planned a national "teach-in" for the environment. Senator Nelson said, "We are not free to decide about whether or not our environment matters. It does matter, apart from any political exigencies. We disregard the needs of our ecosystem at our mortal peril."

On the first Earth Day, ten thousand high schools and grade schools, several thousand communities, and more than twenty million Americans participated in a grassroots demonstration of concern for the environment. Since that first Earth Day, April 22, 1970, it has become an international holiday. In 1990, for the twentieth anniversary, more than two hundred million people from 141 countries participated in the celebration. Around the globe, politicians, celebrities, and activists celebrated the thirtieth anniversary of Earth Day in 2000.

According to The Earth Day Network (www.earthday.net) an international environmental nongovernmental organization that coordinates worldwide activities, Earth Day is now observed in 175 countries and is the largest secular holiday in the world, celebrated by more than a half billion people every year. With the issues of global warming and environmental degradation in the news, Earth Day is more important than ever as a way to focus awareness and teach the tending of our home planet.

Get involved . . . it's your home!

BIOGRAPHY

Regina Ress is an award-winning storyteller, actor, writer, and educator. She has performed and taught for more than thirty-five years in venues from Broadway to Brazil, in English and Spanish, and in settings as varied as grade schools, senior centers, homeless shelters, and prisons, as well as Lincoln Center and the White House. She tells a wide variety of stories: folktales, mythology, and literary and original stories. She has performed and given workshops in schools, theatres, and international festivals across the United States, in Central and South America, and in Europe. She teaches storytelling for New York University's Program in Educational Theatre and produces the storytelling series at the Provincetown Playhouse in New York. Regina is the recipient of a 2004 National Storytelling Network grant for her project, Voices from Washington Heights: Immigrants Tell Stories About and From Their Homelands. She is on the board of directors of the New York City Storytelling Center and is the NYC-Metro area liaison to the National Storytelling Network.

CONTACT

Regina Ress
E-mail: storytellerRRess@aol.com
www.rnrproductions-nyc.com

Retold by

RUTH STOTTER

Each state's Arbor Day celebration initiates the signing of an Arbor Day proclamation by local officials and Arbor Day activities related to trees and tree planting. Celebrations are held as early as January and February in some southern states and as late as May in more northern locations. National Arbor Day is observed on the last Friday in April. Consult http://forestry.about.com/cs/urbanforestry/a/arbor_day_date.htm.

Why the Evergreens Keep Their Leaves in the Winter

INTRODUCTION

This is my retelling of an old story originally published in *A BOOK OF NATURE MYTHS* by Florence Holbrook (1902). Several other versions can be found in *HOW TO TELL STORIES TO CHILDREN* by Sara Cone Bryant (Houghton Mifflin, 1905; George Harrap, 1934) and in *GOOD STORIES FOR GREAT HOLIDAYS* by Frances Jenkins Olcott (1914).

STORY SCRIPT

It was winter and all the birds were getting ready to fly south. "Come on, Little Bird," they called. "It is time to leave."

"I can't fly," Little Bird told them. "My wing is broken."

"We have to leave, Little Bird. Maybe you can hop along with us. Good-bye Little Bird. Take care of yourself. We will see you in the spring." And all the birds flew away.

Poor Little Bird. It was so cold. He hopped over to Maple Tree. "Maple Tree, would you please help me? Would you please keep me warm through the winter?" "NO, Little Bird. I like peace and quiet. You would make too much noise."

Poor Little Bird!

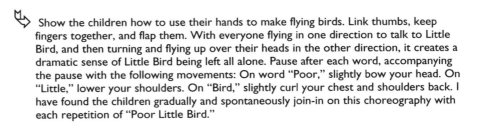

Show the children how to use their hands to make flying birds. Link thumbs, keep fingers together, and flap them. With everyone flying in one direction to talk to Little Bird, and then turning and flying up over their heads in the other direction, it creates a dramatic sense of Little Bird being left all alone. Pause after each word, accompanying the pause with the following movements: On word "Poor," slightly bow your head. On "Little," lower your shoulders. On "Bird," slightly curl your chest and shoulders back. I have found the children gradually and spontaneously join-in on this choreography with each repetition of "Poor Little Bird."

Little Bird saw Oak Tree. "Oak Tree, would you please help me? Would you please keep me warm through the winter?" "NO, Little Bird. I am afraid you might break one of my brittle branches."

 To entice more participation, when Oak Tree says, "NO," you can ask the children why they think Oak Tree did not want Little Bird to stay in its branches. You can use these reasons for the other trees, or repeat this with Maple Tree and Birch Tree.

Poor Little Bird!

Little Bird saw Birch Tree. "Birch Tree, would you please help me? Would you please keep me warm through the winter?" "NO, I don't like Little Birds. Go away."

 I have found that children usually mimic a strong "go away" gesture—using one hand and pushing away.

Poor Little Bird!

Then he heard someone calling. It was Pine Tree. And Juniper Tree. And Fir Tree.

"Little Bird, Little Bird, come here! You can use our needles to make a nest. You can eat juniper berries. We will protect you from the winter cold."

Little Bird hopped up into Fir Tree and made a little nest. He ate Juniper Tree's berries and stood close to Fir Tree when the North Wind came. The North Wind blew and blew.

He blew all the leaves off of Maple Tree.

He blew all the leaves off of Oak Tree.

He blew all the leaves off of Birch Tree. But then he stopped. "I will not blow the leaves off of Juniper and Fir and Pine," the North Wind said, "because they are taking care of Little Bird."

When the other Birds came back in the spring, they called, "Little Bird, Little Bird. Are you here?" And they heard Little Bird, chirping away, saying, "Here I am! I am fine! Fir and Juniper and Pine took care of me. And, look. My wing has mended!"

 I put my hands on my shoulders and flap both my elbows as if they were wings. The children, now used to joining in on the gestures, usually spontaneously do this with me.

"Look, I can fly again!"

And that is the way it happened and is still happening today. Every winter Maple and Oak and Birch lose their leaves—but Juniper and Fir and Pine have remained always green—evergreen. And now you know why!

RELATED STORIES: JOHNNY APPLESEED

Consult the Internet for "Johnny Appleseed" to find numerous references.

RELATED BOOKS

1. *HIDDEN STORIES IN PLANTS: Unusual and Easy-to-Tell Stories from Around the World Together with Creative Things to Do While Telling Them* by Anne Pellowski, illustrated by Lynn Sweat (Macmillan, 1990).

2. *SEEDS AND STORIES* (Story Lovers, P.O. Box 446, Sonoma, CA 95476; www.story-lovers.com).

3. *THE EMPTY POT* (picture book) by Devi (Henry Holt, 1990).

ACTIVITIES

1. This is a fun story to have children act out. You can add other deciduous trees and ask the children to provide reasons why they do not show compassion. Remember, you can have several children play any one of the tree species in the story. Also, along with Little Bird, three children could portray the other birds, and three children could play each tree. With the North Wind, many children can participate in the dramatic presentation of this tale. When the North Wind blows, the trees can shiver and have leaves in their hands that fall to the ground!

2. *String Stunt: Make a Tree.* Hand a loop of string to each child. I usually use multicolored yarn (five feet, ten inches) tied with a strong square knot. I recommend ordering string loops in bulk from string master David Titus at the String Figure Store: www.StringFigureStore.com; (String Figure Store, 130 SW "B" Avenue, Lawton, OK 73501-4040).

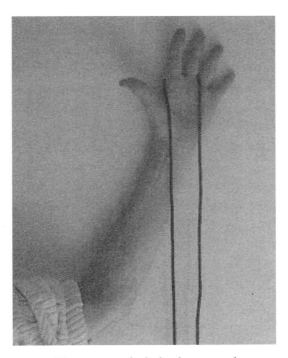

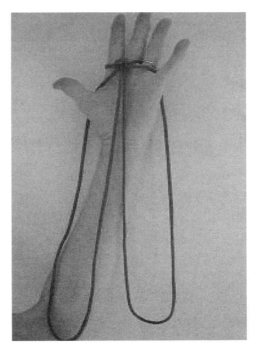

There was a hole in the ground.
Put the string on your left hand behind your
pointer and middle fingers.
A large loop will appear in front of your palm.

A seed was planted. With your right hand,
enter the large loop from the back.
With your pointer finger of your right hand,
take the piece of string that is between your
pointer and middle fingers and pull it
straight down in front of your palm.

Roots began to grow. Reach from behind the loop again. This time, take both strings that are between your pointer and middle fingers and pull them down in front of your palm. You now have two smaller loops. Take the outer edge of one and put it over your little finger. Take the outer edge of the other and put it over your thumb to make the roots. Open your hand wide to show the roots.

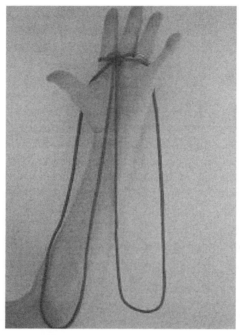

And there was a tree! Pull on the horizontal small piece of string up by your middle finger and pointer finger. As you pull, the tree will take shape.

OTHER LANGUAGES FOR THE SAME STORY

Perhaps you would like to tell this story in another language? (Remember the translation is the same for all languages.)
"A hole in the ground
Plant a seed
Roots
A tree"

French
Un trou dans le sol
La plantation d'une semence
Racines
Un arbre

Italian
Un foro (un bucco) nella terra
Plantare un seme
Radici
Un albero

German
Ein loch im boden
Pflanzen sie einen samen
Wurzem
Ein Baum

Spanish
Un hoyo en la tierra
Siembra una semilla
Raices
Un arbol

Norwegian	Russian
En hull I grunnen	Yamka vee zemie
planter en samen	Zermishka posageno
rotter	Virastaet
en tre	Derevo!

Filipino
Isang bu'tas sa lu'pa
Magtani'm ng (pronounced nang bu'til)
Mga uga't (pronounced ma-nga)
isang kahoy

3. *Making a Paper Tree:* Lay three pieces of newspaper fully opened on the floor, each slightly overlapping the previous one. Roll them up into a tube. Then tear the tube in half from the top to about one-third of the way down on four sides. Now, if you reach in and pull one of the inside cut strips in half, the paper will open up to become a long paper tree! (See Stotter book *SMILES!* in the SPECIALIZED BIBLIOGRAPHY at the end of this book.)

4. *Making Leaf Prints:* These can be used for art objects, a record of leaves you have identified, or to decorate a useful item like stationary, greeting cards, or bookmarks. Leaf prints on fabric have been used for curtains and scarves. Whatever use you make of them, they are fun to make. You might like to try "Crayon Prints," one of several activities described in Stotter's book *Little Acorns.*

Supplies: Crayons (with outer paper removed), paper, straight pins.

Procedure:

A. Pin the leaf on a piece of paper, vein side up, and place it on a smooth board or table.

B. Put your printing paper on top of the leaf and rub the crayon sidewise over the leaf, making sure all your strokes go in the same direction.

HOLIDAY BACKGROUND INFORMATION

When J. Sterling Morton moved to the Nebraska Territory in 1854, the region was a treeless plain. Morton and his wife planted trees and shrubs on their property. When he became editor of Nebraska's first newspaper, Morton wrote articles and editorials enthusiastically encouraging Nebraska residents to plant trees. He pointed out that not only were trees beautiful, but that they also served as a windbreaker to keep the soil in place, provided shade from the sun, and provided wood for building and fuel.

Morton established the first Arbor Day on April 10, 1872. Prizes were given to Nebraska counties as well as to the people who planted the largest number of trees. The result was a big success. More than a million trees were planted!

In 1885, April 22, J. Sterling Morton's birthday, was designated as Arbor Day in Nebraska and declared a legal holiday. Soon, other states passed legislation to make Arbor Day an official holiday as well. Most chose the last Friday of the month as the official date.

By 1907, Arbor Day was celebrated in every state. Today, the last Friday of the month is most commonly celebrated as Arbor Day.

In its beginning years, Arbor Day was primarily promoted in schools, where children were encouraged to plant trees on Arbor Day as an act of patriotism and to acknowledge that planting trees is a sound investment to community beautification.

Today, Arbor Day is a day to appreciate and celebrate trees and to encourage their planting everywhere.

J. Sterling Morton once wrote: "Every generation takes the earth as a trustee. We ought to bequeath to posterity as many forests and orchards as we have exhausted and consumed."

Do you know there are approximately 60,000 species of trees?

For more information about the history of Arbor Day, consult: http://www.arbor-day.net, www.arborday.org, or 1 (888) 448-7337.

BIOGRAPHY

Ruth Stotter is convinced that teaching is in her DNA. She conducts workshops on storytelling skills, adapting stories, and storytelling with props as well as critique clinics. Ruth has performed at numerous storytelling festivals and has been invited to perform in Malaysia, Australia, Great Britain, France, and Portugal as well as throughout North America. She is the author of *About Story, More About Story, Smiles, The Golden Axe,* and *You're On!* She is the former Director of the Dominican University Storytelling Program in San Rafael, California. See more about Ruth at http://www.writeonspeakers.com/ruth_stotter.htm and other sites.

CONTACT

Ruth Stotter
2244 Vistazo Street East
Tiburon, CA 94920
E-mail: r.stotter@comcast.net

May

May Day—May 1—is the time of year when warm weather begins and flowers and trees start to blossom. May 1 is Lei Day in Hawaii and Law Day in the United States. In days past, people exchanged "May baskets"—little baskets of flowers—on May Day. May 1 is also International Worker's Day and celebrated as a holiday in some countries (see "Holiday Background Information" later in the chapter).

The Garden Rainbow

INTRODUCTION

Bruno Bettelheim said, "While the fantasy is unreal, the good feelings it gives us about ourselves and our future are real, and these real good things are what we need to sustain us."

NOTE: See section "About the Story" at the end of the script for performance tips.

STORY SCRIPT

Long ago, when the bumble bees still sang lullabies to the flowers and the flowers could pick their roots right up out of the ground and dance, there lived a little girl who never smiled. She was very sick and had been sent to bed for what seemed like the longest time.

She didn't like to stay in bed. There was nothing to do. She had no toys, no books.

All she could do, lying in bed, was look out the window, high up on the wall. All she could see out of her window was the sky. Sometimes a cloud floated by, but that was hardly enough to make her smile.

What she yearned to do was to go outside and see the garden dance. Her Nana had told her that every morning the flowers and creatures who lived in the garden would dance. But she wasn't allowed outside. She wasn't even allowed out of bed. She was too sick.

Her Nana had also told her that if you wish for something long enough, you *might* get it. So she began to wish . . . "Wish I might, wish I may, see the garden dance today." Her room became *filled* with wishing, but no one heard her. She was alone.

Now that little girl was right: The garden *did* dance! It started each morning at sunrise when the sun awoke the little black spider asleep in the rose bush. He would bounce up and down, up and down, on his web until the dewdrops fell off his web onto the flowers, waking them up with the sprinkles.

> 🤚 Use one hand to bounce your fingers up and down like spider legs. Then sprinkle your fingers downward like droplets. Twirl your head in a circle. Stretch out your arm. Encourage audience to participate in movements with you.

First to wake up was the tulip, who twirled her red petaled head and stretched her green leaves. Then a violet nodded its purple face and winked at the flowers.

A daisy pulled its roots right up out of the ground and cart-wheeled across the garden.

> Continue to match movement to word pictures.

Suddenly, a yellow buttercup leaped over a brown garden toad. The toad leaped over the buttercup. Buttercup over toad, toad over buttercup. Back and forth until there was a game of leap-toad around the garden.

The lilies of the valley, which look like tiny white bells, shimmered and shook. You could almost hear their bells ring.

> Dangle fingers like bells. Shake them quickly like bell clappers. Hold them to your ear to hear them.

The blue pansies pirouetted on their toes. The poppies pranced about with their orange petals, flashing while the bright yellow daffodils bobbled and bounced.

> With palms facing the floor, cup hands and prance them forward like lively steps. Bobble and bounce head.

The purple petunias sacheted and swished their floppy petal skirts. Yellow and blue butterflies fluttered then dipped and dived.

> Wiggle and shake open fingers then drive them downward.

A pink rose bud jumped off the vine and chased after a green-backed beetle.

Soon the whole garden was dancing. It looked like colored ribbons blowing in the breeze.

> Continue to use movements as desired to accompany your word pictures.

But inside the house, the little girl was still in her bed wishing . . . "Wish I might, wish I may . . . See the garden dance today."

Do you think if you sang it with me, it might make her wish stronger? I'll sing it first. Then let's try it together! [See music at the end of story.]

> Teller sings music with lyrics.
> The audience repeats the music with lyrics.
> Wish I might . . . Wish I may . . . See the garden dance today.

Wish I might, Wish I may, See the garden dance today.

Down in the garden, a wind caught hold of a small blue butterfly and took it up in the sky higher than it had ever been before. On the thrust of the wind, the butterfly flew right next to the girl's window. It heard her wishing. It heard her singing. What was she singing? Can you guess?

> **Audience repeats:** "Wish I might . . . Wish I may . . . See the garden dance today."

When the wind went away, the blue butterfly drifted back down to the garden and told the tulip about the little girl's wish. The tulip told the daisy, the daisy told the spider, who told the beetle, who told the rose, who told the toad. Soon the whole garden knew about the little girl's wish. And they decided they wanted to show the little girl their dance.

But there was a problem—a big problem! There was that window . . . ohhhh, soooo high! Toad could jump, but not that high. The butterflies could fly but not the flowers. How could they get up to her window?

They tried to make a ladder climbing one on top of another, but they only toppled down. As hard as they tried, they couldn't find a way to get up to the little girl's window. They didn't know what to do.

> Stack your fists one on top of the other moving higher and higher. Begin to sway your stacked fists. Open hands and shake fingers as you lower them.

Finally, the little black spider remembered that Mother Nature lived in the old oak tree next to the garden. All together, they went to her for help.

Mother Nature listened as the colors of the garden explained why they wanted to show the little girl their dance. Mother Nature nodded her head and sprinkled magic droplets on each of the colors of the garden. They began to spin in a circle, faster and faster. Lifting higher and higher into the sky. Till the colors of the garden danced across the sky in rows of color and made . . . a rainbow.

> Continue to match movement to word pictures.

When the little girl looked out her window and saw the rainbow of dancing colors, she smiled. The colors stayed in the girl's heart and memory and she smiled often.

Ever since that day, Mother Nature has been putting rainbows in the sky to make all of us smile.

See the Garden Dance

Lyrics & Music by Linda Marchisio

NOTE: Transcribed courtesy of The Guitar Lab, Evansville, IN 47715. Lyrics and Music by Linda Marchisio.

ABOUT THE STORY

1. The repeated refrain of this story can be either sung or chanted. When I chant the refrain, it is in a half-whisper tone.

2. If the audience size is small, I encourage participation in the movements of the flowers by stretching, shaking, bouncing, winking, shimmering, and fluttering to match the word pictures from the story. These movements can be accomplished with the upper body while still seated on the floor or in a chair.

3. When I sing the song, I accompany my voice with a kantele, a Finish lap harp with ten strings. I also use the kantele to make the sound effects of the flowers and creatures as they dance in the garden. My kantele is tuned to the D-pentatonic scale (B, A, G, E, D). Many other instruments would make suitable options for accompaniment including electric keyboard, autoharp, and the xylophone.

    Kanteles can be purchased through the mail: Song of the Sea, 47 West Street, Bar Harbor, Maine 04609; (207) 288-5653; E-mail: mail@songsea.com. Or use a search engine to locate other "music-by-mail" sources.

ACTIVITIES

1. The following traditional Mother Goose story is fun to share. It can be demonstrated with an artificial daffodil.

    | "Daffy-down-dilly | (Hide the flower behind your back.) |
    | Has come to town | |
    | In a yellow petticoat | (Show the flower and point to the yellow petals.) |
    | And green gown." | (Turn the flower upside down and show the green outer petals.) |

2. Sing "Inch by Inch," originally by Arlo Guthrie. It's a wonderful, easy-to-sing-along song about the garden growing.

DEDICATION

My mother, my Aunt Letty, and my Nana were all growers and keepers of flowers. They each had a desire to cultivate the magic in flowering plants.

Nana grew wild flowers carefully removed from under forest boughs. She had a nurturing way of growing the "wild ones" in tamer settings so they could be cherished every day.

My Aunt Letty grew and grew and grew flowers—everywhere. My childhood eyes saw the tangled maze of flowers and bushes as a magical, mystical secret world. Walking under her rose-covered trellis, I knew that I had passed through a gate to Mother Nature's kingdom.

I can remember my mother's quiet morning moments surveying her garden, the grass still heavy with dew. Checking each plant's growth, she pulled away the weeds. Often, she spent a moment conversing with a brown garden toad. Her quiet passion for the garden was passed along to me during the frequent tours she guided me through.

This story is dedicated to Mom, Letty, and Nana. They showed me that the garden can dance. The image of the garden's colors often made me smile when I was sick and sent to bed.

RELATED BOOKS

1. *MAY DAY: A Crowell Holiday Book* by Dorothy Les Tina (Thomas Crowell, 1967).

2. *A FESTIVAL OF THE ENGLISH MAY* by Doleta Chapru (Folklore Village Publications, 1977).

3. *FLOWER FAIRIES ALPHABET* by Cicely Mary Barker (Serendipity Books, 2003).

4. *A LEI FOR TUTU* by Rebecca Nevers Fellows (Albert Whitman & Company, 1998).

HOLIDAY BACKGROUND INFORMATION

Some people believe May Day celebrations began with the Druids' celebration of first spring. Other people believe May Day celebrations developed from ancient festivals in Rome or India. In ancient Rome, flowers were gathered on May Day to honor Flora, the goddess of flowers. They held flower parades similar to the floats in our modern parades.

In medieval times, May Day became a popular holiday in England. People decorated their homes and churches with flowers. They danced around a tall May pole holding colored ribbons that looped and wrapped around the pole as they danced.

To celebrate May Day in Switzerland, young men chop down pine trees and plant them under the windows of their sweethearts. They decorate the trees with flower blossoms and colored streamers that blow in the wind. In Spain, the May tree is decorated with ribbons, eggshells, and beads. Men and women dance around the tree and sing *mayos* or *mayas*—May songs.

In France, it is a religious day, sacred to the Virgin Mary. France also celebrates May first as a Valentine's Day called Fete des Muguets. Muguets—lilies of the valley—are picked during the early morning and given to the one you love.

In Italy, Switzerland, and Czechoslovakia, May Day is a day for sweethearts and courting. In various places in America and parts of Europe, May Day is celebrated by dancing around a May pole. Ribbons that twist the pole in an array of colors are held while dancing, as in medieval times.

May Day is also a day of magic. It is said that if you roll naked in the predawn dew on May first, you will receive luck, beauty, and health. In Ireland, on May first, they say you can discover the color of your future love's hair by finding the first morning trail of a small grey slug: A white trail is blonde hair; a black trail is dark hair. They also say that evil spirits are kept at bay when you receive a gift of a May basket.

When my mother was a child in Massachusetts during the 1920s, it was their custom to decorate baskets with paper flower petals, fill them with a flower or a sweet treat, and give them anonymously to a friend or an elderly neighbor confined to the house. Children would place their handmade baskets on the front porch, ring the doorbell and run away and hide. When the person answered the door, they received that basket of May Day joy!

May Day has a more serious side—freedom. In the United States, since 1958, May first has been designated Law Day. The laws of the United States support equal freedom for everyone. Our laws help protect us from people who attempt to remove our freedoms with their actions and words.

In Russia, May Day is a day to honor the workers, a labor day. It was May 1 in 1889 that the Russians decided to support the Labor Movement of the United States in their demands for an eight-hour work day. May first was then designated Labor Day. Today it is still celebrated in Russia and other socialist and communist countries.

Many countries around the world now celebrate the coming of spring and May Day with symbols of flowers, colored ribbons, dancing, and the magic of dawn and dew drops at sunrise on the first of May. Edgerton School in New London, Connecticut, celebrates each and every May first with an annual school-wide celebration which includes a spectacular May pole with dancers.

For me, May Day means the freedom of fantasy. I can use my imagination to "see the garden dance today." I have the freedom of dancing across the sky with the rainbow colors.

For more information on May Day, search the Web. You will find wonderful examples at:

- www.woodlands-junior.kent.sch.uk/customs/questions/mayday.htm

- http://en.wikipedia.org/wiki/May_Day

In my own garden is a sign that reads:
"The earth laughs in flowers." —Ralph Waldo Emerson

BIOGRAPHY

Linda Marchisio loves dancing, storytelling, and hiking to waterfalls. She is currently a teacher of gifted education, a certified library media specialist, and a storyteller. Linda won the 2003 Connecticut Wilbur Cross Award Champion of Children's Reading for her creation of original booktalk programs for children and parents.

CONTACT

Linda Marchisio
E-mail: LjcLsj@cox.net

V. J. RICHEY

Memorial Day, A United States federal holiday, is observed on the last Monday of May to commemorate those who died in the service of their country.

Kelly's Memorial Day Parade

INTRODUCTION

Memorial Day parades have been a tradition in towns across the United States for well over a century. It is an opportunity for Americans of all ages and generations to gather and honor those who sacrificed so much while serving in the U.S. military. The event celebrates all those who served in uniform since the American Revolution.

Many years ago in a small New York town, a little girl attended a Memorial Day parade and became inspired to lead one. What happened next is the essence of this story.

As the storyteller, you will lead the audience in a parade by having participants march in place at their seats or in single file around the room. You will need a silver whistle.

STORY SCRIPT

This is a true story about a girl who loved parades . . . especially the sound of marching feet. To tell this story, I'll need you to start from where you are sitting or standing. You must know your left foot from your right foot.

Any questions about that? Let's start with our left foot. And remember to stop when you hear the command, "Company halt!" Try it with me.

> March in place, saying, "Left, right, left, right, left, right . . ." Encourage audience to participate. When ready, raise one hand in air to signal STOP.

Company, Halt!

Great! You sounded like marching soldiers!

This story happened in a small town a few days before Memorial Day. On this day, we remember all the soldiers who fought in a war or who are still fighting. Americans and veterans who are home from wars march in parades in towns and cities everywhere.

As it happened, Kelly and Kim were identical twins. It was fun, except for one thing.

Their mom insisted that they dress exactly alike.

"Here come Kelly and Kim, the look-alikes!" kids at school teased.

When Kelly and Kim complained, their Mom said, "You're twins! It looks nice when you're dressed alike."

One beautiful Friday morning in May, Kelly and Kim left for school. As usual, they looked exactly alike. Navy blue skirts and white polo tops. Red jackets. White socks and sneakers. Hair tied back with white ribbons. Only one thing made Kelly feel better. She was wearing white underwear. Kim was wearing pink.

To get to school, they walked by the VFW Post. Kelly had gone there all that week after dinner to watch the veterans practicing for the big parade on Monday, Memorial Day. She loved watching them march to the rum-tum-tum of the band.

When Kelly and Kim got to the schoolyard, Kim ran to play jump rope with her friends. Kelly spotted Miss Buxton, the *meanest* teacher in the whole school. She was on schoolyard duty. Kelly decided to march around the schoolyard.

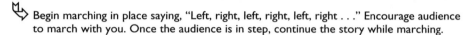 Begin marching in place saying, "Left, right, left, right, left, right . . ." Encourage audience to march with you. Once the audience is in step, continue the story while marching.

She marched past Miss Buxton.

 Left, right, left, right, left, right . . .

Kelly called to friends. "Do *you* want to be in my Memorial Day parade? Everybody, come join the parade . . . for our soldiers!"

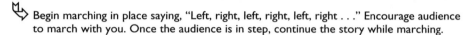 Invite audience, or a few participants to join the parade and form a line behind you. Continue marching along. Lead audience participants in a circle around the room. Lead parade wherever it is safe.

The line grew longer and longer. Kelly's knees went higher. Soon the line was in step. The sound of marching feet grew louder. Kelly was actually leading a parade!

They marched past Miss Buxton. Her silver whistle flashed in the sunlight. Kelly turned away and marched toward another corner of the schoolyard.

 At every turn, Kelly thought about where she would lead her parade. Just marching around the schoolyard got boring. She spotted an open gate. "Go! Go for it!" said a voice inside of her.

Kelly glanced at her twin sister, Kim, jumping rope in the schoolyard. "Kim would never leave the schoolyard." she thought. "It's against the rules."

Left, right, left, right, left, right . . .

Kelly looked for Miss Buxton. Her back was turned toward Kelly.

Left, right, left, right, left, right . . .

"Oh! The whole world must see my parade!" Kelly thought. And she led the parade right through the gate.

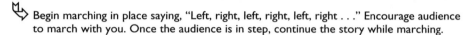 Continue marching, now stronger. Be proud. Chin up. Chest out. Big, beaming smile.

Left, right, left, right, left, right . . .

They marched to the front of the school on the sidewalk by Victory Boulevard. People in cars, buses, and trucks watched the parade as it marched in perfect step.

Kelly shouted above the street noise. "Left, right, left, right, left, right . . ."

Then Kelly got an idea. "I'll lead the parade past the Post. The *veterans* will see my parade!"

➪ Increase voice volume and tempo.

Left, right, left, right, left, right . . .

The parade marched faster and faster. It rounded the corner towards the Post. A veteran came out of the building. His uniform was decorated with metals and stripes. He stopped when he saw the children and waited until they were almost near him. "Company halt!" he shouted.

➪ Stop marching. Audience will stop. If not, repeat the command in the voice of the veteran. This should bring the audience to a halt. Continue the story even if there are one or two stragglers.

The parade stopped. The kids stood still. "Who is in charge here?" the veteran asked, his face quite serious. Kelly's stomach flipped and flopped like a flag in the breeze. The kids behind her were silent. In a wee tiny voice, Kelly said, "I . . . I . . . I am!"

"What is your name?" he asked sternly.

"Kelly."

"Kelly? Just Kelly?"

"Kelly McGowan, Sir." Her cheeks were on fire. "We're honoring all the brave soldiers. I didn't mean to do anything bad. We'll go back to the school yard now." Kelly turned to leave.

➪ Turn as if to run away.

"Halt!" he commanded. "About face, Kelly McGowan!"

Slowly, she turned around. The veteran looked even more serious.

"I've seen you watching us practice here at the Post every evening, Kelly McGowan." His face broke into a big smile.

➪ Make a big smile.

"How would you like to have your Corps march in *our* Memorial Day parade on Monday?"

Kelly could hardly believe her ears. The kids jumped up and down, whooping, "Yes! Yes! Yes!"

➪ Raise arm each time "yes" is said.

Kelly nodded.

"Be here," said the veteran, "at seven o'clock on Monday morning. Ask for me, Captain Baines. We'll have small flags for your group to carry and red poppies for everyone to wear. Till then, Kelly McGowan, shoulders back and chin up." He saluted Kelly, turned around sharply and went back into the building.

➪ Demonstrate the swift salute and sharp turn of a soldier.

"Yes!" Kids yelled, jumping up and down.

Then Kelly called out, "Left, right, left, right, forward MARCH."

ꕳ Begin marching, leading audience participants in line back to their seats. Continue marching.

ꕳ Audience marches in place at their seats.

One by one, kids got in line and marched back to the schoolyard. The sound of their feet was louder than ever. When they arrived, Miss Buxton came toward them blowing hard on her silver whistle.

ꕳ Stop marching and raise hand in air, signaling STOP.

Kelly stopped short. Kids behind her bumped into each other.

"You know you're not supposed to leave the schoolyard!" Miss Buxton's voice shot through the air. "Come here, right now!" Kelly's heart beat like a big bass drum.

Just then the bell rang. Kids ran from everywhere to get on their class lines. Kelly's parade broke up and ran past her, helter-skelter. Miss Buxton lost sight of her in the kid blizzard.

"Whew. Saved by the bell!" Kelly whispered and ran to her class line. Then she heard that whistle again. Kelly turned around.

ꕳ As Miss Buxton, you blow on a silver whistle.

"Against the fence!" Miss Buxton ordered, pointing her finger. But not at Kelly, at *Kim!*

Kelly gasped. "Oh, no! Poor Kim!" The ever-obedient Kim walked toward the fence.

Kelly raced toward her saying, "Miss Buxton thinks you're *me*!"

" Wait 'til I tell Mom!" Kim began to cry.

"Oh, Kim, I'm sorry!" Kelly apologized.

Miss Buxton blew her whistle again.

ꕳ Blow on the silver whistle again.

This time at *Kelly*. "Why aren't you on your class line?" she demanded. Kelly froze in place.

"Did you hear what I said?" the teacher barked.

Kelly opened her mouth as if to speak. But before she could say a word, Miss Buxton commanded, "Get in your class line *now*!"

Kelly did, wondering what would happen to Kim. "What should I do?" she thought. "*I* should be punished, not Kim."

When Kelly and Kim got home from school, Kim ran to tell Mom how and why she had been sent to the principal's office. Mom immediately scolded Kelly. "A parade's a nice idea, Kelly, but *you* broke a school rule. When you get back to school after Memorial Day, you must go to the principal and tell the truth."

"Okay!" Kelly scowled. "But I *did* try to tell Miss Buxton!"

110

"And for breaking the school rule," Mom continued, "you're grounded until you speak to the principal!"

"Oh, no! Not on Memorial Day, Mom! Captain Baines at the Post is expecting my school Corps. We're going to be in the big Memorial Day parade!"

Then Kelly gathered up her courage, and finally sputtered, "Kim got into trouble today because you make us dress alike. Miss Buxton couldn't tell us apart. Nobody *can!*"

Mom's eyes grew big and round. She stared at Kelly. Then at Kim. At last, she broke the silence. "You're right, Kelly," she said slowly. "Maybe what happened today is *partly* my fault. Kim took the blame for your actions, and I believe that you tried to tell the truth."

Mom put her arms around Kelly and Kim. She nodded, "From now on you don't have to dress alike unless you want to."

"Gee, thanks, Mom!" Kim said.

Kelly and Kim looked at each other and smiled. They knew they'd *never* forget Kelly's Memorial Day parade. And they never did.

. . . Oh! I bet you're wondering whether Mom allowed Kelly to lead her friends in the Memorial Day parade that Monday. Well, she did. Kelly kept her Corps in step the whole time—even when she saw Miss Buxton in the crowd.

ABOUT THE STORY

This really happened to the author. Today she and her sister still talk about how their mom used to dress them exactly alike, and especially about the day of the schoolyard parade.

RELATED BOOKS

1. *THE WALL* by Eve Bunting, illustrated by Ronald Himler (Reading Rainbow Book, 1992). A contemporary and realistic children's story about the impact of losing a loved one in war.

2. *MEMORIAL DAY SURPRISE* by Theresa Martin Golding, illustrated by Alexandra Artigas (Boyds Mills Press, 2004). A heart-warming, multicultural story and picture book that introduces children, ages five and up (Grades K–2) to the true meaning of Memorial Day.

3. *LET'S GET READY FOR MEMORIAL DAY* by Lloyd G. Douglas (Rosen Book Works, 2003). Get ready for the holiday by making flags. (Editor's note: See *The Freedom Flag*, an origami story by Gay Merrill Gross, later in this volume.)

4. *MEMORIAL DAY* by Mir Tamin Ansary (Heinemann, 2006). A nonfiction read-aloud book that introduces Memorial Day to children ages six to nine years.

5. *REMEMBRANCE: A TRIBUTE TO AMERICA'S VETERANS* by Robert B. Fletcher, illustrated by Robert A. Fletcher (Iron Mountain Press, 2007). A touching tribute to America's fallen dead, portraying scenes of military and veteran funerals from the Revolutionary War to the Afghanistan War. Historical text and inspirational quotes and poems accompany forty-four detailed watercolor paintings and nineteen pencil drawings.

ACTIVITIES

I. Memorial Day Ceremonies

1. Look for Memorial Day ceremony announcements in public media. Organize a field trip to attend one, especially if it is near a memorial, which may be a building (such as a museum), a monument or statue, or a simple plaque that names a battle or lists the names of those that died in a particular battle. Many memorials bear interesting inscriptions or epitaphs.

2. Visit the war memorials at the Arlington National Cemetery, Virginia, or attend Memorial Day services in our nation's capital. See http://www.mdw.army.mil.

   One service is the wreath-laying ceremony at the Tomb of the Unknowns, in Arlington National Cemetery. See http://www.arlingtoncemetery.org.

3. Visit local or regional cemeteries to place flags or flowers on the graves of fallen heroes, remembering all those who sacrificed their lives for the United States.

4. On Memorial Day, participate in a "National Moment of Remembrance" at 3 P.M., wherever you are.

II. Memorial Day Parades

1. Find a local Veterans of Foreign Wars (VFW) post at: http://emem.vfw.org/findpost.aspx.

   Visit the VFW post and get to know the VFW Post Commander. Ask for the name of the person or group sponsoring a Memorial Day parade. Find out if you can participate in it. If there are no plans for a parade, start one. Contact scoutmasters, schools with or without a band, religious centers, civic organizations, Gold Star Mothers, and so on. The VFW Post Commander may also know of a war veteran who may enjoy coming to your Memorial Day picnic. Oh, the stories you will hear!

III. The U.S. Flag

1. On Memorial Day, fly the U.S. flag half-staff until noon.

2. On Memorial Day, fly the Prisoner of War/Missing in Action (POW/MIA) flag.

IV. Troops, War Veterans, and Loved Ones of Fallen Heroes

1. Send letters or postcards to our troops and war veterans. See http://www.memorialdayfoundation.org for vintage Memorial Day postcards, as well as buttons and bouquets.

2. Pledge to care about widows, widowers, and orphans of our fallen heroes and to provide aid for the disabled veterans.

3. Find and send Memorial Day poems to families of fallen heroes. See http://www.funmunch.com.

V. The American Legion

1. Invite a member of the American Legion to come and show the American Legion's DVD/video, "For Which It Stands."

2. Ask about the American flag's history and symbolism, as well as the proper etiquette and respect for the flag.

3. Ask for a demonstration on flag folding.

4. Discuss the origin of the Pledge of Allegiance and "The Star- Spangled Banner."

5. Discuss the meaning of the words in the "Pledge of Allegiance."

6. For more information on the American flag and the DVD/video, go to the "Americanism" page at the American Legion's Web site: http://www.legion.org/.

VI. Memorial Day Flowers

1. The poppy continues to serve as a perpetual tribute to those who gave their lives for the nation's freedom. It is called the "flower of remembrance." Veterans produce and sell artificial poppies that can be used to obtain donations to help countless veterans and their widows, widowers, and orphans. For the history of the poppy flower as it relates to Memorial Day, see the U.S. Department of Veterans Affairs Web site: http://www.va.gov/.

2. Read aloud Linda Garfield's picture book, *IN FLANDERS FIELDS,* illustrated by Janet Wilson (A Doubleday Book for Young Readers, Delacourte Press, 1995).

3. Create a Memorial Day poppy (*STAR-SPANGLED CRAFTS* by Kathy Ross, illustrated by Sharon Lane Holm (Millbrook Press, 2003).

VII. Memorial Day Poems

1. Read aloud John T. Bird's poem "Last Monday in May," which may be found at the White House Commission on Remembrance Web site: http://www.remember.gov/.

2. For other Memorial Day poems, including the following, go to http://www.pa-roots.org/~memorialday/.

   • "Mother of A Soldier" by Folger McKinsey

   • "Memorial Day" by Eula Gladys Lincoln

   • "The Bivouac of the Dead" by Theodore O'Hara

   • "The Blue and the Gray" by Francis Miles Finch

   • "The Blue and the Gray" (author unknown)

   • "Where are You Going, Great-Heart?" by John Oxenham

   • "In Flanders Field" by John McCrae

VIII. Memorial Day Music

1. Listen to the White House Commission on Remembrance's anthem, "On This Day," composed by Charles Strouse. The song honors America's fallen and the families left behind. It inspires American pride and patriotism. Lyrics, music, and MP3 versions may be found on the Commission's Web site: http://www.remember.gov/.

2. Listen to *Rememberance, a* CD by Rob Fletcher (Iron Mountain Press, 2007). Songs include "God Bless America," "Rally Round the Flag," "Soldier's Joy," "I'll Be with You in Apple Blossom Time," "Amazing Grace," and many more. The CD features readings by Pulitzer prize–winning poet Louis Simpson, and "The Welder" by Irene Carlisle (a.k.a. "Rosie the Riveter"). The CD may be purchased at www.veterantribute.com/store.

HOLIDAY BACKGROUND INFORMATION

Memorial Day, or Decoration Day as it was first known, had its beginnings after the American Civil War (1861–1865) when Union soldiers of the North fought Confederate Southern soldiers. They were fighting over whether the United States should remain one country.

A wide rift had developed between the Northern and Southern states because of slavery and states' rights. People in the North felt it was morally wrong for one human being to own another. They wanted slavery abolished in the South. When the abolitionists helped slaves escape to Canada, Southern cotton and tobacco planters became angry. They felt that abolitionists were stealing their property and threatening their livelihood. The same Southerners who opposed the abolitionists wanted no interference by the federal government in their state affairs. They thought they had the legal right to reject any federal laws they did not like and to secede from the Union. And they did.

On November 6, 1860, Abraham Lincoln, who had spoken against the spread of slavery in new territories, was elected president, and with that several Southern states seceded and formed the Confederate States of America. In a short time, the American Civil War broke out between the Confederate states and the states of the Union. The war began on April 12, 1861, and ended on April 9, 1865.

After the war, the worn-out and injured soldiers returned to their homes and families. About 620,000 soldiers had died on the battlefields (the Union lost 360,000; the Confederates lost 260,000).

The origins of Memorial Day are remote and mixed, but two men are given credit as its originators: Henry C. Welles and General John B. Murray from Waterloo, New York. They wanted to do something to honor the soldiers who fought so hard in the American Civil War. They decorated the graves of the fallen soldiers with flowers and flags. To honor the soldiers who had returned, the veterans had a parade on the way to the cemetery. The first Decoration Day was May 5, 1866.

Another man, John A. Logan, who led the Grand Army of the Republic (GAR), a large group of veterans in the North, had the same idea as Welles and Murray. He wanted to decorate the graves of Northern soldiers every year on May 30. By 1882, the GAR wanted to remember the dead from *all* wars and so changed "Decoration Day" to "Memorial Day." By this time, the Southern states had a holiday for honoring their Confederate dead, although the date for the holiday was different in every Southern state.

In 1971, America's thirty-seventh president, Richard M. Nixon (1913–1994), declared Memorial Day a national holiday. Today many organizations march in military parades and take part in special programs.

We not only remember the soldiers who fell in wars but also our dead relatives. Many people have picnics, reunions, revivals, or sporting events on that day. National events held on Memorial Day include the Indianapolis Speedway automobile race.

On Memorial Day, soldiers at army bases fire rifles. To honor those soldiers who died at sea, navy sailors set tiny ships filled with flowers afloat or throw flowers into the ocean. Families and veteran posts place flowers and flags on the graves of those who died to keep freedom alive. Veterans also sell small, red artificial poppies to help disabled veterans (see Activities earlier in this chapter).

More information on Memorial Day may be found at the History Channel's Web site: http://www.history.com. Find the link to Memorial Day for a complete history of Memorial Day, a timetable of America's wars, Memorial Day videos, battle maps, and more.

Also consult the following organizations:

1. The Veterans of Foreign Wars (VFW): http://www.vfw.org/.

   The VFW is an American organization of current or former members of the United States armed forces, founded in 1899. Its mission is to "honor the dead by helping the living." It seeks to develop comradeship among its members, assist needy veterans and their families, organize memorial services for deceased veterans, and promote patriotism. Headquartered in Kansas City, Missouri, there are 2.4 million members in approximately 9,000 Posts worldwide as of this writing.

2. The American Legion: http://www.legion.org/.

   The American Legion is an organization of veterans of the U.S. armed forces. It was founded in 1919 after World War I by veterans returning from Europe. Headquartered in Indianapolis, Indiana, the Legion consists of nearly 3 million men and women, as of July 2007, who were honorably discharged from the war.

3. The White House Commission on Remembrance: http://www.remember.gov/.

   The White House Commission on Remembrance was established by Congress to promote the values of Memorial Day by acts of remembrance throughout the year. The major initiative of the Commission is the National Moment of Remembrance. The Web site includes information on Taps and John T. Bird's song, "Last Monday in May." You can also sign up to receive the Commission's newsletter.

4. No Greater Love (NGL): http://www.ngl.org/.

   NGL was founded in 1971. It is the only humanitarian, educational, nonprofit organization in the United States solely dedicated to providing annual programs of friendship and care for those who lost a loved one in the service to our country or by an act of terrorism. NGL has created many memorials at Arlington National Cemetery to remember those Americans who have died in wars, conflicts, and terrorist attacks. Search the NGL Web site for a list of the memorials.

5. The Memorial Day Foundation: http://www.memorialdayfoundation.org.

   The Memorial Day Foundation was founded to increase awareness and respect for Memorial Day because it was about to become a forgotten holiday in America. Memorial Day buttons and vintage postcards, as well as bouquets for graves, may be purchased at their Web site.

BIOGRAPHY

V. J. RICHEY, Ph.D., a professional storyteller for several years, drew from her previous careers as an educator and businesswoman to develop repertoires that fit every occasion and every age group. As an author of children's stories and poems, VJ became the first Regional Advisor in Sweden for the Society of Children's Book Writers and Illustrators (1994–1995). At the present time, VJ resides in the Lowcountry of South Carolina, serving as a consultant for new business ventures.

CONTACT

Dr. V. J. Richey
VJRichey@embarqmail.com

The Buddha's birthday is celebrated on the full moon of the sixth lunar month, any day between May and June.

The Buddha's Birthday in Thailand

INTRODUCTION

For non-Thai storytellers, before performing this story, be sure to practice non-English terms, such as names of people and places. For other Buddhist and Thai terms, storytellers could use their own discretion whether or not to use them. A glossary of non-English terms may be found following the story.

STORY SCRIPT

Once King Suddhodana Gautama of the Sakya clan ruled the city called Kapilavastu. He was married to Princess Sirimahamaya of Devadaha, and they lived happily together, ruling Kapilavastu. People could often be heard to say,

"Long live our Great King and Queen."

Would you repeat that with me?

"Long live our Great King and Queen."

> **Audience responds:** Long live our Great King and Queen.

This was usually uttered at least three times. In keeping with the tradition, let's repeat it two more times.

> **Audience responds:** Long live our Great King and Queen.
> Long live our Great King and Queen.

When she was at her tenth lunar month of pregnancy, the queen asked for a royal leave to return to her home city to deliver her child according to the customary rite. It was the day of the full moon in the sixth lunar month when she gave birth to her first son, Lumbini Park, halfway between Kapilavastu and Devadaha. After giving birth to her first son, the future Buddha, the queen returned to Kapilavastu city. The king was filled with joy and held a naming ceremony for the prince. He was called Siddhartha, which means "one with every wish fulfilled." The entire congregation chanted its joyful acceptance,

117

"sathu, sathu, sathu," which means something like amen in Christianity. Will you chant that with me? Remember that the *u* vowel sounds like the *u* in suit.

Audience responds: *Sathu, sathu, sathu.*

One day the queen became very ill. After seven days, she passed on to be reborn in *Dusita* heaven, which in Buddhist cosmology means a heaven for deceased virtuous people. All the seers came and gave the royal predictions.

"The prince will be the most powerful emperor," said one.

"The prince will grow up to be the most meritorious religious leader," said the other.

The king was delighted with the first prediction. He tried every way to prevent the prince from seeing birth, suffering, old age, and death, which could be the motivation for the prince to resign to the religious life. The prince was married to Princess Phimpayasodhara at the age of sixteen and had a son named Rahula at the age of twenty-nine.

At this point, he had learned all about the life cycle of birth, suffering, old age, and death. He decided to leave his worldly possessions in order to follow a religious life in the forest. He was seeking the truth of freeing himself and other living creatures from the suffering of the life cycle.

The king was filled with sorrow for shattering his dream of having the royal son as the most powerful emperor in the universe. The dream was gone.

The royal son spent six years of learning with different masters, from meditation to self-mortification. Only dry skin and bones were left in his body, but he still did not discover the truth. That night the god Indra came from heaven to play music on a *phin*, a string instrument, for the future Buddha, or Bhodhisatta.

The first song was played on the tightest strings, which broke before any beautiful music could be heard. The second song was played on the loose strings, which produced droning sounds. The third song was played on the strings that were neither too tight nor too loose. And the music that came to the royal ears was splendid and heavenly.

The Bhodhisatta then came to realize that it was the middle path that would lead him to the discovery of truth. He began to nourish his body with food and his mind with peaceful reflections. He sat under the Bhodi tree along the Neranchara riverbank to meditate. On the day of his enlightenment, the day of the full moon in the sixth lunar month, a young maiden named Sujada came with young rice cooked in milk called *mathupaayaad* to offer to the Bhodhisatta. After the meal, he put the tray in the river and made a wish. If he were to discover the Truth, the tray would float upstream. And the tray did float upstream.

Before achieving enlightenment, Mara's army—enemy of people—came to attack the Bhodhisatta, tempting him to leave and threatening to take his life. But the Bhodhisatta remained calm until Nang Thoranee, the earth goddess, came to rescue the future Buddha by squeezing water from her long tresses to flood Mara's army. Sounds of disapproval came from all creatures:

Shame, shame, shame to Mara. (Using the English word for "shame.")

Will you say it with me—three times?

> **Audience responds:** Shame, shame, shame to Mara.
> Shame, shame, shame to Mara.
> Shame, shame, shame to Mara.

That very night, the Bhodhisatta became enlightened with the four noble truths. He became the Buddha. He stayed at the tree for seven weeks. On the fifth week, Mara's daughters, named Tanha (Desire), Rakha (Passion), and Oradee (Pleasure), came to tempt the Buddha, but in vain. Thus, the Bhodhisatta has become the enlightened one, or the Buddha. After the seventh week, the Buddha went out to teach others, who sang praise for his compassion. Three times, they chanted. If you are Buddhists, you might want to chant with me. "We take refuge under the Buddha's royal protection."

> **Audience responds:** We take refuge under the Buddha's royal protection.
> We take refuge under the Buddha's royal protection.
> We take refuge under the Buddha's royal protection.

The Buddha's first sermon was on the full moon of the eighth lunar month. His first disciples were the five Brahmins. And his teaching continued until *Maakhabucha Day,* which fell on the full moon of the third lunar month. His 1,250 enlightened disciples came to pay homage to the Buddha. So, he gave the sermon called *Owaadpaatimok,* which is the heart of Buddhism—to avoid evil deeds, to do good deeds, and to purify one's mind. Thus, all living creatures sang praise of the Buddha's Teachings. If you like, you may chant with me three times, "We take refuge under the Buddha's Teachings."

> **Audience responds:** We take refuge under the Buddha's Teachings.
> We take refuge under the Buddha's Teachings.
> We take refuge under the Buddha's Teachings.

With the appearance of his 1,250 enlightened disciples, there came another element in Buddhism, the *Sangha,* the Buddha's Disciples. Thus, the living creatures sang out their praise again, three times. If you like, you may chant with me three times. "We take refuge under the Buddha's Disciples."

> **Audience responds:** We take refuge under the Buddha's Disciples.
> We take refuge under the Buddha's Disciples.
> We take refuge under the Buddha's Disciples.

At this time, Buddhism had achieved the three gems in Buddhism—the Buddha (the religious leader), the *Dhamma* (the Buddha's Teachings), and the *Sangha.* The Buddha continued to teach others for forty-five more years before his *nirvana* (the total extinction of existence) at the age of eighty. On the full moon of the sixth lunar month, the Buddha attained *nirvana.*

And now we have the three most important elements in Buddhism to which we take refuge and chant in humbleness. Here is the chant. Again, if you like, you may chant with me.

"We take refuge under the Buddha's royal protection."

"We take refuge under the Buddha's Teachings."

"We take refuge under the Buddha's Disciples."

> **Audience responds:** We take refuge under the Buddha's royal protection.
> We take refuge under the Buddha's Teachings.
> We take refuge under the Buddha's Disciples.

On the day and night of the full moon in the sixth lunar month, Thai Buddhists pay homage and commemoration to the Buddha's Birth, Enlightenment, and *Nirvana*. The king, queen, the royal family, and the officials lead the people to offer food to the monks; to listen to the sermons on the life of the Buddha and other sacred texts; and to walk around the temples three times in a clockwise direction with fresh flowers, lighted candles, and incense sticks in their hands.

In villages, men and women wear white and take the five precepts, vowing not to kill or harm others' lives, not to steal or to appropriate things that do not belong to them, not to lie or to say hurting and inappropriate words, not to have intimate relations, not to commit adultery or sexual harassments, and not to drink any intoxicating beverages.

During the three nights, the night before the full moon, the full moon night, and the night after the full moon, lanterns are hung around temples and people's houses to remind them of the light of the Buddha's teachings. All of us are taught to remember to pay homage to the Buddha, to follow his teachings of Buddhism—to avoid evil deeds, to do good deeds, and to purify one's mind—and to honor the Buddha's disciples, the *Sangha*. And all of us chant in peaceful contentment the three gems in Buddhism. Can you remember them? I surely hope so. Repeat them with me for one last chant, if you like.

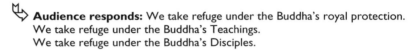 **Audience responds:** We take refuge under the Buddha's royal protection.
We take refuge under the Buddha's Teachings.
We take refuge under the Buddha's Disciples.

ABOUT THE STORY

The Buddha's Birthday in Thailand is called *Wan Wisakha Bucha* (*Wan* means day; *wisakha* means the full moon of the sixth lunar month; *Bucha* means to worship or pay homage). It is the day that Thai Buddhist people commemorate the Buddha's Birthday, Enlightenment, and *Nirvana,* as all three events miraculously happened on the same day. This is the Buddha's birth story from my recollection as it is shared in Thailand.

GLOSSARY OF NON-ENGLISH TERMS USED AS THEY APPEAR IN THE STORY

NOTE: Thai language has been much influenced by Pali and Sanskrit. Thai people borrow many Sanskrit words to use in the spelling of their names, but when they pronounce these words, they use Thai pronunciation. For example, the word to mean the greatest king is Maha Raja, but the Thai people would pronounce it as "maha racha."

Non-English Words	Meanings
Suddhodana	Prince Siddhartha's father
Gautama (*Kho-ta-ma*)	King Shuddhodana's family name
Sakya, Shakya (*sak-ya*)	King Shuddhodana's clan
Kapilavastu (*ga-bin-la-pat*)	King Shuddhodana's city in the south of present-day Nepal
Sirimahamaya (*si-ri-ma-haa-maa-yaa*)	The Buddha's mother

Non-English Words	Meanings
Devadaha (*the-wa-tha-ha*)	Queen Sirimahamaya's home
Lumbini (*lum-phi-nii*)	The garden where Prince Siddhartha was born
sathu (*saa-thu*)	Accepting, approving sounds, similar to "amen" in Christianity
Indra	A Hindu god
Dusita (*du-sit*)	One of the seven levels of heaven in Buddhist cosmology
Phimpayasodhara (*phim-phaa-ya-soo-tha-raa*)	Name of Prince Siddhartha's wife
Rahula (*raa-hun*)	Name of Prince Siddhartha's son; it means "fetter"
Phin (*pin*)	Thai/Lao string musical instrument
Bodhisatva or Bhodhisatta (*pho-thi-sat*)	A being seeking Buddhahood
Neranchara (*ne-ran-cha-laa*)	The river where the Buddha floated his food tray to make a wish and where he meditated; other names of the river include the Nilajan or Lilajan rivers
Sujada (*su-cha-da*)	The maiden who presented the young rice cooked in milk to the Buddha the day he was to attain enlightenment
Mathupaayaad (*ma-thu-paa-yaad*)	Young rice cooked in milk
Nang Thoranee (*nang-tho-ra-nii*)	*Nang* refers to a woman's title; *thoranee* means earth; the Earth Goddess
Mara (*maan*)	The demon who threatened to kill the Buddha on the night of his attainment of enlightenment
Tanha (*tan-haa*)	Desire, craving; Mara's first daughter
Rakha (*raa-kha*)	Passion; Mara's second daughter
Oradee (*Or-ra-dii*)	Pleasure; Mara's third daughter
Makhabucha Day (*maa-kha-buu-chaa*)	*Maakha* means the full moon of the third lunar month; *bucha* means to worship, to pay homage; the day the 1,250 enlightened disciples came to pay homage to the Buddha by chance and the day the Buddha gave the first sermon on the heart of Buddhism—to avoid evil deeds, to do good deeds, and to purify one's mind
Owaadpaatimok (*oh-waad-paa-ti-mok*)	The first sermon the Buddha gave to his 1,250 enlightened disciples on the full moon of the third lunar month or Maakhabucha Day Patimokkha (*paa-ti-mok*) can also refer to the basic code of monastic discipline, consisting of 227 rules for monks and 310 for female monks
Sangha (*sang-gha*)	A Buddhist community of *gha* monks, the Buddha's disciples; these monks vow to practice the 227 rules
nirvana (*nip-phaan*)	"Total extinction of existence," the ultimate Buddhist goal of obtaining peace by extinguishing the illusion of ego and desire

More information on the Buddhist terms and pronunciations can be found on the following sample Web sites:

http://www.accesstoinsight.org/glossary.html

http://www.mahidol.ac.th/budsir/glossary.htm

http://ias.berkeley.edu/orias/visuals/buddha/Buddha_gloss.html

OTHER STORIES ABOUT THE BUDDHA

1. *PHYA KHANKHAAK, THE TOAD KING: A Translation of an Isan Fertility Myth in Verse*, translated by Wajuppa Tossa; original transcription by Phra Ariyanuwat (Associated University Presses, 1996).

2. *THE THREEFOLD REFUGE IN THE THERAVÂDA BUDDHIST TRADITION*, by John Ross Carter, editor, (Anima Books, 1982).

3. *TEN LIVES OF BUDDHA,* by M. L. Manich Jumsai (Chalermnit, 2000).

4. *TEN LIVES OF THE BUDDHA: Siamese Temple Paintings and Jataka Tales,* by Elizabeth Wray, Clare Rosenfield, and Dorothy Bailey; photographs by Joe D. Wray (Weatherhill, 1996).

5. *TALES AND TEACHINGS OF THE BUDDHA: The Jâtaka Stories in Relation to the Pâli, Canon* by John Garrett Jones (Allen & Unwin, 1979).

For information about video recordings, e-mail Wajuppa Tossa (wajuppa@yahoo.com).

RECOMMENDED BOOKS

1. *ESSAYS ON CULTURAL THAILAND* by Phrayâ Anuman Rajadhon, editor (Bangkok, Thailand: Office of the National Culture Commission, Ministry of Education, 1992).

2. *REFLECTIONS ON THAI CULTURE: Collected Writings of William J. Klausner* (Siam Society, 1987).

3. *THE RELATIONSHIP BETWEEN THE ART AND HISTORY OF THE THAI PEOPLE,* Na Pâknam Nô, translator; Sudhiporn Vidhyanukorn, editor (Office of the National Culture Commission, MI, Cellar Book Shop, distributor, 1985).

4. *THAILAND: A Short History* by David K. Wyatt (Yale University Press, 2004).

THAI/LAO FOLKTALES

1. *LAO FOLKTALES* by Wajuppa Tossa and Kongdeuane Nettavong, Margaret Read MacDonald, editor (Libraries Unlimited, 2008).

2. *THAI TALES* by Supaporn Vathanprida (Libraries Unlimited, 1994).

3. *THE GIRL WHO WORE TOO MUCH*, retold by Margaret Read MacDonald; Thai text by Supaporn Vathanprida; illustrated by Yvonne Lebrun Davis (August House, 1998).

4. *HUSH! A THAI LULLABY* by Mingfong Ho, illustrated by Holly Meade (Orchard Books, 1996).

5. *PHADAENG NANG AI: Translation of a Thai/Isan Folk Epic in Verse* by Wajuppa Tossa (Bucknell University Press, 1990).

BACKGROUND INFORMATION

Visit these Web sites for more information:

http://www.thai-experience.org/festival-calendar.html

http://www.un.or.th/thailand/holidays.html

http://www.tourismthailand.org/

http://www.seasite.niu.edu/Thai/default.htm

http://www.urbandharma.org/udharma3/holidays.html

http://ias.berkeley.edu/orias/visuals/buddha/life.html

http://www.mahidol.ac.th/budsir/MenuEng.htm

BIOGRAPHY

Dr. Wajuppa Tossa is an associate professor of English and American Literature at Mahasarakham University, Thailand. Her translations of the Isan folk epics *Phadaeng Nang Ai* and *Phya Khankhaak, The Toad King* were published by Bucknell University Press in 1990 and 1996, respectively. Her new book, working in cooperation with Lao National Library Director Kongdeuane Nettavong, titled *Lao Folktales* (edited by Dr. Margaret Read MacDonald), was published by Libraries Unlimited in 2008. Dr. Wajuppa Tossa is also a storyteller, touring and giving storytelling performances in Thailand and other countries, including Malaysia, Laos, Myanmar, the Philippines, Singapore, Hong Kong, China, Australia, The Netherlands, and the United States. She delights her audiences, students, and workshop participants by sharing her love of folktales and the art of storytelling in her presentations. She is particularly keen on the use of folktales and storytelling in her career as a teacher and facilitator. (Many websites about Dr. Tossa's activities can be found through an Internet search engine.)

CONTACT

Dr. Wajuppa Tossa
Associate Professor of English and American Literature
Western Languages and Linguistics Department
Humanities and Social Sciences Faculty
Mahasarakham University
Khamriang, Kantharawichai
Mahasarakham 44150, Thailand
E-mail: wajuppa@yahoo.com

June

An "Origami" Story
GAY MERRILL GROSS

Flag Day, a legal holiday, is celebrated June 14 in the United States of America.

The Freedom Flag

INTRODUCTION

Pass out to each member of the audience a blank sheet of paper, 8.5 x 11 inches. On the storyteller's sheet, you will have printed "A Free Family Lives Here" as diagramed below. Ask your audience to follow your instructions on the blank sheet of paper.

STORY SCRIPT

Position your paper so the long sides are at the top and bottom.

History is not always written in the pages of a book, or printed in a newspaper.

Fold your paper in half like a book, bringing the short sides together (demonstrate—see diagram A).

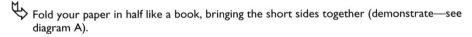

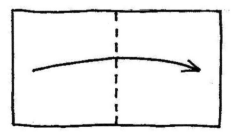

Diagram A

☝ Fold the paper in half again, bringing the bottom edges up to the top edges (see diagram B).

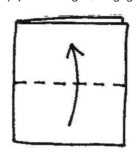

Diagram B

Some people's stories of freedom are very small but no less important. So, let's open our minds.

☝ Storyteller demonstrates how small the paper can become. See diagrams C and D.

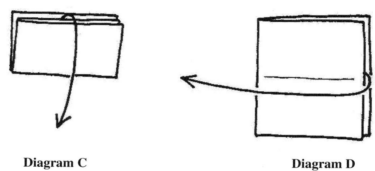

Diagram C   **Diagram D**

☝ Completely open your paper back to your original rectangle. (On your flag, the writing still faces you in the top corner.) Please put the paper down now, or hold it out of sight until it is mentioned again in the story.

In this story, a young boy named Luke was alone at home when he heard the sound of men approaching on horses. He knew his country was at war. Was this the enemy's army? Were these men sent to force him and his family to live according to their rules? Or were they from his family's side? Perhaps they were standing up to the people, trying to tell them how to live their lives? As the young boy peeked out of the window, he could not make out the faces of the people on the horses. But then he saw something that made his heart jump with joy. He saw someone in the group carrying a long stick with a piece of material showing the colors and symbols of this group.

Luke didn't have any colored material, but he ran and got a large sheet of paper and tore it halfway down the center on one side.

☝ Now pick up your paper and lift it up (see diagram E).

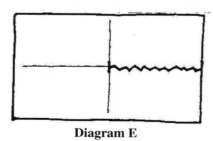

Diagram E

☝ Lift up the paper again. Tear the paper along the crease of the right side of the paper. Follow me along with this.

☝ Tear as far as the vertical centerline. If you have made sharp creases, the paper will be easier to tear. (Remember to keep your writing hidden from the audience.)

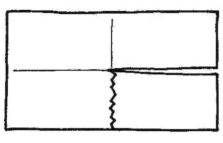

Diagram F

☝ Tear along the vertical crease, from the bottom edge up to the horizontal centerline. (See diagram F.) Remove the smaller rectangle you have torn off from the larger one. Then roll the side up into a stick. (Demonstrate per diagram G.)

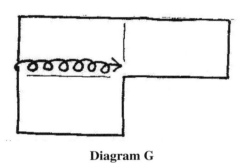

Diagram G

As the group on horses came nearer to his house, he rushed outside and held up his own flag so that all could see his message . . .

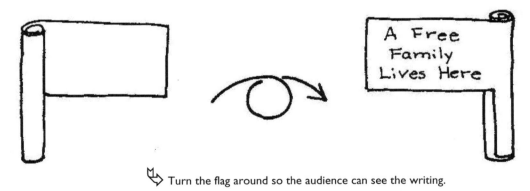

☝ Turn the flag around so the audience can see the writing.

A Free Family Lives Here!

Now write your message on your flag, *whatever you feel in your heart.*

ABOUT THE STORY

THE FREEDOM FLAG was never previously published. It was created especially for this book.

Gay Merrill Gross has written many stories combining origami and storytelling. Her first two stories were published in *THE FAMILY STORYTELLING HANDBOOK,* edited by Anne Pellowski (Simon & Schuster, 1988).

OTHER BOOKS ABOUT ORIGAMI

Several self-published origami storybooks are available from the author. Contact Gay at paperteller@hotmail.com.

Other introductory books include:

1. *MINIGAMI: Great Projects for Origami Greetings, Decorations and Pockets* by Gay Merrill Gross (Firefly Books, 2005).

2. *ORIGAMI: The Art of Paperfolding* by Gay Merrill Gross (Laurel Glen, 2004).

3. *ZOOGAMI: An Origami Menagerie at Your Fingertips* by Gay Merrill Gross (Barnes & Noble Books, 2005).

4. *ORNAGAMI: An Origami Christmas at Your Fingertips* by Gay Merrill Gross (Barnes & Noble Books, 2005).

5. *ORIGAMI: Easy-to-Make Paper Creations* by Gay Merrill Gross (Barnes & Noble Books, 2001).

6. *EASY ORIGAMI: Step-by-Step Projects That Teach Across the Curriculum* by Gay Merrill Gross and Tina Weintraub (Scholastic Professional Books, 1996).

For more information on origami, contact: OrigamiUSA, 15 West 77th Street, New York, NY 10024; Phone: (212) 769-5635; www.origami-USA.org.

BOOKS ABOUT FLAGS

1. *THE AMERICAN FLAG* by Vera Rollo (The Maryland Historical Press, 1989). Contains up-to-date information on the New Flag Code, the pledge of allegiance and its history, a description of state flags, flag etiquette, and so on.

2. *FLAGS OF THE WORLD:* www.crwflags.com/fotw/flags/. Contains more than 34,000 pages and over 64,000 images of flags.

3. *WORLD FLAGS:* www.worldflags101.com. Geographical regions and nations, and many symbols of other walks of life.

4. *FLAG DAY:* www.holidayinsights.com/other/flagday.htm. Contains proper display of our flag, how to "retire" it by burning, and so on.

5. *THE FLAG OF THE UNITED STATES OF AMERICA:* www.usflag.org. Contains Mike Dalka's dedication, the history of Flag Day, current flags of America, patriotic writings, and much more.

6. *NATIONAL FLAG DAY FOUNDATION:* www.nationalflagday.com/default.asp. Contains the first Flag Day observance, the Pledge of Allegiance, current events.

HOLIDAY BACKGROUND INFORMATION

Until the global war on terrorism, the following poem, author unknown, shows the shallow contempt for the flag under which some Americans functioned.

"I AM YOUR FLAG"

"Some people call me Old Glory, others call me the Star Spangled Banner, but whatever they call me, I am your flag—the flag of the United States of America.

"Something has been bothering me, so I thought I might talk it over with you, because you see, it is about you and me.

"I remember some time ago, people lined up on both sides of the street to watch a parade and, naturally, I was leading every parade proudly waving in the breeze. When your daddy saw me coming, he immediately removed his hat and placed it against his left shoulder so that his hand was directly over his heart—remember?

"What happened? I'm still the same old flag. Oh, I have a few more stars and a lot more blood has been shed since those parades of long ago.

"But now I don't feel as proud as I used to. When I come down your street and you just stand there with your hands in your pockets, I may get a small glance and then you look away. Then I see children running around and shouting – they don't seem to know who I am.

"I saw a man take his hat off, then look around. He didn't see anybody else with theirs off, so he quickly put it back on. And what about that night at the ballgame, when they played the "Star Spangled Banner" and I waved so proudly in the breeze, but nobody bothered to sing?

"Oh, they stood up all right, as sort of a mild patriotic gesture—but then they talked among themselves about the game and weather, but they did not sing. I felt hurt.

"Is it a sin to be patriotic? Have you forgotten what I stand for and where I have been? Anzio, Guadalcanal, Korea, Vietnam, in deserts overseas, and in many other battles. Take a look at the memorial honor rolls sometime—names of those who never came back—who gave their lives to keep this republic free.

"One nation, under God." When you salute me, you are saluting them.

"I may not be coming down your street for a long time. It seems that patriotic parades are a thing of the past. But when I do, will you do me a big favor?

"Stand up straight, place your right hand over your heart, and if they play the "Star Spangled Banner," sing out loud and clear. I will salute you by waving back.

"Show me you remember.

"I AM YOUR FLAG."

BIOGRAPHY

Gay Merrill Gross has been turning scraps of paper into whimsical origami figures since the age of nine. She has written seven introductory books on origami and has taught this magical art at museums, libraries, schools, colleges, and corporations.

Gay has been a guest teaching artist in Italy, Germany, Canada, and the United States. She especially loves sharing with teachers her ideas for integrating origami into classroom curriculum as a creative art and hands-on learning activity. By combining origami with storytelling, she creatively folds enchantment into the learning process.

Gay has appeared on *Martha Stewart Living* (CBS), *The Carol Duvall Show* (HGTV), and *Home Matters* (Discovery Channel). She is a founding and active member of OrigamiUSA. For further book information, consult http://www.allbookstores.com/author/Gay_Merrill_Gross.html.

CONTACT

E-mail: paperteller@hotmail.com

July

ANDREA BIELECKI, TERESA MILLER, AND OTHER PATRIOTIC STORYTELLERS

On July 4, Americans celebrate the signing of their Declaration of Independence in 1776.

Fourth of July Holiday

INTRODUCTION

On July 4, 2007, National Public Radio (NPR) had the Declaration of Independence read in its entirety by various staff members. One voice at a time took turns uttering one sentence of the Declaration. What a great audience-participation story this could make! Think of members of your audience becoming part and parcel of a truly historical moment! To enable this to happen, we are passing out copies of what we are going to use. The storyteller speaks the first sentence. Then, those of you who wish to stand up to indicate your willingness to be a voice for freedom can help. All right, then, let's see who is standing for freedom.

Wait for the audience to indicate their cooperation. If the group or room is large, pass out wireless microphones for audience responses, being sure you are in control of your own mike.

NOTE: This performance may be done in a classroom, in a library, in a theatre or in an auditorium. If a guitarist or a small band or a large band can be part of the program, you might want to advertise it as a *CONCERT FOR FREEDOM.*

STORY SCRIPT

When in the course of human events, it becomes necessary for one people to dissolve the political bands which have connected them with another and to assume among the powers of the earth, the separate and equal station to which the Laws of Nature and of Nature's God entitle them, a decent respect to the opinions of humankind requires that they should declare the cause which impel them to the separation.

[Storyteller moves from left to right section of audience seeing that each speaker passes the traveling mike on to next speaker.]

(Speaker 1)
We hold these truths to be self-evident, that all men are created equal, that they are endowed by their Creator with certain unalienable Rights, that among these are Life, Liberty and the pursuit of Happiness.

(Speaker 2)
That to secure these rights, Governments are instituted among Men, deriving their just powers from the consent of the governed.

♪ (Speaker 3)

That whenever any form of Government becomes destructive of these ends, it is the right of the People to alter or to abolish it, and to institute new Government, laying its foundation on such principles and organizing its powers in such form, as to them shall seem most likely to effect their Safety and Happiness.

♪ (Speaker 4)

Prudence, indeed, will dictate that Governments long established should not be changed for light and transient causes.

[After the fourth speaker, and again after the eighth, and the twelfth, and the sixteenth has spoken, storyteller speaks again, this time saying:]

A thought: You have heard that Americans have the worst voting record in the world. Think of this—every time you don't vote, you are giving power away to undeserving individuals.

♪ (Speaker 5)

Accordingly, all experience hath shown that man-kind are more disposed to suffer, while evils are sufferable, than to right themselves by abolishing the forms to which they are accustomed.

♪ (Speaker 6)

But when a long train of abuses and usurpations, pursuing invariably the same Object, evinces a design to reduce them under absolute Despotism,

♪ (Speaker 7)

It is their right, it is their duty, to throw off such Government, and to provide new Guards for their future security.

♪ (Speaker 8)

Such has been the patient sufferance of these Colonies; and such is now the necessity which constrains them to alter their former Systems of Government.

Every time people don't vote, they are keeping us an impoverished nation. **VOTE!**

♪ (Speaker 9)

The history of the present King of Great Britain is a history of repeated injuries and usurpations, all having in direct object the establishment of an absolute Tyranny over these States. To prove this, let Facts be submitted to the candid world.

♪ (Speaker 10)

He has refused his Assent to Laws, the most wholesome and necessary for the public good.

♪ (Speaker 11)

He has forbidden his Governors to pass Laws of immediate and pressing importance, unless suspended in their operation till his Assent should be obtained, and when so suspended he is utterly neglected to attend to them.

(Speaker 12)

He has refused to pass other Laws for the accommodation of large districts of people, unless those people would relinquish the right to Representation in the Legislature, a right inestimable to them and formidable to tyrants only.

Before I go on, it behooves me to remind you that we are great friends today with the people of England, so you won't hear any judgmental comments on anything going on politically right now.

(Speaker 13)

He has called together legislative bodies at places unusual, uncomfortable, and distant from the depository of their public Records, for the sole purpose of fatiguing them into compliance with his measures.

(Speaker 14)

He has dissolved Representative Houses repeatedly, for opposing with manly firmness his invasions on the rights of the people.

(Speaker 15)

He has refused for a long time to cause others to be elected; whereby the Legislative powers, incapable of Annihilation, have returned to the People at large for their exercise.

(Speaker 16)

The State remaining in the mean time is exposed to all the dangers of invasion from without and convulsions from within.

Now, our laws are written by representatives for whom we vote.

VOTE!

(Speaker 17)

He has endeavoured to prevent the population of these states; for that purpose obstructing the Laws for Naturalization of Foreigners; refusing to pass others to encourage their migrations hither, and raising the conditions of new Appropriations of Lands.

(Speaker 18)

He has obstructed the Administration of Justice, by refusing his Assent to Laws for establishing Judiciary powers.

(Speaker 19)

He has made Judges dependent on his Will alone, for the tenure of their offices, and the amount and payment of their salaries.

(Speaker 20)

He has erected a multitude of New Offices, and sent hither swarms of Officers to harass our people, and eat out their substance.

Every American has representation for citywide, countywide, state and national legislative offices.
VOTE!

(Speaker 21)

He has kept among us, in times of peace, Standing Armies without the Consent of our legislatures.

(Speaker 22)

He has affected to render the Military independent of and superior to the Civil power.

 (Speaker 23)

He has combined with others to subject us to a jurisdiction foreign to our constitution, and unacknowledged by our laws; giving his Assent to their Acts of pretended Legislation.

 (Speaker 24)

For Quartering large bodies of armed troops among us: for protecting them, by a mock Trial, from punishment for any Murders which they should commit on the Inhabitants of these States. . . .

We will not be too tired to exercise our right to vote. **VOTE!**

 (Speaker 25)

For cutting off our Trade with all parts of the world, for imposing Taxes on us without our Consent. For depriving us in many cases, of the benefits of Trial by Jury. For transporting beyond Seas to be tried for pretended offences.

 (Speaker 26)

For abolishing the free System of English Laws in a neighboring Province, establishing therein an Arbitrary government, and enlarging its Boundaries so as to render it at once an example and fit instrument for introducing the same absolute rule into these Colonies.

 (Speaker 27)

For taking away our Charters, abolishing our most valuable Laws, and altering fundamentally the Forms of our Governments.

 (Speaker 28)

For suspending our own Legislatures, and declaring themselves invested with power to legislate for us in all cases whatsoever.

The people, all the people, have a right to vote. **VOTE!**

 (Speaker 29)

He has abdicated Government here, by declaring us out of his Protection and waging War against us.

 (Speaker 30)

He has plundered our seas, ravaged our Coasts, burnt our towns, and destroyed the lives of our people.

 (Speaker 31)

He is at this time transporting large Armies of foreign Mercenaries to complete the works of death, desolation, and tyranny, already begun with circumstances of Cruelty & perfidy scarcely paralleled in the most barbarous ages, and totally unworthy of the Head of a civilized nation.

👆 (Speaker 32)

He has constrained our fellow Citizens taken Captive on the high Seas to bear Arms against their Country, to become the executioners of the friends and Brethren, or to fall themselves by their Hands.

Our duly elected representatives will voice our concerns on immigration, only if we vote. **VOTE!**

👆 (Speaker 33)

He has excited domestic insurrections among us, and has endeavoured to bring on the inhabitants of our frontiers, the merciless Indian Savages, whose known rule of warfare, is an undistinguished destruction of all ages, sexes, and conditions.

👆 (Speaker 34)

In every stage of these Oppressions We have Petitioned for Redress in the most humble terms. Our repeated petitions have been answered only by repeated injury.

👆 (Speaker 35)

A Prince, whose character is thus marked by every act which may define a Tyrant, is unfit to be the ruler of a free people.

👆 (Speaker 36)

Nor have We been wanting in attentions to our British brethren. We have warned them from time to time of attempts by their legislature to extend an unwarrantable jurisdiction over us.

The administration of true justice depends on elected officials who represent all the people. All of us must vote. **VOTE!**

👆 (Speaker 37)

We have reminded them of the circumstances of our emigration and settlement here. We have appealed to their native justice and magnanimity.

👆 (Speaker 38)

We have conjured them by the ties of our common kindred to disavow these usurpations, which, would inevitably interrupt our connections and correspondence.

👆 (Speaker 39)

They too have been deaf to the voice of justice and of consanguinity. We must, therefore, acquiesce in the necessity, which denounces our Separation, and hold them, as we hold the rest of mankind, Enemies in War, in Peace Friends.

👆 (Speaker 40)

We, therefore the Representatives of the United States of America, in General Congress, Assembled, appealing to the Supreme Judge of the world for the rectitude of our intentions, do, in the Name, and by Authority of the good People of these Colonies, solemnly publish and declare, That these United Colonies are, and of the Right ought to be Free and Independent States.

Judges are appointed by those we vote for.

VOTE!

⇨ (Speaker 41)
That they are Absolved from all Allegiance to the British crown, and that all political connection between them and the State of Great Britain, is and ought to be totally dissolved.

⇨ (Speaker 42)
As free and Independent States, they have the full power to levy War, conclude Peace, contract Alliances, establish Commerce, and to do all other Acts and Things which Independent States may of right do.

⇨ (Speaker 43)
And for the support of this Declaration, with a firm reliance on the protection of divine Providence, we mutually pledge to each other our Lives, our Fortunes and our sacred Honor.

[If music and a singer are available, suggest the CONCERT FOR FREEDOM begin with the singer urging audience participation with the chorus for such songs as "This Land Is Your Land" and other patriotic songs that call for a chorus from the audience.]

ABOUT THE STORY

The one multitalented storyteller-musician-writer whom I had envisioned carrying this off with *éclat* sent a lovely "thanks, but no thanks," citing many reasons for his inability to work this into his already heavily committed schedule.

My daughter, visiting with me at the time his e-mail arrived, could see my obvious disappointment at his decision.

"But, Mummy," said she, "this would appeal to *any* patriotic storyteller." Thus was "born" the author for the Fourth of July holiday. So PATRIOTIC STORYTELLERS it is.

Immediately, my daughter's fertile imagination went into orbit. Andrea could see placards with only the word **VOTE** printed thereon in huge letters. The **VOTE** signs could be held in strategic places within the room, library, or auditorium by friends of the storyteller who elect to use the material set forth above. Friends could hold the sign up over their heads whenever the storyteller used the word **VOTE**.

Then in a rush came her other bons mots. (Every so often, my three years of high school French comes in handy.) "Maybe whoever does this can add their own comments, such as:

"Our laws are written by representatives we *vote* for . . . **VOTE!**"

"Every American has representatives—citywide, countywide, in every state, in our nation—for whom we vote . . . **VOTE!**"

And so on.

My daughter, Andrea (Miller) Bielecki, carries the weight of her chosen profession. She teaches special education and loves every challenging minute of it. Feel free to use her carefully chosen expressions of your own.

Isn't it wonderful that all of our voices count? We can be heard when we vote . . . **VOTE!**

ACTIVITIES

For suggested activities, consult: http://www.enchantedlearning.com/crafts/july4/
or http://www.apples4theteacher.com/holidays/fourth-of-july/kids-crafts/index.html.
For local or regional displays of fireworks, consult your local newspaper.

BIOGRAPHY

Andrea Bielecki has appeared as a nanny, art student, massage therapist, secretary, administrative assistant, project leader, classroom volunteer, Sunday school teacher, Daisy Girl Scout leader, teacher assistant, substitute teacher, special education teacher, and carpool driver. Two of her formative role models were Mary Poppins and the character Dickon in Sarah Hodgson Burnett's book, *The Secret Garden.* Right now, she enjoys her life as a special eduction teacher. She is a member of the Council on Exceptional Children.

CONTACT

Teresa Miller
P.O. Box 5756
Evansville, IN 47715-4185

Andrea Bielecki
E-mail: aebielecki@gmail.com

September

CATHY SPAGNOLI

Ramadan occurs during the ninth month of the Islamic calendar, which begins in the Gregorian calendar on September 13. It celebrates when the Qur'an was revealed. The Qur'an, also known as the Koran, is the book of sacred writings of Islam.

Charity

INTRODUCTION

In the small, wealthy country of Bahrain, the first Gulf country to export oil, is a beautiful museum of the holy Qur'an (often referred to as the Koran). In the striking building are priceless copies of the holy book, from various places and times, many with matchless calligraphy and ornate decorations. The teachings of Islam are shared in the Qur'an as well as through the sayings of the Prophet Muhammad. Ramadan is a time to reflect on and share these important teachings.

Mohammed Taib Bin Mohamed, a learned Muslim librarian, told this author, "Ramadan is a blessed month as it is during the month that the devils are tied and the angels roam freely." As such, Allah bestowed upon the Muslim to grab the opportunity by doing good deeds so as to get Allah's blessing. Any wrongdoing on the part of Muslim in Ramadan should not be blamed on the devil but always be put to themselves.

This small chain story sharing the important value of charity, practiced during Ramadan and throughout the year, is drawn from the words of the Prophet.

STORY SCRIPT

One day, they say, the angels asked Allah, "O Allah! Is there anything of Your creation stronger than rocks?"

Allah answered, "Yes, iron is stronger than rocks. For iron breaks rocks."

> **To audience:** Can you remember that? Say it with me:

> **Audience responds:** Yes, iron is stronger than rocks. For iron breaks rocks.

The angels then asked, "O Allah! Is there anything of Your creation stronger than iron?"

Allah replied, "Yes, fire is stronger than iron; for fire melts iron."

> **To audience:** Say it with me:

> **Audience responds:** Yes, fire is stronger than iron; for fire melts iron.

Then the angels asked, "O Defender! Is there anything of Your creation stronger than fire?" Allah replied, "Yes, water is stronger than fire. Water overcomes fire, putting it out."

> **To audience:** Can you say that with me?

> **Audience responds:** Yes, water is stronger than fire. Water overcomes fire, putting it out.

So the angels asked "O Allah! Is there anything of Your creation stronger than water?"

Allah said, "Yes, wind is stronger than water. It moves it and pushes it as it wills."

> **To audience:** Let's say that together.

> **Audience responds:** Yes, wind is stronger than water. It moves it and pushes it as it wills.

Now the angels asked, "O Our Cherisher! Is there anything of Your creation stronger than the wind?"

Allah said at last, "Yes, O children of Adam. Giving charity is stronger still than the wind."

> **To audience:** Let me hear you say that much:

> **Audience responds:** Yes, O children of Adam. Giving charity is stronger still than the wind.

There's more you want to remember and here it is: "Those who give with their right hands and conceal it from their left, they overcome all."

> **To audience:** Could I hear that?

> **Audience responds:** Those who give with their right hands and conceal it from their left, they overcome all.

Allah said, "That is all correct!"

ABOUT THE STORY

I first read this well-known story in *THE SAYINGS OF MUHAMMAD* (New Delhi: Goodword Books, 1997). Since then, I've also heard it from several Asian friends. So I happily shared it at the Asian Congress of Storytellers in Singapore one year, not realizing that it was Ramadan time. Sometime after that, I was in Malaysia at the Malaysian Congress of Storytellers. Mohamed Taib Bin Mohamed then thanked me for sharing this story and said how much he was moved when I told that tale during Ramadan, because it shared such an important value of the holiday.

ACTIVITIES

Teaching Plates (an activity for any time of the year): In many parts of the world, plates are decorated with lovely designs and colors. But a more unusual form of decoration is found in the Muslim cultures of Central and West Asia. These proverbs and sayings in elegant Arabic calligraphy have long graced plates and bowls there. The beauty of the letters add strength to the simple teachings often shared. The shapes of the English alphabet do not lend themselves as elegantly to a circular calligraphy as does Arabic, but students can try their own adaptations of traditional sayings.

Materials you will use include traditional sayings, paper or paper plates, and pencils.

Method:

A. Write the sayings that follow on the board, or dictate them to audience.

B. Describe the concept of a plate with writing on it (usually around the rim, but at times in the center as well), meant to share wisdom.

C. Have students cut out large circles or use paper plates.

D. Ask students to choose one saying, and try to write it, as artistically as possible, around the outer edge of the plate.

E. Display the plates on the wall.

These are some of the traditional sayings:

• Those content with their own opinion, run into danger.

• He who speaks, his speech is silver, but silence is a ruby.

• Prosperity and peace: Planning before work protects you from regret.

• He who professes the faith will excel.

• Blessings.

An example can be found at: http://www.metmuseum.org/toah/ho/06/nc/ho_65.106.2.htm.

HOLIDAY BACKGROUND INFORMATION

In Syria, the *hakawati* storyteller also tells in a coffeehouse, sitting or standing in front, book in one hand, cane or sword in the other, reading the text or reciting from memory and interjecting poems, jokes, and commentary. In its heyday, a known teller could pack a house of 200 and use accents with great facility.

Because listeners came night after night, the *hakawati* was close to many in the crowd, and often helped to keep their spirits up. They say that a famous *hakawati,* Abu 'Ali Abouba, once went to a new doctor, complaining of melancholy. The doctor, not recognizing him, said, "You need to see the *hakawati* Abouba, who will cheer you up." "But," said the patient sadly, "I *am* Abouba!"

The *hakawati* tells tales of heroes: Sultan Baybars, the Banu Hilal, Prince Antar, and others. Today, the art suffers as the coffeehouses that supported it lose their regular audiences or shut down completely. The government helps by sponsoring festivals and performances during Ramadan, but it may not be enough.

(This activity and storyteller profile are adapted from Spagnoli's book, *THE WORLD OF ASIAN STORIES*, Tulika Publishers, 2007.)

HOLIDAY BACKGROUND INFORMATION

It is during Ramadan that Muslims observe the Fast of Ramadan, which lasts for an entire month (consult www.holidays.net/ramadan/). For more reading about Ramadan and why Muslims fast, see www.holidays.net/ramadan/story.htm. Ramadan is the month during which the Qur'an was revealed, providing guidance for the people, clear teachings, and the statute book (www.submission.org/ramadan.html).

BIOGRAPHY

In her search for stories, Cathy Spagnoli has slid through Indonesian rice fields, sipped sake with Japanese epic singers, met with Korean monks in high mountain temples, hiked the Himalayas with Tibetan dancers, marveled at Kamishibai festivals, and shared tea with warmhearted Southeast Asian refugees.

As she explained in "About the Story" above, she told the Ramadan chain story at the Asian Congress of Storytellers and again in Malaysia at the Malaysian Congress of Storytellers. She has published sixteen books and is working on more. For more information on Cathy, consult http://www.cathyspagnoli.com/index.htm.

CONTACT

Cathy Spagnoli
27225 97th Avenue SW
Vashon, WA 98070
cathy.spagnoli@gmail.com

Retold by
NORMA E. CANTÚ

México celebrates Independence Day on the September 15 and 16.

El Grito de Dolores
(Cry of the City of Dolores)

INTRODUCTION

This story is repeated every sixteenth of September when México celebrates Independence Day. México had been under Spanish rule since the Spanish conquered the Aztecs in 1521. While others had sought independence before, it was not until 1810 that the war of independence began in earnest. (Although the story talks of a bell ringing, no real bell is needed.)

It would be very appropriate to tell *EL GRITO DE DOLORES (Cry of the City of Dolores)* in Spanish.

STORY SCRIPT

The people of México had been preparing to declare independence from Spain for a long, long time. But their well-laid plans had been discovered, and they needed to change plans.

It was late on the night of September 15 in 1810, when a group of conspirators met to decide their next steps. "What shall we do?" asked Doña Josefa Ortiz de Dominguez, wife of the Corregidor of Queretaro.

Doña Josefa was one of the leaders of the plot to overcome the Spanish colonizers. The group, including Ignacio Allende and hundreds of others, realized that it didn't have the arms necessary to lead the uprising from Queretaro, but they decided that they must act quickly. "We must take action," they all agreed.

A messenger bearing the news that their plot had been discovered was sent to the town of Dolores, where a Catholic priest, Don Miguel Hidalgo y Costilla, awaited word from the group. Padre Hidalgo, an active proponent of Mexican Independence, had the backing of many people.

> Show the children how to gallop in place. One child can be selected to act as the messenger who is going to alert the people in Dolores.

> The one child selected to act as messenger keeps galloping through the story script until he or she hears the words . . . "Issue the call for independence."

It was dawn when the messenger arrived. The priest received the news and quickly decided to issue the call for independence.

> ⇨ Child messenger stops galloping.

He rang the church bells, calling all the townspeople to the plaza in front of the church.

> ⇨ The storyteller rings the imaginary bell—Ding dong, Ding dong, Ding dong—pausing after each peal of the bell, accompanied by the following movements: On the word "Ding," pull down as if ringing a church bell, and crouch down; on the word "dong" let the rope go up and stand on tiptoes.

When the townspeople had gathered, Padre Hidalgo explained, "México is ready to declare its independence from the Spanish Crown!" Raising his arm he shouted, "Viva México!" three times. To which those around him answered, "Viva México!"

> ⇨ The storyteller says "Viva México!" three times, pausing each time for the audience response. If necessary, invite the audience to repeat. "Viva México!" Wait for the pause after each response.

Viva México!

> ⇨ **Audience replies:** Viva México!

Viva México!

> ⇨ **Audience replies:** Viva México!

Viva México!

> ⇨ **Audience replies:** Viva México!

Father Hidalgo led the mass of Indians, Mestizos, and Criollos. They all marched forward, gathering supporters along the way. From the city of Dolores, they were all going toward México. This was the beginning of the Mexican revolution. A few days later, Hidalgo was executed by the Spanish government.

Thus, in commemoration of Father Hidalgo's "Cry of Dolores," every fifteenth of September at around 11 P.M., Mexican people celebrate that one courageous act by reenacting the event. The sixteenth is a national holiday, and signs of the celebration are everywhere.

The green, white, and red of the Mexican flag shows proudly everywhere as the whole nation celebrates with parades, rodeos, fiestas, and concerts.

The celebration also occurs in the areas that were once part of México and are now in the United States, in large cities and small towns, wherever Mexican people live. Los Angeles, for example, has one of the most lavish celebrations.

All over the world as night falls on the fifteenth of September, people gather to hear the highest functionary in plazas and courtyards. He may be the president (in México City), the governor (in every state of the Mexican Republic), the mayor of a town, or the ambassador in a foreign country. Whoever it is, he or she gives forth the now famous shout, "Viva México!"

Let's hear it again.

Viva México!

⤷ **Audience:** Viva México!

Viva México!

⤷ **Audience:** Viva México!

Viva México!

⤷ **Audience:** Viva México!

ABOUT THE STORY

It was adapted from the traditional telling of the declaration of Mexican Independence, which I learned as a child.

NOTES ON A FEW OTHER TELLERS OF LATIN-AMERICAN STORIES

1. **Olga Loya:** See www.olgaloya.com/olgastory.html and http://store.augusthouse.com/. Her book *MAGIC MOMENTS* contains stories in both English and Spanish (August House, 1977).

2. **Charles David Kleymeyer:** See "Silent Night, 1914—The Peace Message for Christmas" (featured later in this book). While living and traveling in the Andes in support of economic development for the Latin American, he developed several stories in Spanish and English.

3. **Antonio Sacre:** Sacre is an international traveling writer and storyteller. See www.antoniosacre.com.

RELATED BOOKS

1. Margot Zemach's *LOS TRES CERDITOS* (The Three Pigs), translated by Rita Guibert (Farrar, Straus & Giroux, 1988). Written completely in Spanish.

2. *TOMASA THE COW (LA VACA TOMASA)* by Pietrapiana (Piñata Books, 1999). Tells in both English and Spanish of Tomasa's decision to take risks, to seek freedom in her unusual ways.

3. *QUOMODO INVIDIOSULUS NOMINE GRINCHUS* by Christi Natalem Abrogaverit. Translated from *"How the Grinch Stole Christmas"* (Bolchazy-Carducci Publishers, 1999). Illustrated; text completely in Spanish.

4. *SPANISH-AMERICAN FOLKTALES* by Teresa Pijoan de Van Etten (August House, 1990).

BOOKS RECOMMENDED BY NORMA CANTÚ

1. *STORIES OF MEXICO'S INDEPENDENCE DAYS AND OTHER BILINGUAL CHILDREN'S FABLES* by Timothy L. Sawyer, Jr. and Eliseo "Cheo" Torres, editors; illustrated by Herman Ramirez (University of New Mexico Press, 2005). See especially "Sixteen: A Story about Mexico's Independence."

2. *THE LATINO HOLIDAY BOOK: From Cinco de Mayo to Día de Los Muertos: The Celebrations and Traditions of Hispanic-Americans* by Valerie Menard (Marlowe, 2000).

3. *CELEBRATIONS: Holidays of the United States of America and Mexico/Celebraciones: Días feriados del los Estados Unidos y México* by Nancy Maria Grande Tabor (Charlesbridge, 2004).

ACTIVITIES

1. This is an informative story that children can act out. In many schools, the story is dramatized, and the exact words that are said by the president of México and other dignitaries are repeated while the larger group answers: Viva!

2. Draw a flag of México or color it in.

GREEN　　　　BRONZE EAGLE　　　　RED

Supplies: Construction paper, scissors, sticker of the image of the eagle, crayons to color drawn image.

Procedure: Cut equal sized 3-inch strips of red and green construction paper. Glue onto the narrow edges of an 8½ x 11 inch white background cardstock to form the flag. Draw or paste a previously cut-out image of the eagle perched on a prickly pear cactus holding the serpent in the middle white section.

NOTE: The Mexican flag was created in 1821 at the conclusion of the War for Independence and is celebrated on México's Flag Day, February 24.

3. An additional story to complement this one would be the Aztec myth of how the Aztecs came from Aztlán (place of white herons in the Nahuatl language—somewhere around Salt Lake City, according to some scholars) to the Valley of México where they found the "sign" that their god Huichilopotli had told them to look for: an eagle perched on a prickly pear cactus with a serpent in its beak. It would add to the story to draw the flag and either paste a sticker with the central image or draw and color it.

HOLIDAY BACKGROUND INFORMATION

When the priest Miguel Hidalgo y Costilla called his fellow Mexicans to arms against the Spanish on September 16, 1810, he set in motion a revolution that did not end until eleven years later in 1821 when Spain finally conceded defeat, ending almost 400 years of Spanish rule. Up until that night when Father Hidalgo called out "Mexicanos, Viva México!" (Mexicans, long live México!), México had been known as Nueva España (New Spain).

The revolutionaries marched out from Dolores in the state of Guanajuato to the town of San Miguel de Allende, on to Queretaro and on to México City, gathering supporters along the way and a banner to accompany their cry of Viva México.

The banner is the image of the Virgen de Guadalupe, patron saint of México. To their rallying cry of "Viva México!" they added "Viva La Virgen de Guadalupe!" Because she is said to have appeared to a Mexican Indian, Juan Diego, she was a fitting symbol for a revolution that included the indigenous people of México as well as the mestizos (mixed heritage people) and the criollos, Mexican born people of Spanish descent.

The celebration has been celebrated every year on the night of the fifteenth of September, except in 1847 when México was at war. President Benito Juarez had the bell brought from Dolores to México City where it is rung every September 15 during the ceremony of the "Grito." Originally, the celebration occurred on the sixteenth, but in 1910, it was changed by Porfirio Diaz to the fifteenth at 11 P.M. Every year, from the balcony of the National Place, the president of México recreates the Grito de Dolores: He rings the bell and gives the cry "Viva México!"

To find out about a local celebration of El Grito de Dolores, contact the nearest Mexican consulate or Embassy. Also consult various Web sites, including http://www.sanmiguelguide.com/tour-el-grito.htm.

BIOGRAPHY

Norma E. Cantú has published extensively in folklore and literary studies as well as in the poetry and fiction genres. She is the editor of a book series, Rio Grande/Rio Bravo: Borderlands Culture and Tradition (Texas A&M University Press). Author of the award-winning *Canícula Snapshots of a Girlhood en la Frontera* (New Mexico University Press, 1995 and 2000), she edited *Flor y Ciencia: Chicanas in Mathematics, Science and Engineering* (Adelante Project, 2006) and has coedited *Chicana Traditions: Continuity and Change* (Illinois University Press, 2002) and *Telling to Live: Latina Feminist Testimonios* (Duke University Press, 2001).

Having finished her novel, *Cabañuelas,* Norma Cantú is currently working on another novel tentatively titled *Champú, or Hair Matters.* She is also working on an ethnography of the Matachines de la Santa Cruz, a religious dance drama from Laredo, Texas, and a collection of poetry. She has published widely on Chicana/o culture and traditions along the U.S.–México borderlands.

As a folklorist and writer, she serves as professor of English and U.S. Latina of literature at the University of Texas at San Antonio. Consult http://galenet.galegroup.com/servlet/BioRC?vrsn=149&OP=contains&locID =evan14908.

CONTACT

Norma E. Cantú, Ph.D.
12310 Stable Square Drive
San Antonio, TX 78249
E-mail: Normaelia@aol.com

National Constitution Day is observed annually on September 17 in the United States.

The Constitution Jive

INTRODUCTION

Most people think of the Fourth of July as America's most important day, but in many ways, Constitution Day is just as important. It is the day that celebrates the creation of the Constitution of the United States. The U.S. government is governed or ruled by the Constitution. One unique aspect of the Constitution is the three-branch system of government. The executive (president), judiciary (judges), and legislative (Congress) branches balance the powers of each other. Let's celebrate the United States with a jazzy beat and a hand jive.

1. Before beginning the story, teach the audience to call and respond. You say a line, and they repeat it back to you. Use this technique for the refrain and the long refrain. Say the verse on your own without the call and respond. Use any rhythm or beat that is comfortable for you as the storyteller. My personal favorite is to use a quirky, slightly syncopated beat where the emphasis is not on the first beat.

2. Teach the audience the repeating refrain "Executive, Judiciary, Legislature" and also the Hand Jive movements before you begin.

   E-xe 'cu-tive, ju-di 'ci-ary, leg - 'is la-ture.

Hand Jive

1. Place one hand at head level with palm flat facing away from body and fingers spread. Place other hand palm facing back at hip level. Shake both hands while saying "executive."

2. Switch hands and shake while saying "judiciary."

3. Both hands shake in front of the face with palms facing away from body and move to circle up and out ending near by sides while saying "legislature."

Throughout the rest of the verses, lead the audience in fingers snaps, or thigh slaps.

STORY SCRIPT

⇨ Teller repeats refrain.

E-xe 'cu-tive, ju-di 'ci-ary, leg - 'is la-ture.

⇨ Hand jive with call and respond.
Follow musical beat above.

E-xe 'cu-tive, ju-di 'ci-ary, leg - 'is la-ture.

> Hand jive with call and respond.
> Follow musical beat above.
> Teller repeats refrain.

E-xe 'cu-tive, ju-di 'ci-ary, leg - 'is la-ture.

> Hand jive with call and respond.
> Follow musical beat above.

E-xe 'cu-tive, ju-di 'ci-ary, leg - 'is la-ture.

> Hand Jive with call and respond.
> Follow musical beat above.

Our Constitution is the oldest of its kind. Since seventeen hundred and eighty-seven, the Constitution tells us how to govern. The first ten amendments are the Bill of Rights.

> Keep up the beat with finger snap or thigh slap while explaining what happens.

E-xe 'cu-tive, ju-di 'ci-ary, leg - 'is la-ture.

> Hand jive with call and respond.
> Follow musical beat above.

E-xe 'cu-tive, ju-di 'ci-ary, leg - 'is la-ture.

> Hand jive with call and respond.
> Follow musical beat above.

E-xe 'cu-tive, ju-di 'ci-ary, leg - 'is la-ture.

> Hand jive with call and respond.
> Follow musical beat above.

E-xe 'cu-tive, ju-di 'ci-ary, leg - 'is la-ture.

> Hand jive with call and respond.
> Follow musical beat above.

The delegates arrived by coach and saddle. Some arrived early, and some arrived late. Ben Franklin came in a sedan chair, carried by prisoners from the penitentiary.

> Keep up the beat with finger snap or thigh slap while explaining what happens.

E-xe 'cu-tive, ju-di 'ci-ary, leg - 'is la-ture.

> Hand jive with call and respond.
> Follow musical beat above.

E-xe 'cu-tive, ju-di 'ci-ary, leg - 'is la-ture.

> Hand jive with call and respond.
> Follow musical beat above.

E-xe ′cu-tive, ju-di ′ci-ary, leg - ′is la-ture.

> ♫ Hand jive with call and respond.
> Follow musical beat above.

E-xe ′cu-tive, ju-di ′ci-ary, leg - ′is la-ture.

> ♫ Hand jive with call and respond.
> Follow musical beat above.

The delegates met in the Pennsylvania State House with windows closed and doors locked tight. The weather was hot and very sweaty, but the Constitution was kept a secret.

> ♫ Keep up the beat with finger snap or thigh slap while explaining what happens.

E-xe ′cu-tive, ju-di ′ci-ary, leg - ′is la-ture.

> ♫ Hand jive with call and respond.
> Follow musical beat above.

E-xe ′cu-tive, ju-di ′ci-ary, leg - ′is la-ture.

> ♫ Hand jive with call and respond.
> Follow musical beat above.

E-xe ′cu-tive, ju-di ′ci-ary, leg - ′is la-ture.

> ♫ Hand jive with call and respond.
> Follow musical beat above.

E-xe ′cu-tive, ju-di ′ci-ary, leg - ′is la-ture.

> ♫ Hand jive with call and respond.
> Follow musical beat above.

The delegates, how they disagreed! Some hollered "States" should rule themselves.

Some yelled "National" should rule us all. No one wanted another King. "State"—"National"—"Who's in charge?"

> ♫ Keep up the beat with finger snap or thigh slap while explaining what happens.

E-xe ′cu-tive, ju-di ′ci-ary, leg - ′is la-ture.

> ♫ Hand jive with call and respond.
> Follow musical beat above.

E-xe ′cu-tive, ju-di ′ci-ary, leg - ′is la-ture.

> ♫ Hand jive with call and respond.
> Follow musical beat above.

E-xe 'cu-tive, ju-di 'ci-ary, leg - 'is la-ture.

> Hand jive with call and respond.
> Follow musical beat above.

E-xe 'cu-tive, ju-di 'ci-ary, leg - 'is la-ture.

> Hand jive with call and respond.
> Follow musical beat above.

Thanks to Edmund Randolph and the Virginia Plan, a three-branch government would do the trick. Executive, Judiciary, Legislature—each with separate powers to keep us safe.

> Keep up the beat with finger snap or thigh slap while explaining what happens.

E-xe 'cu-tive, ju-di 'ci-ary, leg - 'is la-ture.

> Hand jive with call and respond.
> Follow musical beat above.

E-xe 'cu-tive, ju-di 'ci-ary, leg - 'is la-ture.

> Hand jive with call and respond
> Follow musical beat above.

E-xe 'cu-tive, ju-di 'ci-ary, leg - 'is la-ture.

> Hand jive with call and respond..
> Follow musical beat above.

E-xe 'cu-tive, ju-di 'ci-ary, leg - 'is la-ture.

> Hand jive with call and respond.
> Follow musical beat above.

Roger Sherman and the Connecticut Plan was a Great Compromise that ended the fight, with a House of Representatives based on population. But the Senate is based on equal vote.

> Keep up the beat with finger snap or thigh slap while explaining what happens.

E-xe 'cu-tive, ju-di 'ci-ary, leg - 'is la-ture.

> Hand jive with call and respond.
> Follow musical beat above.

E-xe 'cu-tive, ju-di 'ci-ary, leg - 'is la-ture.

> Hand jive with call and respond.
> Follow musical beat above.

E-xe 'cu-tive, ju-di 'ci-ary, leg - 'is la-ture.

> Hand Jive with call and respond.
> Follow musical beat above.

E-xe ′cu-tive, ju-di ′ci-ary, leg - ′is la-ture.

> Hand jive with call and respond.
> Follow musical beat above.

The Founding Fathers, all fifty-five, wrote the Constitution, but not all signed. When nine out of thirteen states voted "Yes," we had our Constitution! Success!

> Keep up the beat with finger snap or thigh slap while explaining what happens.

E-xe ′cu-tive, ju-di ′ci-ary, leg - ′is la-ture.

> Hand jive with call and respond.
> Follow musical beat above.

E-xe ′cu-tive, ju-di ′ci-ary, leg - ′is la-ture.

> Hand jive with call and respond.
> Follow musical beat above.

E-xe ′cu-tive, ju-di ′ci-ary, leg - ′is la-ture.

> Hand jive with call and respond.
> Follow musical beat above.

E-xe ′cu-tive, ju-di ′ci-ary, leg - ′is la-ture.

> Hand jive with call and respond.
> Follow musical beat above.

Our Constitution is the oldest of its kind. Since seventeen hundred and eighty-seven, the Constitution tells us how to govern, and the first ten amendments are the Bill of Rights.

> Keep up the beat with finger snap or thigh slap while explaining what happens.

E-xe ′cu-tive, ju-di ′ci-ary, leg - ′is la-ture.

> Hand jive with call and respond.
> Follow musical beat above.

E-xe ′cu-tive, ju-di ′ci-ary, leg - ′is la-ture.

> Hand jive with call and respond.
> Follow musical beat above.

E-xe ′cu-tive, ju-di ′ci-ary, leg - ′is la-ture.

> Hand jive with call and respond.
> Follow musical beat above.

E-xe ′cu-tive, ju-di ′ci-ary, leg - ′is la-ture.

> Hand jive with call and respond.
> Follow musical beat above.

ABOUT THE STORY

I created the original version of this verse in 1987 to celebrate the bicentennial of the Constitution. It has gone through several transformations including the most recent one when my fifth-grade class at Henry A. Wolcott Elementary School (West Hartford, Connecticut) performed it for Constitution Day 2006. I found history boring as a child, so I selected the facts that interested me and arranged them with an upbeat rhythm that made me want to dance.

RELATED BOOKS AND WEB SITES

1. *SHH! WE'RE WRITING THE CONSTITUTION*, by Jean Fritz, illustrated by Tomie dePaola (G. P. Putnam's Son, 1987).

2. *BEN'S GUIDE TO U.S. GOVERNMENT FOR KIDS*: http://bensguide.gpo.gov.

3. *THE NATIONAL CONSTITUTION CENTER*: www.constitutioncenter.org/explore/ForKids/index.shtml.

ACTIVITIES

1. Joke: Where was the Constitution signed? At the bottom!

2. Which State First? (Game)

Write the first thirteen states on index cards. Give one card to each person. Have the participants try to put themselves in the correct order based on which state entered the Union first. For the first thirteen states, this is the same order ratified for the Constitution. You can expand this game to include all fifty states.

1	Delaware	December 7, 1787
2	Pennsylvania	December 12, 1787
3	New Jersey	December 18, 1787
4	Georgia	January 2, 1788
5	Connecticut	January 9, 1788
6	Massachusetts	February 6, 1788
7	Maryland	April 28, 1788
8	South Carolina	May 23, 1788
9	New Hampshire	June 21, 1788
10	Virginia	June 25, 1788
11	New York	July 26, 1788
12	North Carolina	November 21, 1789
13	Rhode Island	May 29, 1790

HOLIDAY BACKGROUND INFORMATION

In 1952, President Harry Truman signed a Bill proclaiming September 17 as "Citizenship Day," a holiday that honored everyone who had become a U.S. citizen during that year. Citizenship Day quickly waned in popularity, and the September 17 date became Constitution Day.

Constitution Day is a new school and federal holiday. As passed by the 108th Congress, starting with the 2005 school year, all schools that receive federal funds must "hold an educational program pertaining to the United States Constitution on September 17 of each year." Why September 17? On September 17, 1787, the Constitution was signed by 39 of the 55 original framers, but that is only part of the story.

When the United States won the war for independence from Great Britain (1783), it was still a loose group of thirteen states. It wasn't until the delegates wrote the Constitution that the United States actually became united under one governing law. The Constitution has told us how to govern for more than two hundred years.

The process of writing the Constitution was full of debate, arguing, and anger. People were afraid a strong government would be like having a king. Many wanted to keep a state government rather than to chance a national government, which they feared might become too much like Great Britain's style of governing. Luckily, Edmund Randolph from Virginia suggested dividing the powers of government into three branches: Executive, Judicial, and Legislative. Each branch has its own powers and limits, a system called checks and balances. In brief:

1. The Executive Branch consists primarily of the president, vice president, and the cabinet members who enforce the laws.

2. The Judicial Branch consists of the Supreme Court, which interprets the laws.

3. The Legislative Branch consists of the Congress, which makes the laws.

Another point of contention was how the legislature should be structured. Some delegates wanted it based on population but others wanted equal representation. Roger Sherman from Connecticut devised the Great Compromise with the House of Representatives based on population and the Senate based on equal vote.

In the end, only thirty-nine of the fifty-five framers signed the Constitution on September 17, 1787. Some delegates refused to sign because there was no bill of rights. The first ten amendments to the Constitution, called the Bill of Rights, did not go into effect until 1791.

There are many interesting tidbits about the creation of the Constitution.

• At the time of its creation, Benjamin Franklin was ill and was carried to the Pennsylvania State House in a chair lifted by prisoners.

• Throughout the summer, the delegates met secretly in the Pennsylvania State House. The windows were closed, and the heat was unbearable for the men dressed in wool, which was standard apparel for the time.

• There is at least one spelling error in the Constitution. Pennsylvania is spelled "Pensylvania" above the signatures.

• The U.S. Constitution is the oldest written constitution—and the shortest with 4,440 words. The Constitution is considered a living document because it can and has been amended. Franklin D. Roosevelt stated, "The United States Constitution has proved itself the most marvelously elastic compilation of rules of government ever written."

• The order in which the state quarters are released as currency is the same order that that state ratified the Constitution or became officially a state of the union.

Following is the preamble of the Constitution:

"We the people of the United States, in order to form a more perfect union, establish justice, insure domestic tranquility, provide for the common defense, promote the general welfare, and secure the blessings of liberty to ourselves and our posterity, do ordain and establish this Constitution for the United States of America."

BIOGRAPHY

Linda Marchisio loves dancing, storytelling, and hiking to waterfalls. She is currently a teacher of gifted education, a certified library media specialist, and storyteller. Linda won the 2003 Connecticut Wilbur Cross Award as a Champion of Children's Reading for her creation of original booktalk programs for children and parents.

CONTACT

Linda Marchisio
E-mail: LjcLsj@cox.net

RUTHILDE KRONBERG

The International Day of Peace is celebrated on September 21.

The Boy Who Called the King a Fool

INTRODUCTION

More than 3,500 events in two hundred countries join the worldwide movement to create a Global Ceasefire and day of peace and nonviolence. Consult www.internationaldayofpeace.org.

STORY SCRIPT

Long ago the king of Laquay invited the king of Sinsabarra to hunt in his forest. The hunt was a great success. The banquet that followed was even better. There was food and wine in abundance. Maybe if there had not been so much wine, the crown prince of Laquay and the crown prince of Sinsabarra would not have gotten into a fight. Before anyone could stop them, they grabbed their swords and killed each other.

Kneeling next to the bodies of their sons, their grief-stricken fathers blamed each other's sons for the tragedy. They vowed they would avenge both deaths on the battlefield. On the day the Laquyen soldiers assembled to ride to the appointed battlefield, their king addressed them: "Soldiers of Laquay, I challenge you to avenge the death of your crown prince. Be on your way, and when you return victorious, you will get your just rewards."

The soldiers cheered, but their cheering stopped when a group of women entered the courtyard. The women had come for a last goodbye to their beloved husbands and sons and had heard the king's words. They rushed up to the king, and cried, "And what will happen if our soldiers are defeated?"

The king glared at them and shouted furiously, "Go home to your kitchens where you belong. If they return defeated, they will end up in the death camp of Orreply."

Without another word, he turned and walked back into his castle.

Everyone was stunned. Criminals were sent to the death camps, not soldiers! But no one had the courage to follow the king and tell him that what he planned to do was evil. So when the drummer boy began to beat the drum, the soldiers started to ride towards the battlefield.

> ⇗ Begin to mime the beating of a drum as he chants, "Barr-room boom, boom"—"Barr-room boom, boom."

163

Would you follow the call of the drum, now?

 Audience chants the sound of the drum with the teller:
Barr-room boom, boom—
Barr-room boom, boom
Barr-room boom, boom
Barr-room boom, boom

 Audience chants the sound of the drum with the teller:
Barr-room boom, boom
Barr-room boom, boom
Barr-room boom, boom
Barr-room boom, boom

During the first hours of their journey, the soldiers talked mostly about the battles they had fought and won. But as the day passed on, they began to worry about the king's words. Would he really send them to the death camp of Orreply if they did not win this battle?

They had heard rumors that this had been done by other kings. Finally, a respected veteran soldier, who was known by all for his heroism in driving invaders out of the king's country, said calmly, "We must fight the king's battle, because we swore allegiance to the king. However, if we don't win this battle, the death camp of Orreply cannot be worse than a war. They rode on silently, each occupied with his own thoughts.

After a while, they passed an old farmhouse. A ragged-looking farm boy, who was sweeping the yard, stared at the soldiers' beautiful red and gold uniforms. Suddenly, he threw his broom down and came running after them, yelling, "Please take me with you! I want to come with you!"

The soldiers tried to send him back, but he would not listen. Finally, the army cook gave in. He allowed the boy to ride on one of the provision carts.

When evening came, the farm boy helped the soldiers to set up camp. He helped to cook their meals. Later on, when they sat around the fire, the conversation returned to the king's words. Shaking his head, the veteran soldier said, "I fought in many battles. Most of them were caused by the high and mightiest hunger for power. But this one is the craziest of them all. . . . It doesn't make sense that men will have to die because two drunken fools, who happen to be of royal birth, killed each other."

A young recruit, who had just recently joined the king's army, laughed and said, "What if the kings had to fight their own battles?"

His sergeant, sitting behind the young soldier, heard those words. He looked at him sternly and warned, "If you want to go back to your family, you had better learn to hold your tongue, or you will end up in the death camps of Orreply. It doesn't pay to criticize kings."

Their conversation stopped when a corporal joined them. "I heard you picked up a boy," he said. "Our drummer boy got sick, and we have to replace him." All excited, the boy, who had been listening, cried, "I'll take his place! Please let me be your drummer boy!"

The corporal grinned and replied, "Good! Actually, you look old enough to handle the job of a drummer boy. I can teach you the signals. Now listen carefully. The one who beats the drum must not lose heart. No matter what is going on around him, he must continue to beat the drum. Beat the drum, remember!"

"I promise," said the boy. And he left with the corporal. The following evening, the soldiers reached the battlefield. Next morning came when the sun came out, they met the enemy.

Again mime the beating of a drum and chant almost to oneself, "Barr-room boom, boom"—
The audience does not help this time.

Barr-room boom, boom

Barr-room boom, boom—

Follow the call of the drum

Barr-room boom, boom

Barr-room boom, boom

Within minutes, the soldiers rushed at each other, and the air was filled with the screams of men and horses. The drummer boy had never seen anything like it. He watched with horror as the men mowed each other down like wheat stalks. But he kept on beating his drum. Out loud he shouted,

Barr-room boom, boom

Barr-room boom, boom—

Barr-room boom, boom

Barr-room boom, boom

 Audience follows the call of the drum and chants it as long as they hear it:
Barr-room boom, boom
Follow the call of the drum
boom, boom.
Barr-room boom, boom

Suddenly a heavy blow hit the boy's right shoulder. He fell down. Remembering the words of the corporal—"He who beats the drum must never lose heart . . ."—he kept on beating the drum. Barr-room boom boom. Follow the call of the drum . . .

But after a while, the pain got so bad that he fainted. When he regained consciousness, he found himself lying on the bank of a river. Because he was terribly thirsty, he struggled to his feet. Now what he saw made him sick in his stomach.

The battlefield had become a graveyard. Not a single man nor a single horse was stirring. All of them were dead. Pulling all his strength together, the boy staggered down to the river. When he bent down to drink, he saw that the water was stained from the blood of dead men. A feeling of horror swept over him, and he remembered the words of the veteran soldier, "Two drunken fools killed each other and a hundred had to die."

Whose fault was it? The soldiers? The king's? THE KING! Someone had to tell the king what had happened. Stumbling over and around dead bodies, the boy managed to reach the road that led to the king's castle. Weakened from the loss of blood, he almost gave up when he saw a man on a horse galloping toward him.

When he reached the boy, the man got off of his horse and asked anxiously, "Are you coming from the battlefield?"

The boy replied, "Yes."

"Tell me who won," said the horseman.

The boy whispered, "Nobody. They are all dead." The horseman threw up his arms and moaned, "THEY ARE ALL DEAD?"

The boy wiped away a tear and sobbed, "I have to go and tell it to the king. Maybe he won't ever declare war again."

"Don't go!" shouted the horseman. "Don't you know the ones who return defeated will be sent to the death camps of Orreply?"

But the boy shook his head, "I know, but I have to go anyway. Someone will have to tell the king that no one ever wins a war."

The horseman shook his head and mumbled sadly, Don't bet your life on it. "Don't you know that power corrupts? Once they reach the top, they think they are God! But if you must go, let me help you. I will lend you my horse. Otherwise you won't make it."

He helped the boy to mount the horse and the boy rode off to the castle. By the time he arrived, the boy was so exhausted that those who saw him thought he would fall off the horse at any moment. But the boy didn't. He sat up straight and began to beat his drum.

Barr-room boom, boom

Barr-room boom, boom

Listen to the call

of the drum boom boom

Listen to the call of the drum!

The minute the king heard the drum, he rushed outside to greet his soldiers. But when he saw no one but the drummer boy, surrounded by a group of very anxious women and children, he turned pale and cried, "Are you coming from the battlefield?"

The boy nodded his head.

The king frowned and shouted, "Have you lost your tongue? Tell me what happened!"

The boy took a deep breath and replied, "I beat a dead skin, and it called the living to die."

The king stamped his foot and thundered, "I did not ask you what you *did,* I asked you to tell me what you *saw!*" shouted the king.

The boy shuddered and replied, "I saw precious mixed with precious but it had no value," replied the boy.

Now the king was really angry. He yelled, "Don't talk to me in riddles! I order you to tell me what happened."

The boy closed his eyes. Slowly but clearly he said, "Two fools declared war and a hundred men had to die. How can you sleep at night, King Laquay?" whispered the boy with his last strength. With that, he fell off the horse. Two women had to carry him away.

The king gasped for breath and whispered, "My soldiers lost the battle." He staggered toward his castle. But before he got there, a young woman, who realized that she had become a widow and her children were now orphans, picked up the drum and began to beat it. She sang out:

"Barr-room boom, boom. Don't follow the call of the drum. It called our loved ones to die. Help us bury the dead, oh mighty king of Laquay."

The king looked like he was about to lose his mind. He sobbed, "I don't want to bury anyone . . ." He ran off into the woods.

Years later he returned, a changed man. An advocate for peace and justice, he visited many countries and told his story. Some listened and joined him. Others just shrugged their shoulders. Children who heard his story asked questions and learned from him. So there is still hope for all of us.

ABOUT THE STORY

Ruthilde Kronberg, a veteran storyteller, has written extensively about the individual's interest in bringing about peace through peaceful means. "This," says she, "is my contribution to the antiwar efforts. War overshadowed my childhood, and one can never disconnect oneself. It always pops up."

RELATED BOOKS

There are plenty of stories, articles, novels, television movies, plays, documentaries and so forth written about war. Consult the Internet. A few suggestions:

1. *A MAN WITH NO BRAIN* by Mohammed Bel Halfaoui, translated from the French by Cathryn Wellner (Reprinted by the Seattle Storyteller's Guild, P.O. Box 45532, Seattle, WA 981455-0532).

2. "How the Beldys Stopped Fighting" from *FOLKTALES OF THE AMUR: Stories from the Russian Far East,* by Dmitri Nagashkin (Harry Abrams, 1980). Two highly respected twins stopped war by pretending to favor it but changed the rules to make war impossible.

3. "The Singing Tree," from the book by the same name by Kate Seredy (Viking Press, 1940). Tells of an incident that occurred in Hungary on the battlefield during World War I.

4. *THE BIG BOOK FOR PEACE.* Ann Durrell and Marilyn Sachs, editors (Dutton Children's Books, 1990). Stories, poems, songs, and illustrations for a peaceful world. The publisher's profits and royalties go to five organizations working for world peace.

5. *PEACE TALES: World Folktales to Talk About* by Margaret Read MacDonald.

Suggestion: Why not select a date and time for the creation of a powerful Thought-Image of Peace——one that can have a profound effect on the attitudes and motivation of millions of others through subconscious communication? One way to achieve this is through the power of prayer. Another involves meditation and visualization of a sane peaceful loving world.

AMERICAN WAR CASUALTIES

American Revolution—4,435	War of 1812—2,260
Mexican-American War—13,283	American Civil War—505,978
Spanish-American War—2,446	World War I—116,516
Pearl Harbor—2,300	World War II—405,399
Korean War—54,246	Vietnam War—90,209
Gulf War—2,094	September 11, 2001—3,000
Iraq—ongoing at the time of the writing; 4,130 Americans as of August 4, 2008	Afghanistan—ongoing at the time of the writing; 566 Americans as of August 4, 2008

Sources: http://infoplease.com/ipa/A0004615.html, http://www.antiwar.com/casualties/, and http://www.cnn.com/SPECIALS/2003/iraq/forces/casualties/.

And that says nothing about the thousands upon thousands of wounded veterans dating back to World War I. Nor does it include other thousands still missing in action and never accounted for or all non-American casualties.

Seen on a memorial plaque at a cemetery:

If tears could build a stairway, and memories a lane,

I'd walk right up to Heaven and bring you home again.

BIOGRAPHY

Ruthilde Kronberg has been telling stories in the St. Louis and County school districts since 1971. She has been a guest lecturer in several universities and a feature teller at the St. Louis Storytelling Festival, Missouri River Story Festivals, Shakespeare Festivals, and Fourth of July Festivals. Ruthilde also told stories in various parks and in St. Louis County churches and temples. She is the author of *A PIECE OF THE WIND* (Harper and Row, 1990), *CLEVER FOLK: Tales of Wisdom, Wit and Wonder* (Libraries Unlimited, 1993). Ruthilde had a story in *JOINING IN,* an anthology of audience participation stories, and is coauthor of *THE BIBLE TELLS ME SO* (Concordia, 1979).

CONTACT

Ruthilde Kronberg
608 Bacon Avenue
St. Louis, MO 63119

October

United Nations Day is celebrated internationally on October 24.

The Magic Paint Box

INTRODUCTION

I tell this story as a Socratic dialogue, urging the audience to participate by answering my questions.

STORY SCRIPT

While working at the United Nations' summer camp, I became friendly with three boys: Sean from Belfast, Shakib from Beirut, and Yacov from Tel Aviv. Each had come to attend a UNICEF program that brought together children from war-torn parts of the world. Each was asked to speak about and practice peace. These three boys—Catholic, Moslem, and Jew—became best friends.

Do you ever go away on vacation or go to camp? Did you make good friends? Where did they come from?

> 🖒 Wait for audience responses. Answer them.

When summer ended and it was time to say goodbye to my three friends, the boys were brokenhearted. Would they ever see each other again? They promised to write. They promised to remain best friends, but we all knew how hard it would be after thousands of miles separated them.

I tried to make them feel better by offering to buy each of them a souvenir present from the United States. So one morning, we all set off to a huge toy store. The boys ran up and down the aisles trying to choose: Play Station programs, model airplanes, rollerblades. They looked at everything.

What would you choose? What would be a good souvenir of America?

> 🖒 Wait for audience responses. Answer them.

Sean chose a science lab, and Shakib found a telescope, but Yacov couldn't decide. Up and down he searched, up and down. As he was moving down again, he heard, "Choose me. Choose me." Yacov turned, looking for the voice. Who was calling? Where was the voice coming from? Again he heard,

"Choose me! Choose me!" It seemed to be coming from a wooden box buried way back of the shelf in front of him.

Yacov reached for it and opened it. Colors and light seemed to spring up and out. At the bottom of the box was the most beautiful set of paints Yacov had ever seen. Different shades of green and gold like flowers and leaves, pinks and browns, yellows and tans.

All the colors of the world seemed to be in that box. "This is the perfect gift to take back from America," said Yacov. "I will send my friends pictures of Israel and all the people who are waiting for me at home."

When Yacov got home to Tel Aviv, he felt very lonely. His brother Ari was away in the army. Ari was on patrol in the West Bank where Palestinians and Israelis were fighting. Yacov wished his brother were home. He wished people would not fight each other. If only he could make his wishes come true!

Did a member of your family ever go away for a long time? Maybe Mom or Dad on business? Or someone in the Army? What was it like when they came home? How did you celebrate? If none of your family or friends ever goes away, how would you celebrate?

↳ Wait for audience responses. Answer them.

Yacov opened the wooden box of paints from New York and began to paint the scene he wished could happen soon: His brother in his soldier's uniform running up the front steps of their house. Suddenly, a knock on the front door stopped Yacov. He put down his brush, ran downstairs, and opened the door and—"Ari! Ari! You're here! You've come home!" Yacov sprang up into his brother's arms, shouting, "I brought you home. I painted a magic picture and wished it would come true!"

The soldier laughed at his brother's chatter. "Could be, for all I know! I can't figure out how I got here. One second I was in my Jeep in Hebron, and then I'm here. May be magic at that! I've got to get to a phone. My unit will think something happened to me."

Yacov's mind was working furiously. "If I can make magic once, why not again? And again, and again!!"

How many of you think magic really happened? What is magic?

↳ Wait for audience responses. Answer them.

Yacov hurried to his room to paint a picture for his friend Sean.

What kind of picture would you paint of the war in Northern Ireland? How would you help your Irish friend if you were Yacov?

↳ Wait for audience responses. Answer them.

The Belfast that Yacov painted was the city of his magic dreams. It showed Protestants and Catholics dancing together, working together, and playing together. In the middle of the picture, held high up on the shoulders of the crowd, was Sean, waving the blue and white flag of the United Nations as the people jubilantly roared, "Peace! Peace has broken out!"

Next morning, all the newspapers, radios, and televisions were filled with the report. Peace had broken out in Northern Ireland!

The next day, Yacov set to work again. This time, he painted Christians and Moslems in Beirut tearing down the barbed wire that separated their neighborhoods. People were working side by side to rebuild their city while his friend Shabik handed out blue and white flowers of peace and United Nations' flags. That afternoon, news flashes and computer networks reported, "Peace has broken out in Beirut!"

How many of you think magic can happen? What about the magic of friendship and brotherhood? Can you think of some way you can help others to live and work together?

☞ Wait for audience responses. Answer them.

Listen—if each of us will do what I know Yacov and his friends are also doing—trying and trying and trying again and again—peace can happen. How wonderful, if we could cause Peace to break out all over the world!!

ABOUT THE STORY

One day, many storytellers were loading our cars following a stirring peace conference organized by the Storytelling Center of New York and the Jewish Storytelling Center.

A woman came up to me to say, "You must hear this story!" Then, she pulled me over to a friend, also packing her car. "Tell it to him!" she demanded. "Tell him the Magic Paint Box!"

I do not know the name of the woman in the parking lot, but she created a spell of binding, memorable inspiration for me to hold out the hope of world peace to other storytellers. I pass it on to you—not exactly as told to me, but you can change it, too, and pass it on.

RELATED BOOKS

1. *THE PEACE BOOK* by Todd Parr (Little Brown Young Readers, 2005).

2. *JEWISH TALES: One Generation Tells Another* by Peninnah Schram (Jason Aronson, an imprint of Rowman & Littlefield, 1987).

3. *ONE DAY WE HAD TO RUN* by Sybella Welkes (Evans Brothers, 2000).

ACTIVITIES

1. Can anyone you know make a financial contribution to the United Nations Children's Fund (UNICEF)? Address such checks to the United States Committee for UNICEF, 333 East 38th Street, New York, NY 10016; telephone: (212) 686-5522.

2. UNICEF has a catalog depicting various suggestions for gifts, greeting cards for various holidays, 12-month Art Wall Calendars, day planners, coffee mugs, and so on. Call or write to UNICEF, P.O. Box 1500, Louisiana, MO 63353; telephone: 1 (800) 553-1200; shop online at www.unicefusa.org/shop.

3. When I was a little boy, the Halloween holiday and UN day made a happy coincidence. We would dress up in costumes from all over the world and go trick-or-treating for UNICEF. We would take metal collection boxes from door to door, reminding neighbors of our connection to children all over the world. "Trick-or-Treat for UNICEF" began in 1950 when American kids raised much money for children in postwar Europe. Shop online for gift ideas at www.unicefusa.org/shop.

HOLIDAY BACKGROUND INFORMATION

The United Nations officially came into existence on October 24, 1945, when its charter had been ratified by the governments of a majority of its signatories. Therefore, that date was designated throughout the U.S. and worldwide as a day to inform people of all nations of the aims, purposes, and achievements of the UN. It is the highlight day of a weeklong celebration of the founding of the United Nations with educational events and cultural activities to inform the public of its ongoing work.

In 1956, the American committee for the United Nations officially promoted the celebration of United Nations day by noting, "The success of the United Nations in promoting world peace depends on all of us." UN Day is celebrated in many schools in various countries, and the latest information (2007) cites that:

- In Costa Rica, it is a national holiday.

- In Denmark, Finland, and Sweden, it is a flag day.

- In Norway, it is celebrated in many kindergartens and primary schools.

- In Mexico, it is a national holiday.

- In America, the president voluntarily issues a proclamation. UN Day is often marked in American schools with international festivals including songs, dance, and food from around the world.

Source: Retrieved from http://en.wikipedia.org/wiki/united_Nations_Day.

BIOGRAPHY

Gerald Fierst is a performer, writer, and teacher who has appeared throughout America, in England, and in Asia as a storyteller of traditional Jewish and world folklore. He has performed as an actor in film, television, and regional theatre, conducting workshops for teachers and students in writing and performance. He has served as artistic director of the Jewish Storytelling Center at the 92nd Street Y in NYC and as a member of the Board of the New York City Storytelling Center.

Fierst is a graduate of Yale University with Certification as a Teaching Artist from Teachers College, Columbia University. Fierst has been featured at the National Storytelling Association's Festival and is a Parent's Choice Honoree. He is a recipient of a New Jersey State Council Fellowship in Playwriting for his musical *Dancing with Miracles,* based on Yaffa Eliach's *Hasidic Tales of the Holocaust* (Oxford University Press, 1982). His audio recordings *Monstrous Mischief* and *Tikun Olam: Stories to Heal the World* are Parents Choice Silver Medal winners. For more information on Gerald, consult http://www.geraldfierst.com.

CONTACT

Gerald Fierst
259 Park Street
Upper Montclair, NJ 07043
E-mail: Gerald@geraldfierst.com

Halloween is celebrated each year on October 31 in many Western countries.

The Halloween Pumpkin

INTRODUCTION

Before beginning the telling of this story, see the "About the Story" section. TIP: If masks are used, the teller removes a jack-o'-lantern mask from "prop" bag as she reaches down pretending to carve a face, etc. and places the mask on a chair on stage or in front of the audience.

I wrote "The Halloween Pumpkin" for my son, Jonathan, on his seventh Halloween.

STORY SCRIPT

This is a story about a pumpkin, a pumpkin that came to life one Halloween.

There is a part in this story just for you. I will teach you the refrain in the story so that you can say it along with me each time. Here is the refrain:

Thump, thump, thump!

Woo—OW, woo—OW, woo-OW!

I'll eat you up!

Ho, hum, that was fun!

Now, let's do it together.

⇗ **Audience responds:**
Thump, thump, thump!
Woo—OW, woo—OW, woo-OW!
I'll eat you up!
Ho, hum, that was fun!

That was very good. First, we'll use a lower, slower pacing for the jack-o'-lantern's scary voice. Then, we'll add gestures to what we are saying. Follow along with me: "Thump, thump, thump!"

⇗ The teller indicates to the audience how to make the sound of a fence post hitting the ground, by stamping one foot on the floor three times, saying, "Woo—OW, woo—OW, woo—OW!"

175

The teller puts up both arms and makes round circular hand motions; left hand moves clockwise and right hand moves counterclockwise. While doing so, the teller says, "I'll—eat—you—up!"
On the word "up," the teller opens his or her mouth wide to exaggerate a swallowing motion and says, "Ho, hum, that was fun!"
The teller indicates to the audience to make a scary face at that point.
The audience uses a lower, slower pacing for the jack-o'-lantern's scary voice and then adds gestures to what is being said. The teller says, "Follow along with me: Thump, thump, thump!"
The audience stamps one foot on the floor three times.

"Woo—OW, woo—OW, woo—OW!"

 The audience puts up both arms and makes round, circular hand motions; the left hand moves clockwise, and the right hand moves counterclockwise.

"I'll—eat—you—up!"

 On the word "up," audience members open their mouths wide to exaggerate a swallowing motion.

"Ho, hum, that was fun!"

 The audience makes a scary face.

There once lived an old woman in a tumbledown shack high on a hill. She had pale white skin and spider-web hair that fell down to her waist. Her eyes were as green as a cat's.

It was early on Halloween morning, when the earth was filled with magic. The old woman was walking down a road when she came upon a pumpkin patch. She saw a round, fat, orange pumpkin that would be just right for the jack-o'-lantern she wanted to carve. She bent over, wrapped her twig-like arms around the pumpkin, snapped it from the vine, and took it home.

Boldly, she began to carve a face on it that was twisted and scary. Stretching up on the tips of her toes, she lifted up the pumpkin and sat it high on a wooden fence post to scare away the goblins and ghosts.

Darkness came, and a full moon hung in the sky. Everything went still. She gazed out into the night. Then, that jack-o'-lantern began to shake and make a terrible sound, which sounded like "Woo—OW, woo—OW, woo—OW!"

 The teller motions to the audience to repeat the refrain along with him or her, including the gestures, in a lower, slower pacing for the jack-o'-lantern's scary voice.

 Audience responds:
"Thump, thump, thump!
Woo—OW, woo—OW, woo—OW!
I'll—eat—you—up!
Ho, hum, that was fun!"

Her heart jumped, for the old woman was frightened. The jack-o'-lantern began to hop, using the fence post as a wooden leg. It sounded like "Thump, thump, thump!"

 Both the audience and teller begin to clap their hands in unison while stamping one foot on the floor three times.

🔾 "Thump, thump, thump!"
The teller gestures to the audience to repeat the refrain along with her or him,
including gestures, in a lower, slower pacing for the jack-o'-lantern's scary voice.
"Thump, thump, thump!
Woo—OW, woo—OW, woo-OW!
I'll eat you up!
Ho, hum, that was fun!"

The jack-o'-lantern swallowed up the old woman—all of her—in *one* gulp, saying, "Ho, hum, that was fun!" And he hopped on his one wooden leg down the quiet, still road.

🔾 If masks are being used, the audience member representing the old woman holds the
mask in front of his or her face and moves behind the teller.

The jack-o'-lantern hopped until he met a boy dressed up like a skeleton, who was on his way to a Halloween party. When the boy saw the jack-o'-lantern hopping toward him, he stood frozen with fear.

🔾 The teller motions to the audience to repeat the refrain along with her, including the
gestures, in a lower, slower pacing for the jack-o'-lantern's scary voice.
"Thump, thump, thump!

Woo—OW, woo—OW, woo—OW!

I'll—eat—you—up!

Ho, hum, that was fun!"

The jack-o'-lantern swallowed the boy whole, saying, "Ho, hum, that was fun!"

🔾 If masks are being used, the audience member representing the boy holds the mask in
front of his face and moves behind the teller.

Under the moonlit sky, he hopped on his one wooden leg down the quiet, still road. Round and about him, not a leaf stirred. A dog, seeing the jack-o'-lantern, barked wildly. He growled and yapped, showing his teeth, but the jack-o'-lantern just kept on hopping toward him. The dog jumped into the air trying to bite the jack-o'-lantern. He skimmed his nose now and again, barking even louder.

"Thump, thump, thump!"

🔾 The teller motions to the audience to repeat the refrain along with her or him,
including the gestures, in a lower, slower pacing for the jack-o'-lantern's scary voice.

🔾 **Audience responds:**
Thump, thump, thump!
Woo—OW, woo—OW, woo—OW!
I'll—eat—you—up!
Ho, hum, that was fun!"

The jack-o'-lantern opened his twisted mouth and swallowed that dog whole, saying, "Ho, hum, that was fun!"

🔾 If masks are being used, the audience member representing the dog holds the mask in
front of his or her face and moves behind the teller.

The jack-o'-lantern hopped on his one wooden leg down the quiet, still road, and he saw a farm in the distance. Slowly, he hopped toward the farmhouse. The farmer, who was working in the barn, heard the "thump, thump, thump" noise. He opened the barn door and lit a lantern to help him see in the night. As he whirled around, he came face-to-face with that jack-o'-lantern. The farmer was so scared, he dropped his lantern. "Thump, thump, thump!"

⇨ The teller motions to the audience to repeat the refrain, including the gestures, in a lower, slower pacing for the jack-o'-lantern's scary voice.

⇨ **Audience responds:**
"Thump, thump, thump!
Woo—OW, woo—OW, woo—OW!
I'll—eat—you—up!
Ho, hum, that was fun!"

In one bite, he swallowed the farmer saying, "Ho, hum, that was fun!"

⇨ If masks are being used, the audience member representing the farmer holds the mask in front of his or her face and moves behind the teller.

The jack-o'-lantern hopped toward the barn and went inside. There he saw an old mule. The mule wasn't scared one bit! The jack-o'-lantern came closer, saying, "Thump, thump, thump!"

⇨ The teller motions to the audience to repeat the refrain including the gestures, in a lower, slower pacing for the jack-o'-lantern's scary voice.

⇨ **Audience responds:**
"Thump, thump, thump!
Woo—OW, woo—OW, woo—OW!
I'll—eat—you—up!
Ho, hum, that was fun!"

But the mule just kicked up his hind legs at that jack-o'-lantern and split him into two pieces.

⇨ Hold hands up together and boldly separate them, saying, "W—o—o—o—sh!"
The teller makes a tumbling motion with hands. Repeats this hand motion four times.

Pumpkin seeds flew in all directions.

Out tumbled the old woman,

Out tumbled the boy,

Out tumbled the dog,

Out tumbled the farmer.

The spell of the Halloween pumpkin was broken.

The boy headed on down the road to his Halloween party. The dog took off into the night, barking at all the shadows. The farmer went about quieting the farm animals for the evening and gave the mule a carrot for saving everyone.

That old woman just giggled as she scooped up the pumpkin and every seed she could find.

⇨ Make a giggling sound; pantomime a scooping motion.

Slowly, she walked back to her tumbledown shack high on a hill.

 Make a walking motion with hands.

There, she baked a fine pumpkin pie and toasted those seeds with just a touch of cinnamon and butter.

Pantomime a stirring motion.

Then she ate and ate until there was nothing left.

Pantomime an eating motion.

She fell back into her chair and laughed and laughed and laughed! Then she whispered, "Ho, hum, that was fun!"

The audience repeats softly in unison with the teller, "Ho, hum, that was fun!"

With thanks to Stephen C. Rood, who did all the technical computer editing and drawing for the activities.

CREATING THE STORYTELLING MASKS

Materials Used

- One 9-inch white paper plate
- One wooden popsicle stick or tongue depressor
- Markers, tape, stapler, hole punch, scissors
- One large cloth "prop" bag big enough to hold all masks created

    1. Cut two slits about 2 inches in length on each side of one paper plate.

    2. Punch two holes for the eyes in the paper plate across from the slits using a hole punch or scissors.

    3. Turn the plate over and decorate the plate by drawing the face of one of the following six characters:

- An old woman
- Jack-o'-lantern
- Boy in skeleton costume
- Dog
- Farmer
- Mule

    4. Using your imagination, color your mask.

    5. Turn the plate over, overlap the slits, and staple closed. This will cause plate to bend or bow outward.

    6. Staple and tape the wooden stick or tongue depressor to the bottom of the plate.

Assembly Diagram

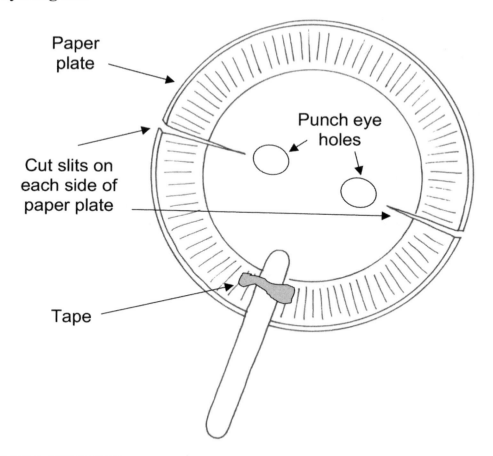

Paper plate

Cut slits on each side of paper plate

Punch eye holes

Tape

ABOUT THE STORY

There are two ways "The Halloween Pumpkin" can be told. In both ways, the audience is told that there is a refrain that the jack-o'-lantern says throughout the story. The teller chants it and teaches it. The audience is asked to chant the refrain each time it occurs in the story as follows:

"Thump, thump, thump!
Woo—OW, woo—OW, woo-OW!
I'll eat you up!
Ho, hum, that was fun!"

Then, the audience members are asked to add gestures to what they have been saying:

1. "Thump, thump, thump!"

   The audience stamps one foot on the floor three times.

2. "Woo—OW, woo—OW, woo—OW"

   The audience puts up both arms and makes round, circular hand motions; the left hand moves clockwise, and the right hand moves counterclockwise.

3. "I'll—eat—you—up!"

   On the word up, the audience members open their mouths wide to exaggerate a swallowing motion.

4. "Ho, hum, that was fun!"

   The audience members make scary faces.

For either way of telling the story, as described further below, have the audience members sit in a circle (if the size of the group numbers twenty-five or less). For larger groups, have the audience sit in chairs or on a rug.

In the first method, the teller narrates the story, and the audience members join in on the refrain and the gestures. The second method includes a greater level of audience participation using visual aids and six masks that need to be prepared ahead of time. See cutouts and directions above.

In the second method, the teller selects five members from the audience to be one of the five characters. The teller has all masks placed in a "prop" bag. The selected audience members each reach into the bag and pull out a mask at random. The mask selected is the character each will be in the story. The teller then takes a couple of minutes individually with the selected audience members to make certain they know and understand what their character is and what they are to do when the teller says, "I'll—eat—you—up! Ho, hum, that was fun!" The teller can also inform the audience members that they will be visually cued as well, explaining the specific cues for each character. When hearing these words or seeing the visual cue, the characters, each at their designated time, raise their mask to hide their face and move behind the teller.

Each selected audience member sits next to the teller in the order that the characters appear in the story (the old woman, boy in skeleton costume, the dog, the farmer, and the mule). Then each audience member places the mask on the floor in front of him or her. The teller narrates the story and becomes the jack-o'-lantern character. As the story unfolds and each character is swallowed up, the audience member representing that character raises his or her mask to hide the face and moves behind the teller. Then the Teller and each character that has been swallowed up line up and circle the room. At the end, they pretend to tumble out of the pumpkin. The old woman character pantomimes scooping up the pieces of pumpkin and seeds. The other characters return to their seats. The old woman character pretends to walk home and pantomimes baking (stirring motion) a pie and eating it up! The entire group whispers the last line, "Ho, hum, that was fun!"

Young children enjoy being "swallowed up" and becoming part of the story. Adapt to your group. For instance, the story can be expanded by having children imagine themselves as additional characters in the story (e.g., the farmer's wife, a cow). Also, children from the audience can be called into the story by describing a particular child (e.g., a blonde-haired girl in a pink dress) or naming a child (e.g., Mike or Sue).

Improvise and have fun!

OTHER VARIANTS OF THE STORY

1. "The Wolf and the Seven Little Goats" by The Brothers Grimm, in *HOUSEHOLD STORIES* (New York: Macmillan, 1954). German folktale.

2. "Sody Sallyraytas" by Richard Chase in *GRANDFATHER TALES* (Boston: Houghton Mifflin, 1948). Tale from the southern United States.

3. "The Cat and the Parrot" by Virginia Haviland in *FAVORITE FAIRY TALES TOLD IN INDIA* (New York: Little, Brown and Company, 1973). Indian folktale.

4. Leydenfrost, Robert. *The Snake That Sneezed* (New York: G.P. Putnam's Sons, 1970). A humorous picture book.

RELATED BOOKS

1. *WITCHES, PUMPKINS, AND GRINNING GHOSTS* by Edna Barth (New York: The Seabury Press, 1972).

2. *HALLOWEEN FUN* by Judith Hoffman Corwin (New York: Julian Messner, 1983).

3. *HOW TO HAUNT A HOUSE FOR HALLOWEEN* by Robert Friedhoffer (New York: Franklin Watts, 1989).

4. *THE VANISHING PUMPKIN* by Tony Johnston (New York: G.P. Putnam's Sons, 1983).

5. *WHEN THE LIGHTS GO OUT: TWENTY SCARY TALES TO TELL* by Margaret Read MacDonald (H.W. Wilson, 1988). Includes Halloween sources (e.g., tales, tale origins and variants, how to tell stories to an audience, etc.).

HOLIDAY BACKGROUND INFORMATION

Halloween is celebrated on October 31 in the United States and Canada. Halloween has a more ancient origin than any other holiday, but it no longer has any serious meanings for most people in today's culture.

Children keep it alive because they love it—dressing up in costumes and masks as ghosts, witches, skeletons, or anything else their imagination takes them. These outfits stand for the ghosts or spirits that frightened people on this same evening hundreds of years before the birth of Christ. Once people offered gifts of food to appease the spirits; today people offer treats to children as they visit door to door crying "Trick or treat!"

Halloween parties remind us of symbols of the harvest—pumpkins, apples, apple cider, popcorn, candy corn, nuts, and cornstalks. The white ghost and the witch's black hat and cloak, with her faithful black cat companion, all have their origins with the Celts who lived more than 2,000 years ago in what is now Great Britain and Ireland. Of the many Celtic gods, one was named Samhain, the god of death. The Celts believed that Samhain came to earth on the evening of October 31 and made the dead, or ghosts, come back to life; he also commanded fairies and goblins walk the earth. The Celts believed, too, that black cats were once people who had been changed into cats by black magic. Samhain's night marked the beginning of winter. It was at this time of the year, with the days growing shorter, the nights longer, and plants having died, that the association of black with death and Halloween took place.

After the Romans conquered the Celts in 43 B.C., they held celebrations for their own gods, one of which was the goddess of fruit, Pomona. To give thanks for a bountiful harvest, they offered Pomona offerings of apples. Over time the festivals of Samhain and Pomona became intertwined. Today Halloween combines ghosts and black cats as well as symbols of the fall harvest.

Many of the customs of the Celts survived even after the rise of Christianity in the fourth century. In the seventh century, the church set aside All Saint's Day on November 1 in memory of early Christians who had died for their beliefs. Another name for All Saint's Day was All Hallows. October 31 was known as All Hallows' Eve, later shortened to Halloween. The Celtic people continued to expect the arrival of ghosts of the departed on the evening of October 31. In the tenth century, the church set aside the date of November 2 as All Souls' Day to remember the souls of all the departed ones.

In the 1800s, people from Great Britain and Ireland moved to the United States. They brought with them the Celtic holiday of Halloween, as well as their customs and traditions for this holiday. The jack-o'-lantern came from Ireland. It originated from a story about a man named Jack. He was barred from entering heaven because he was bad, and the Devil sent him out of hell because he was a trickster. He was forever banished to walk the earth with only his lantern and was known by the Irish as "Jack of the Lantern." The Irish were the first to carve a jack-o'-lantern, although they were originally made from large potatoes or turnips because the Irish did not have pumpkins back then.

Trick-or-treating is also from Ireland. Irish farmers went to wealthy homes asking for food. If the rich people would not give them anything, the farmers would play tricks on them (moving objects or stealing small items). People thought ghosts had played the tricks.

In Scotland, people believed that witches possessed magical powers. They were thought to gather on Halloween night. It was believed that they flew to their meetings on broomsticks, often accompanied by a black cat.

Bonfires have also played an integral part of Halloween. In the early times, they were lit by the Celts to honor Samhain. Later, the people of Great Britain and Ireland lit fires to scare away evil witches and ghosts. The Scottish people lit torches for the same purpose.

In America, Halloween is celebrated with costume parties, trick-or-treating, houses decorated with lights, practical jokes, fortune-telling, bonfires, pumpkin-decorating contests, prizes for the largest baked pumpkin pie, apple bobbing, and the telling of scary stories.

BIOGRAPHY

Stephanie Mita is a storyteller, performing artist, and teacher who researches traditional tales and also writes her own. She is storyteller-in-residence at P.S. 105, Bronx, New York. Her performances have included the Metropolitan Museum of Art; the Hudson River Museum; the "New York Is Book Country" festival; the Arts in Education Conference at Skidmore College; the New York State Writing Conference at SUNY, Albany, New York (presenter); the Sleepy Hollow Festival; St. Paul's Church National Historic Site in Mt. Vernon, New York; and Shanghai and Soochow, China.

She wrote an original adaptation of *Pinocchio* and created a one-woman show combining song, acting, movement, and the spoken word based on Carlo Collodi's masterpiece. At the Westchester Italian Cultural Center, Stephanie has performed Italian folktales as well as her own original works. She created "Hoop and a Tale," a program of original stories focusing on exercise and healthy foods while exercising with a hula-hoop. She conceived "Storytelling in the Park" performances at thirty park locations for the City of Yonkers, New York. Stephanie has also contributed to the New York State guide for *Italian Americans: Looking Back—Moving Forward*.

CONTACT

Stephanie Mita
183 Boulder Ridge Road
Scarsdale, NY 10583
E-mail: smitta@optonline.net

November

JOSEPH BRUCHAC

In 1990, the first President Bush approved a resolution that declared November as our "National American Indian Heritage Month."

Gluskonba and the Maple Trees

INTRODUCTION

1. This is a traditional Abenaki story. Abenaki is spelled as it sounds. Vowel sounds are consistent, unlike English.

   A: ah, as in Ma

   E: eh, as in Bet

   I: ee, as in Beet

   O: oh, as in Go

   U: uh, as in But

   W: aw, as in Caw, but nasalized (as in *Wliwini* meaning "thanks")

   Unusual sounds: "Nd" at the start of a word (as in *Nda,* meaning "no" or in Ndakinna, meaning "Our land"); the same as the "nd" sound in the word "under."

2. Note on "Ho?" and "Hey": One of the old traditions in a Northeastern woodlands storyteller is the use of a set of call and response words. Although not literally translatable, "Ho?" serves as a question or a request for the audience to respond, thus showing that they are listening intently. The audience response of "Hey!" (pronounced as a nasal "Henh!" among Iroquoian peoples) indicates that they are awake and following the story. "Ho?" and "Hey!" may also be used to pick up the pace of a story by a rapid repetition of the two words.

STORY SCRIPT

Kwai, kwai, nidobak, which means "Hello, my friends." Can you handle that?

 **Audience responds, with laughter:**
Hello, my friends.

Well, you simply say right back to me "*Kwai, kwai, nidobak*!" Try that.

 **Audience responds:**
Kwai, kwai, nidobak.

187

In the old days, stories were often told around a fire late at night. Sometimes, when people sit around a fire late at night, they start to fall asleep. But you must stay awake to hear this story. So it was that long ago—and today, as well—we storytellers would check to make sure that everyone was awake and listening by saying, "Ho?" Then everyone still awake had to respond by saying "Hey!" "Ho?"

 **Audience responds:**
Hey!

Also, if you agree with something I say and I ask you a question, the right way to respond in Abenaki is with this word, "Unh-hunh!" I'll say it again. "Unh-hunh!" That means "yes" in Abenaki. Do you understand?

 **Audience responds:**
Unh-hunh!

Wli, which means "good." Now, if you do not agree with something I say, then you have to say the Abenaki word for "No." That word is "*Nda!*" Try that.

 **Audience responds:**
Nda!

Do you all want to go home now?

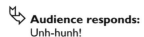 **Audience responds:**
Nda!

Wli. Good. Now my story can begin.

Ho?

Audience responds:
Hey!

A looooooooooooooooooooooooooooong time ago. [Hold the "ooo" for as long as you can.] Was that a long time ago?

Audience responds:
Unh-hunh!

Long ago, some things were not the same as they are today. Back then, pure sweet syrup flowed all year through the maple trees. Do you all know what maple syrup is?

Audience responds:
Unh-hunh!

Is it sweet to taste?

Audience responds:
Unh-hunh!

Back then, it was even sweeter. All you had to do to get maple syrup was to break a twig and then catch the syrup in a carved wooden cup or a basket made of folded birch bark. Not only that, maple syrup flowed all year round from those trees. Wasn't that a wonderful gift from Ktsi Nwaskw, the Great Mystery?

> Pause, wait for answer.

> **Audience responds:**
> Unh-hunh!

However, sometimes when things are too easy, we human beings begin to take those things for granted. Is that not so?

> Pause, wait for answer.

> **Audience responds:**
> Unh-hunh!

And so it was with the gift of maple syrup.

Back then, long ago, Gluskonba was out walking around. Do you know who Gluskonba is?

> Pause, wait for answer.

> **Audience responds:**
> Nda!

Ah, Gluskonba is the one who was given the power to change things by the Great Mystery. And he often used that power to help the human beings. And so it was that, as Gluskonba was out walking around, he decided to visit the Abenaki people. Ho?

> **Audience responds:**
> Hey!

However, when Gluskonba came to their village, it seemed that something was very wrong. The village was empty of people. The wigwams were falling apart. Saplings were starting to grow up in the pathways. Gluskonba became very worried. "Where have my people all gone?" Gluskonba said. "Has some monster come and taken them away? I must find them!"

So Gluskonba began to search for the people. He walked out of the village, looking with his eyes, listening with his ears. He listened very carefully, just like this

> Cup your hands behind your ears, then ask the audience to do the same.

Try it.

> Audience mimics teller's actions.

This way, your ears are like those of the deer. You can focus your hearing by keeping your hands behind your ears and moving your hands so that your palms face the direction in which you want to listen.

As soon as Gluskonba did this, he heard a sound. It was like this.

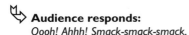 Make a heavy sighing sound, followed by smacking your lips. *Oooh! Ahhh! Smack-smack-smack.* [To audience.]

Try making that sound.

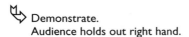 **Audience responds:**
Oooh! Ahhh! Smack-smack-smack.

Wli! Good.

Now if I hold my right hand out—go ahead, hold out your right hand.

Demonstrate.
Audience holds out right hand.

Wli! Good.

And if I raise my hand while I am holding it out, make that sound louder.

Oooh! Ahhh! Smack-smack-smack!

 Demonstrate.
Audience holds out right hand and says more loudly.
Oooh! Ahhh! Smack-smack-smack!

Wli! Good.

Now if I lower my hand [demonstrate] that will make the sound softer. Go ahead and try it.

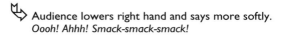 Audience lowers right hand and says more softly.
Oooh! Ahhh! Smack-smack-smack!

Wli! Good.

Now, keep your left hand behind your ear and use your right hand to direct the audience as you imitate Gluskonba trying to locate that sound.

Gluskonba went toward the direction of the dawn land, the east,

 Hold out hand and lower it.

but the sound grew fainter. He tried going to the direction of the winter land, the north.

Hold out hand and lower it.

But the sound grew fainter still. He tried the direction of the summer land, the south.

Hold out hand and lower it.

There, too, the sound grew fainter. It was only when he walked in the direction of the sunset land, the west, that the sound grew louder.

Hold out hand and raise it.

The further he went in that direction, the louder the sound grew. Finally, he found himself sitting on top of a hill looking down on a big grove of maple trees. The sound was coming from beneath those trees!

☝ Pull your hand back in. Stop making the *"Oooh. Ahhh. Smack-smack-smack"* sound.

All the people were there, and what do you think they were doing?

☝ Pause and see if anyone gives you an answer and respond according to whatever might be said with either "Yes" or "No."

The answer was actually "not exactly," and let me tell you why. Because. Because all the people in the village were there on their backs, each beneath a maple tree.

They had broken twigs, so that sap was dripping down into their open mouths. And as they drank that sap, they said,

☝ Hold out hand to audience.

☝ **Audience responds:**
Oooh! Ahhh! Smack-smack-smack!

Those people had been there for so long, drinking that sweet syrup, they had all become fat! Grass was growing between their fingers and toes! Field mice had made nests in their hair!

"This is not good," said Gluskonba. "The people have become fat and lazy. Our Creator did not mean for human beings to live this way."

So Gluskonba carefully peeled some bark from a birch tree. He remembered to thank the tree for its gift. Then he made a big basket and went down to the river, filled that basket with water, and came back to pour it into the top of the maple trees. He did that many times, until the sap in every tree became very thin and watery.

The people began to say, "Wah-hah!"

Each of you, try saying that as I look your way and nod at you.

☝ NOTE: Do NOT point a finger at anyone. That is regarded as very rude behavior by virtually all American Indians. To point at someone, use your chin or purse your lips in their direction.

☝ Wah-hah. Wah-hah. Wah-hah.

As that sap became so watery and no longer sweet to the taste, each of those people sat up and looked around. "What is wrong with our sweet syrup?" they asked. Ho?

☝ **Audience responds:**
Hey!

Then, Gluskonba spoke to them. "*Nidobak*," he said, "my friends, our Creator did not mean for you all to become fat and lazy. From now on, maple syrup will no longer be easy to obtain. The sap from the trees will only be a little sweet. To get your maple syrup, you must gather much sap in bark baskets. Then you must boil it down until it becomes syrup. You must work hard, gathering dry wood, to keep the fires going. You must clean up the woodlands as you go.

"Not only that, this sweet gift from the trees will only come once a year, just at the time when the snows begin to melt away.

"Then you will remember to be thankful for the maple syrup and thank the trees."

So Gluskonba said, and so it is to this day. Ho?

 Hey!

ABOUT THE STORY

I've been sharing this very old, traditional story with audiences for more than three decades now. Although I have chosen to tell the Abenaki version of the tale, the story is also a prominent part of the traditions of the Anishinabe people, who live to the west of us among the Great Lakes and are regarded as our cousins. In their stories, they speak not of Gluskonba (or Gluskabe), but of Manabozho (or Nanabush).

Among those Abenaki elders who shared stories with me many years ago and helped me understand this tale and many others, I must credit Stephen Laurent (Atian Lolo) and Maurice Dennis (Mdawelasis). Although some have tried to say that maple sugaring was introduced to the American continent by Europeans, this story and numerous others that have been part of our traditions for centuries, indicate that gathering maple sap and making it into syrup is something that we did not have to learn from late arrivals to this land.

RELATED BOOKS

1. By Joseph Bruchac: *TELL ME A TALE* (Harcourt Brace, 1997); *OUR STORIES REMEMBER* (Fulcrum, 2003); *THE WIND EAGLE* (Bowman Books, 1985); *THE FAITHFUL HUNTER* (Bowman Books, 1988); *KEEPERS OF THE EARTH* with Michael Caduto (Fulcrum, 1988).

2. *TRADITIONAL AMERICAN INDIAN LITERATURES: Texts and Interpretations* by Karl Kroeber, Jarold Ramsay, Dennis Tedlock, Barre Toelken, Tacheeni Scott, and Dell Hymes (University of Nebraska Press, 1981).

3. *THROUGH INDIAN EYES: The Native American Experience in Books for Children* by Beverly Slapin and Doris Seale (New Society, 1992).

4. *NATIVE AMERICANS IN CHILDREN'S LITERATURE* by Jon C. Stott (Oryx Press, 1995).

5. *COYOTE AND NATIVE AMERICAN FOLKTALES* by Joe Hayes (picture book) (Mariposa, 1983).

HOLIDAY BACKGROUND INFORMATION

Thanks to the Maples.

While modern American calendars celebrate Thanksgiving only once a year, among the Native peoples of the Northeast, both Algonquian (such as the Abenaki, Lenape, Wampanoag, and others) and Iroquoian (such as the Mohawk, Onondaga, Seneca, and others), there were a number of times during the year when there would be a celebration of thanks for one of Mother Earth's gifts, such as when the strawberries became ripe or when the green corn was ready for picking.

The first big yearly Thanksgiving, though, was for the maple trees, the sap of which begins to flow around the end of February, the time known as Maple Sugar Moon to many native nations.

Thanks would be spoken to the trees, both before and after the harvest of sap. Whole communities in some cases would move out to the forest during this season to tap the trees. Children enjoyed a special treat at this time. A cup made of birch bark would be filled with snow, and then hot maple syrup would be poured into the cup full of snow. (Tapping the trees was done by making a V-shaped cut in the bark and placing a bucket made of folded birch bark—which is watertight—beneath it to catch the sap. Boiling down would be done by pouring the sap into a dugout canoe and then dropping red hot stones into the sap.)

NOTE: For a brief history of the creation of American Indian Heritage Month, consult: www.infoplease.com/spot/aihmorigins1.html. This will also give you links to American Indian Tribes, Glossary of American Indian terms, Navajo Code Talkers, Native American languages, and Sacagawee Golden Dollar. Also consult www.ihs.gov/PublicAffairs/Heritage/index.cfm for national American Indian and Alaska Native Heritage Month information. For information about Plimouth Plantation, consult http://en.wikipedia.org/wiki/Plimoth_Plantation.

BIOGRAPHY

Joseph Bruchac is a poet, writer, and traditional storyteller who often draws on his Abenaki Indian roots for inspiration. He and his family have been involved for more than thirty years in various activities to promote and preserve Abenaki language, music, storytelling, and cultural traditions, as well as supporting contemporary Abenaki communities in the United States and Canada. A former three-time member of the board of the National Storytelling Association, he has performed and done workshops all over the United States, in Europe, and in such different settings as maximum security prisons and senior centers.

His poems, stories, and essays have appeared in more than a thousand publications, and he is the author of more than 120 books, including his recent novels *HIDDEN ROOTS*, which won the 2007 Native American Librarians Association Award, and *GERONIMO*, winner of the 2007 Spur Award from the Western Writers Association. For more information, consult http://www.josephbruchac.com/ and other Web sites that can be found using a search engine.

CONTACT

Joseph Bruchac
P.O. Box 308
Greenfield Center, NY 12833
E-mail: nudatlog@earthlink.net

LARRY JOHNSON

Veterans Day, both a federal holiday and state holiday in all states, falls on November 11, the anniversary of the signing of the Armistice that ended World War I. Consult: www.va.gov/opal/feature/celebrate/vetday.asp. (For Veterans Day UK consult: www.veterans-UK.com/remembrance/nationalceremony.html.)

Eleven Bells

INTRODUCTION

This story, a fictional account based on actual experiences with the author's grandfather, is a call to more strongly honor not only those who served and died, but also to all of LIFE as we continue to struggle with conflict in our communities and the world.

STORY SCRIPT

I shall pass out as many bells as I have, and ask the rest of you to use your voice to "GONG" as we ring the bells eleven times.

I want to tell you a story that begins with the end of World War I, "the War to end all Wars." When it was over, at 11 A.M. on November 11, 1918, many churches in America rang their bells eleven times to honor and remember the many soldiers who died, and to think of a time when people of the world would no longer need to experience such horror. This was the start of what we now celebrate as Veterans Day. Will you now ring your bells or your voice to "GONG" eleven times?

⇗ Lead audience in ringing actual bells or "gong" eleven times.

When I was nine and my brother was seven, we spent the whole summer with my favorite Grandpa. Well, he was my only living Grandpa, but even if I had a lot of Grandpas, he would have been my favorite. He was fun, even when we were working. When he sent us out to bury coffee grounds by Grandma's flowers, he said, "The worms love 'em. It makes the ground feel like a carnival for worms." Then he'd sing some goofy song we'd heard at the amusement park the day before.

When it was time to go fishing, we'd go with Grandpa to the flower garden and dig for worms, away from the flowers. "The worms help the flowers grow better," he told us, "but the flowers don't need all of them. Fish need some too. We'll get eleven." Then we'd dig till we had eleven juicy angleworms in a coffee can for an afternoon of fishing with Grandpa.

One day we came back from a walk to town with Grandma, and Grandpa had mounted a tall pole in the ground. "It's eleven feet tall," he said. "Climb to the top, and there's a silver dollar there for each of you. Some day that dollar will be worth eleven." It took me three days, and my brother a week, to get good and strong enough to make it to the top, but we did. We proudly collected our silver dollars. The next year in school and in the neighborhood, we were the best climbers around.

There were lots of things we remember. But especially on rainy days, we remember my Grandpa's basement. It was the cleanest and brightest I'd ever seen, and it was filled with neat stuff. He had all the license plates from old cars hanging on the wall, right next to political campaign buttons from times I would learn about much later in history classes. There were wonderful model airplanes my uncle had made when he was our age, and an old, old logging-saw Grandpa said he used long before chainsaws. The walls held many mounted deer antlers, along with pictures of Grandpa's "SureShot" hunting gang, and a beautiful, old, carved cuckoo clock from Germany, which had stopped at 11:00 o'clock. Grandpa's Museum was free, but he teased, "I should charge you 11 cents to get in."

One day, my brother and I were "Up Town" with Grandpa. He belonged to an organization called Veterans of Foreign Wars (VFW) and another one called the American Legion. He was taking his turn raising the flag and was showing us how to fold it properly, and how and why to respect it. Suddenly he broke down, almost crying, as he said, "Boys, war is a horrible thing. I was in World War I, and my brother was killed there. I hope neither one of you has to go. Soldiers see things and live through things that no one should have to be a part of."

Then my Grandpa took out a small bell. He rang it eleven times, saying, "Boys, when we came back from the war, they rang the bells eleven times to remember the soldiers who didn't make it home. We called what we did THE WAR TO END ALL WARS." Can we hear those gongs going?

Ring bells or "voice gong" eleven times.

"When I hear those bells," Grandpa continued, "I'm remembering my brother, and I'm asking people everywhere to give the soldiers who come home all the medical treatment they need, and all the training and support they need to do good work in their towns. NO ARGUING!"

I never saw that serious side of my Grandpa again. We just kept on having fun. He died when I was exactly eleven years old. Most people just said, "Your Grandpa got old and died. He lived a good life." His friends, who were with him in the war, said, "It's because of something that happened 'over there.' He was a good man. He should have lived much longer."

All I know is that every year on my Grandpa's birthday, and on Veteran's Day, wherever I am at precisely 11 o'clock in the morning, I stop and I am quiet for eleven minutes. Then I say to whoever is around, "WHEN SOLDIERS COME HOME, GIVE THEM ALL THE MEDICAL TREATMENT THEY NEED, AND ALL THE TRAINING AND SUPPORT TO DO GOOD WORK IN THEIR TOWNS. THEN WE MUST WORK REALLY HARD SO "NATION FIGHTS" CAN BE WORKED OUT WITHOUT HURTING PEOPLE. NO ARGUING!"

May I hear those bells again?

Ring bells or "voice gongs" eleven times.

How about repeating Grandpa's words: "WHEN SOLDIERS COME HOME, GIVE THEM ALL THE MEDICAL TREATMENT THEY NEED, AND ALL THE TRAINING AND SUPPORT TO DO GOOD WORK IN THEIR TOWNS. THEN WE MUST WORK REALLY HARD SO "NATION FIGHTS" CAN BE WORKED OUT WITHOUT HURTING PEOPLE. NO ARGUING!"

 **Audience responds:**
"When soldiers come home, give them all the medical treatment they need, and all the training and support to do good work in their towns. Then we must work really hard so 'nation fights' can be worked at without hurting people. NO ARGUING."

It's time to ring those bells or hear "voice gongs" eleven times.

 (All participate.)

ABOUT THIS STORY

The story, although "fictional," is extremely true and biographical. My own grandfather did all the interesting things mentioned, including the incident at the flagpole and World War I. The only "literary license" is the obsession with the number eleven and the eleven bells being part of the story told by my grandpa. It is true that ringing of the bells eleven times at 11 A.M. on November 11, 1918, happened for some time after the war, but I don't remember my grandfather telling me that. I have it because it's part of many ceremonies done by the Twin Cities chapter of Veterans for Peace I belong to. I also belong to the American Legion because that was Grandpa's group. He was eligible for VFW, but there was no chapter at the time in the little town of Lindstrom where he lived. There is today, and when I took the 61-mile hike through Lindstrom, we had a ceremony at the stunning Veteran's Memorial with local VFW members and some of my VFP friends. Though there were differences about the reasons for and conduct of certain wars, there was absolute agreement on the pressing need for total physical and emotional support for the families of those who die or for those who return from any kind of warfare.

RELATED BOOKS

1. *THE WALL* by Eve Bunting, illustrated by Richard Himler (Houghton Mifflin, 1990). For six to nine year olds, this book is about a visit to the Vietnam War Memorial.

2. *PEPPER'S PURPLE HEART,* written and illustrated by Heather French Henry (Cubbie Blue, 2003). Children learn about our nation's veterans and why we honor them.

HOLIDAY BACKGROUND INFORMATION

Although Veterans Day is still celebrated on November 11, it is done too often with a disconnect on the part of the general public from the genuinely deep sacrifices made by the soldiers and their families.

The original Armistice Day focused on the honoring of soldiers who had died, but also had the element of "to end all wars." The growing body of lessons learned since that first Armistice Day celebration led soldiers of all political and philosophical persuasions to agree on the need for extreme honoring and care in all areas, particularly for soldiers who return to civilian life.

BIOGRAPHY

In 1961, Larry Johnson took a 50-mile hike when President Kennedy, a war hero, asked for a level of fitness in the country.

On August 9, 2007, when he turned 61, he took a 61-mile hike up Highway 61 in Minnesota, and into the small town where his grandfather and uncle, both veterans, are buried. The hike was awareness for better health for all ages, especially a promotion of the thoughts presented in this story.

In the 1960s, Larry became a conscious storyteller, while working with young people, often in gangs, at war with the culture.

In 1970, he was drafted and served as an army medic. Upon his return, his storytelling became a tool for community work in health, education, environment, social justice, and the like.

Larry belongs to both the American Legion (http://www.americanlegion.com/) and Veterans for Peace (http://www.veteransforpeace.org/).

Since 1982, he has partnered in all ways with Elaine Wynne, and they have continued and expanded their work as the Key of See Storytellers. Much of Larry's individual work these days reflects this story. Larry and Elaine have thirteen wonderful grandchildren, all of them good storytellers, and good workers in the world.

CONTACT

Larry Johnson
Key of See Storytellers
Box 27314
Golden Valley, MN, 55427
E-mail: Topstory7@comcast.net

In America, Thanksgiving Day is celebrated on the fourth Thursday in November.

Rabbit, Bobcat, and the Wild Turkeys

INTRODUCTION

This story features turkeys, which are an important element in Thanksgiving Day celebrations. It is a trickster tale that entertains audiences of all ages. Older folk (fourth grade and up) may be shy about vocal participation, but they still like the story, especially the notion of "playing dead." I do not generally rehearse the audience for their roles as "Turkeys." At most, I might advise them that "This story has some parts where I will need your help to make it sound good. I'll let you know what to do."

PERFORMANCE NOTES

Tellers who prefer to "warm up" an audience might want to start by practicing the Turkeys' different emotional states before beginning the story. I have not found it to be necessary. Even kindergarteners can pick up the appropriate tones and inflections from the teller's example, so fast that the prompts ("Let's hear __") don't interrupt the flow or satisfaction of the story. (Lessons about distinguishing among emotions can be pounded in later by those so inclined.)

When doing this story with a very large group, you will need some way to interrupt the Turkey cacophony so that you can get on with the story. If there's no sound system to help your voice override the audience, you'll need to establish a "cut" signal to stop the commotion. This can be practiced ahead of time.

STORY SCRIPT

In the long ago times, Rabbit had a long bushy tail of which she was very proud.

> 🖐 Look behind you at your beautiful tail. Pull around front and stroke it fondly with your paw.

She always spread it out on the grass behind her, when she stopped to nibble the tender green leaves.

> 🖐 Arrange your tail out of the way and nibble a mouthful or two.

One evening Rabbit was in the meadow, busy eating supper, minding her own business. Suddenly Bobcat pounced upon her and said, "At last I have you!"

> 🖐 Pretend to be Bobcat: Loom over someone in the audience.

199

"Rabbit! You will taste delicious!" Rabbit couldn't get away.

> Pretend to be Rabbit: cringe and shiver with fear. Then get a crafty look.

But she could use her wits. "Me? Why would you want to eat skinny little me, when you could have a feast of plump Turkeys. Bobcat said, "Turkeys? Don't joke with me, Rabbit. Those wild Turkeys are so sneaky, I can never catch them."

> Bobcat can be portrayed as not too bright.

"They let me get just close enough to see how fat and tender they are. Then they slip away into the tall weeds. I could never catch a Turkey!"

Rabbit said, "Yes you could, Bobcat. I can help you. You must fool the Turkeys so that they will come close to you. Then you can catch as many as you want. All you have to do is play dead."

"Dead! I don't want to be dead, Rabbit!"

"Not really dead, Bobcat. You just *play* dead. Come with me." They went near the woods, where the weeds grew tall.

"Now lie down on your back with your eyes closed and your mouth open, and put your paws in the air.

> Rabbit shows Bobcat how.

"The Turkeys will think you are dead, and they won't be afraid to come close. Try it: You can play dead." So Bobcat lay down, put his paws in the air, closed his eyes and opened his mouth. He lay very still. He really looked dead.

Let's see you pretend to be dead Bobcats. Lean back, put up your paws, close your eyes and open your mouth.

> Audience mimics dead bobcats.

Yechh, a whole room full of dead Bobcats!

Okay, here's what happened next.

Rabbit said, "That's very good, Bobcat. Now I will go tell the Turkeys, and they will come."

So Rabbit left Bobcat on the ground pretending to be dead, and found the Turkeys in the tall weeds. They were quietly scratching the ground, looking for tasty seeds and bugs to eat.

Now I need you to help me. I need you to be those tricky Turkeys. What noise do Turkeys make? People usually say "gobble gobble," but really it's more like "looble looble." We can make the Turkeys sound different, depending on whether they're happy or nervous or angry.

Let me hear how the Turkeys sound right now, CALM and PEACEFUL.

> Gobble *low* and *slow*, inviting the audience with expression and gesture to gobble quietly, too.
> Audience gobbles.

Rabbit ran up and said, "Bobcat is dead! Bobcat is dead!" The Turkeys were very surprised to hear this. They couldn't believe it.

Let me hear you sound like very DOUBTFUL Turkeys. Gobble a little faster, with a rising inflection.

⟜ Audience responds, acts doubtful.

"Really," said Rabbit. "This is what happened: Bobcat tried to catch me. We had a terrible fight! We struggled and kicked. Bobcat almost got me! But I won, and now Bobcat is dead. Come, see for yourselves." The Turkeys still did not believe Rabbit.

Let's hear how VERY DOUBTFUL they sounded. Slow, rising inflection.

⟜ Audience gobbles in slow, rising inflection.

So they came along to see. And there was Bobcat on the ground, with his paws in the air and his eyes closed and his mouth open. He didn't move at all. He looked very dead.

⟜ Audience may want to play dead again. Proceed after a respectful pause.

The Turkeys stood around looking at Bobcat, feeling very worried. They had never been this close to Bobcat before.

 Let's hear those WORRIED Turkeys.

⟜ Gobble in a tense and higher pitch, with an "uh-oh" inflection. Crane head back and forth in a birdlike manner, looking at Bobcat with one eye at a time.

"Go closer," said Rabbit. "See for yourselves. Bobcat is dead!" The Turkeys went closer, still feeling worried.

"Uh-oh," they said.

But as they got closer and saw that Bobcat really looked *very* dead, they began to believe that it was true. They were SURPRISED.

⟜ Quick rising inflection as if asking, "Dead? Dead?" Broad "aah!" inflection. Audience gobbles with short, high inflection as if exclaiming, "Dead!"

They were RELIEVED. They were HAPPY! Bobcat, their enemy, would never try to hunt them again! They circled around Bobcat, dancing and gobbling. Let's hear those HAPPY Turkeys dance!

⟜ Gobble, bobbing head and shoulders as if feet are moving.

They danced closer and closer. Bobcat waited until the Turkeys were *very* close. Then he jumped up and grabbed the two fattest, tenderest ones. They squawked with fear!!

Let's hear those FRIGHTENED Turkeys squawk!

⟜ Flap wings, eyes wide. Audience responds with a S – Q – U – A –W – K!

Bobcat dragged those two away into the woods. The other Turkeys realized that Rabbit had tricked them. They were very angry.

Let's hear how those ANGRY Turkeys really felt about Rabbit. Gobble with a "grrrr" inflection.

⟜ Audience responds as angry Turkeys again: S – Q – U – A –W – K!

Rabbit ran away laughing, back to the meadow.

ᗏ Smugly settle down again with your tail spread behind you.

Rabbit stretched out her long, bushy tail behind her and started nibbling grass again, thinking how clever she was. She had escaped from Bobcat, and she had tricked the Turkeys. But the Turkeys got together in the tall weeds. They grumbled and mumbled about how Rabbit had tricked them.

Let's hear them GRUMBLE and MUMBLE.

ᗏ Frown and shake head, gobbling in a low and ominous tone.
Audience responds with grumbles and mumbles.

They wanted to teach Rabbit a lesson. They whispered and planned together. Let's hear them.

ᗏ WHISPER with audience and peer around conspiratorially.

When they were ready, they all went together. They crept out of the tall weeds. . . . They snuck up silently behind Rabbit. . . .

Rabbit was happily nibbling grass and not paying attention. She didn't even hear those tricky Turkeys. The Turkeys counted together silently.

ᗏ With one finger over lips, soundlessly mouth, "One . . . Two . . .Three . . ." while
holding up 1-2-3 fingers of other hand. Dramatic pause . . .

Then they all *jumped* on Rabbit with a loud SQUAWK!

ᗏ Point to audience when you reach S – Q – U – A –W – K!

Rabbit was so surprised she leaped away! But she wasn't quite fast enough. The Turkeys didn't land on Rabbit, they just landed on that long, bushy tail stretched out behind her. She pulled and she tugged, but they were all standing on it.

She couldn't get away! She pulled so hard that her tail snapped right off!

ᗏ Mime pulling and tugging your held rump, in a panic. Mime sudden breakaway, pained
expression. Run off holding rump.

Rabbit got away. But the Turkeys had her long, bushy tail. They picked it up and held it over their heads, all in a line, and they did a victory dance with it.

Let's hear how those excited, VICTORIOUS Turkeys sounded.

ᗏ Some audiences like to dance for a while, heads bobbing as if stepping, hands raised
holding tail, chanting, "Gob-ble! Gob-ble! Gob-ble!"

When the dance was over, the Turkeys wondered what to do with that tail. Who would get to keep it? They decided to share it. Each Turkey got a little piece to wear on his chest, to show how they had taught Rabbit a lesson.

ᗏ Mime plucking a piece and sticking it proudly to the center of your sternum.

To this day, wild turkeys have had a little brown tuft sticking out of the middle of their chests. It doesn't look like feathers. It looks like fur. It's called a "turkey beard," but this story says it's really a piece from Rabbit's tail.

And I must tell you that Rabbit has never played tricks on the Turkeys again.

ABOUT THE STORY

This story is largely based on one I have heard from Creek Nation people in Oklahoma. I've heard it with Rabbits and Bobcats of either gender. Some of the motifs also occur in variants told by other tribes. For example:

Playing dead to lure prey: "Raccoon and the Crayfish" (Joe Bruchac's tape *Iroquois Stories*). "How Brer Rabbit Outsmarted the Frogs" (Jackie Torrence, pp. 56–61, in *Homespun*, edited by Jimmie Neil Smith, Crown, 1988. Jackie, whose heritage was African American and Cherokee, heard this story from her grandma.).

Origin of turkey's beard: Made from a scalp stolen from warrior Terrapin (Cherokee: "How Turkey Got His Beard" in *Mini Myths and Legends of the Oklahoma Indians* by Lu Celia Wise, Oklahoma State Department of Education, 1978). Here, Turkey is the trickster. Terrapin gets revenge, shooting Turkey's legs full of those useless splints.

There are, of course, many other tales explaining Rabbit's short tail.

ACTIVITIES

1. *A skit* can develop quite readily after people have heard this story. Review the story's sequence of events. Cast individuals as Rabbit and Bobcat, and pick a flock of Turkeys. (When working in spacious rooms with up to twenty-five kids, I have included the entire group.) The storyteller serves as Narrator for the first run, then someone else can take over.

   Discuss the necessary scenes (Rabbit's grassy meadow; Turkeys' tall weeds; Bobcat's "play dead" spot) and decide where to locate them in the room. "Everyone take your places: GO."

   Some suggestions to avoid mayhem: Bobcat doesn't carry the Turkeys but pulls them offstage, an arm encircling each. Turkeys don't touch Rabbit but land on her tail; her struggles result in its loss.

2. *Illustrate a book or film strip:* This straightforward plot lends itself well to pictorial retelling by a group. Review the sequence and divide the story into as many scenes as there are participants (some scenes may be shown in several stages). Each person picks a different scene and draws one picture. Physically sequence the pictures by asking people to line themselves up in story order without any talking, just by looking at their neighbors' scenes. Then each person can orally rehearse his or her portion of the text by holding up the picture and telling that part of the story.

   After several rehearsals (during which the text tends to get more fluent, complete, and complex), somebody with excellent handwriting can record the finished text from each teller. Bind them together into a book with the text on the left side, facing its picture (text pasted to the back of the preceding picture). Make a "film strip" by attaching alternate text and pictures into a long vertical strip (make the view screen from a cardboard carton).

BACKGROUND NOTES

As in many Native American and Oriental trickster stories, the trickster ends up permanently marked as a result of his or her trickery. Listeners can enjoy the cleverness of the trickster, but they go away warned by the implicit message that tricks backfire on the perpetrator.

Unlike our domesticated birds notorious for their stupidity, wild turkeys are a wary and elusive lot. I can sympathize with Bobcat. Wanting a closer look, I've tried to sneak up on the flocks of wild turkeys that materialize from nothing in the wooded Osage Hills near me. But as soon as they see me, they fade silently back into the weeds.

Since many people may not be familiar with the appearance or behavior of wild turkeys, it can help to bring a picture showing one with his "beard." (Try finding one in wildlife or hunting magazines.)

HOLIDAY BACKGROUND INFORMATION (Provided by Teresa Miller)

The Pilgrims were taken aback when ninety Wampanoag Indians, headed by Chief Massasoit (dead in 1661), arrived to share in the feast they have prepared. Noticing the limited food supply, the Indian visitors sent out hunters who brought in five deer carcasses to augment the otherwise meager food supply. With "firewater," cider, and beer to wash the food down, there was enough nourishment for a three-day feast.

When you hear or read allusions to the good old days of Pilgrim cuisine, remember that they dined mostly on salted fish stew, beef pottage, or Windsor beans.

Thanksgiving in America was started by the Puritans, who were Christians, but they were sharing in a tradition observed by religions around the globe. Contained in the sacred texts of people of faith (the Christian Bible, the Muslim Koran, the Jewish Torah, the Hindu Vedic writings, and others) are commands to give thanks for food. Not just with a sense of obligation, but with joy.

As a holiday, Thanksgiving goes back to the middle of the Civil War. Abraham Lincoln issued a national Thanksgiving Proclamation, inviting "My fellow citizens in every part of the United States, and also those who are at sea, and those who are sojourning in foreign lands, to set apart and observe the last Thursday of November next, as a day of Thanksgiving and Praise to our beneficent Father who dwelled in the Heavens."

In the United States, Thanksgiving is a time for family, food, football Thanksgiving games, puzzles, and crafts. It marks the unofficial beginning to the winter holiday season. Of all the Thanksgiving symbols, the turkey has become the most well known. The wild turkey is native to northern Mexico and the eastern United States.

For more information about Thanksgiving, consult http://wilstar.com/holidays/thankstr.htm or one of the myriad Web sites available from Plymouth Plantation (e.g., http://pilgrims.net/plimothplantation/vtour/ and http://www.intime.uni.edu/multiculture/curriculum/lessons/restructure/thanksgiving.htm).

NOTE: *A Native American's Point of View:* "For an Indian, who is also a schoolteacher, Thanksgiving was never an easy holiday for me to deal with in class. I sometimes have felt like I learned too much about "the Pilgrims and the Indians." Every year I have been faced with the professional and moral dilemma of just how to be honest and informative with my children at Thanksgiving without passing on historical distortions and racial and cultural stereotypes." For your questions and comments, contact Jim Cornish, grade five teacher, Gander Academy, Gander, Newfoundland, Canada. Web site: http://www.stemnet.nf.ca/CITE/themes.html. Last updated in January 2007.

BIOGRAPHY

Fran Stallings (Bartlesville, Oklahoma) has worked as a professional storyteller since 1978, telling traditional tales and original creations nationwide and overseas. She has produced three CDs, published stories and articles, and edited books and magazines. Consult www.franstallings.com

CONTACT

Fran Stallings
1406 Mackyln Lane
Bartlesville, OK 74006-5419
E-mail: fran@franstallings.com

Hanukkah, also called the "Festival of Lights," lasts over a week,
usually between late November and late December.

Reisele's Hanukkah Dream

INTRODUCTION

Before beginning to narrate the sequence of events, the storyteller explains that this is an audience-participation story and asks for seven volunteers whom the teller seats in a half circle facing the rest of the audience. Then assign a number to each volunteer. *Asik* and *Reisele* have the main parts. *Dreidel* and *Menorah* represent fantasy. The charcoal burner, farmer, and grandmother will speak as indicated. The storyteller has prepared in advance a name tag for each volunteer to identify his or her part.

The candleholder used for Hanukkah is called a menorah. It contains eight candles. The dreidel is a kind of spinning top with four sides.

STORY SCRIPT

In a small Eastern European village, there lived a Jewish couple by the names of Asik and his wife Reisele.

> The storyteller places a name label on Asik's shoulder and one on Reisele's shoulder.

Together they owned and operated a grocery store. They were beloved and respected by all their neighbors.

One day, the governor of their province began to persecute the Jews exactly like King Antiochus had done so long ago. He forbade them to practice their religion, confiscated their belongings, accused them of crimes they had not committed, and threw many of them into prison.

Most of those not imprisoned left everything they owned behind and joined friends and relatives in other lands. Reisele and Asik had no one to go to.

Not wanting to end up in prison, they fled into nearby mountains with nothing but a few blankets, a metal pot filled with beans, their Shabbat candle sticks, a cherished old tin dreidel, and an ancient menorah.

> The storyteller places a name tag on the shoulder of the dreidel and another on the shoulder of the menorah.

They honestly did not expect to live through the upcoming winter. But just as it began to freeze, an old mountaineer by the name of Pjotr found them. He remembered Asik and Reisele from the times he had gone into their village to trade his furs for food. He took them back to his mountain cabin.

Glad to be with a true friend, Asik and Reisele helped Pjotr tend his vegetable garden and care for his goats.

When Pjotr grew old and feeble, they nursed him lovingly until he died.

Life was tough in the mountains. Reisele and Asik had to work hard just to stay alive. They never failed to observe the Sabbath. They celebrated all the Jewish holidays.

Years passed. They doubted they would ever see another Jewish face again. But one morning Reisele said, "Asik, I have dreamed three times in a row that we will celebrate the first night of Hanakkuh with our own people."

> ⇨ The storyteller instructs volunteers to repeat their lines. Thus, the volunteer wearing label Reisele is told to say, "Asik, I have dreamed three times in a row that we will celebrate the first night of Hanukkah with our own people."
> **Reisele repeats teller's words:** "Asik, I have dreamed three times in a row that we will celebrate the first night of Hanukkah with our own people."
> The storyeller instructs Asik to ask, "Could you tell me where we would find some Jews?"
> **Volunteer Asik replies:** "Could you tell me where we would find some Jews?!"

Reisele retorted, "Don't ask me! All I know is that when I have the same dream three times in a row, it comes true!"

> ⇨ **Volunteer Reisele repeats:** "Don't ask me! All I know is that when I have the same dream three times in a row, it comes true."

Asik said sadly, "Oi, oi my Reisele, my dear Nashume-le, this dream won't come true."

> ⇨ **Volunteer Asik repeats:** "Oi, oi my Reisele, my dear Nashume-le, this dream won't come true."

Reisele just smiled. The day before Hanukkah, she scrubbed a basket of potatoes for latkes, prepared a big dish of wild berry sauce, and put the menorah and the dreidel on the window sill. When night came, she went to bed, still smiling, and fell asleep.

Poor Asik could not sleep. He lay awake, tossing and turning, worrying how to comfort his dear wife, when once again they had to celebrate Hanukkah by themselves. When he finally fell asleep, the menorah spoke, saying, "Dreidel, listen to me. Reisele's dream must come true. Go to the valley now and find some Jews to celebrate Hanukkah with them."

> ⇨ **Volunteer menorah repeats:** "Dreidel, listen to me. Reisele's dream must come true. Go to the valley now and find some Jews to celebrate Hanukkah with them."

The dreidel replied sadly, "Do you expect me to find Jews when they were all driven away?"

> ⇨ **Volunteer dreidel repeats:** "Do you expect me to find Jews when they were all driven away?"

Times change. Some of the Jews might have come back.

> ⇪ **Volunteer menorah repeats:** "Times change. Some of the Jews might have come back."

Dreidel said, "How will I find my way to the valley? It's pitch dark outside."

> ⇪ **Volunteer dreidel repeats:** "How will I find my way to the valley? It is pitch dark outside."

The Menorah responded, "I shall give you my light."

> ⇪ **Volunteer menorah repeats:** I shall give you my light.

The menorah began to glow, and surrounded the dreidel with its light.

The dreidel was delighted: "I didn't know you could do that. Look, I can see my reflection in the window pane. I am shimmering and glimmering just like you."

> ⇪ **Volunteer dreidel repeats:** "I didn't know you could do that. Look, I see my reflection in the window pane. I am shimmering and glimmering just like you."

Glowing with pride and happiness, she wound herself up and skipped out of the house, down the mountain path.

After a while she came to a charcoal burner's hut. She peeked into his window and saw that he was still awake.

> ⇪ Teller puts a name tag on the volunteer "charcoal burner's" shoulder. Teller has dreidel began to chant.

"If you heard the story of Judah Maccabee, drop what you are doing and come along with me."

> ⇪ **Volunteer dreidel repeats:** "If you heard the story of Judah Maccabee, drop what you are doing and come along with me."

Amazed at the sight of a shimmering, glimmering dreidel who could talk, the charcoal burner came outside and cried, "I have never heard the story of Judah Maccabee. Will you come into my hut and tell it to me?"

> ⇪ **Volunteer charcoal burner says:** "I have never heard the story of Judah Maccabee. Will you come into my hut and tell it to me?"

The dreidel said, "I don't have time. I have to find people who know the story already."

> ⇪ **Volunteer dreidel repeats:** "I don't have time. I have to find people who know the story already."

The dreidel wound herself up again and spun down the mountain path. By the time the morning star rose in the sky, she came to a farmhouse. Glad to see that the farmer and his family were already out in the yard, she stopped and chanted again.

"If you ever heard the story of Judah Maccabee, drop what you are doing and come along with me."

> ⇪ **Volunteer dreidel repeats:** "If you ever heard the story of Judah Macabee, drop what you are doing and come along with me."

Enchanted by the shimmering, glimmering dreidel, the farmer cried, "We would like to come with you, but we don't know the story of the Maccabees. Can you tell it to us?"

> **Volunteer farmer repeats:** "We would like to come with you, but we don't know the story of the Maccabees. Can you tell it to us?"
> Volunteer dreidel says: "I don't have time to tell it. I must find some people who know it already."

She was just about to leave when an old grandmother came hobbling outside and said, "Long ago, my friend told me the story of the Maccabees. But she and all the other Jewish families were driven away."

> Teller puts label on old Grandmother.

The dreidel said, dismayed, "Aren't there any Jews left?"

> **Volunteer dreidel says, dismayed:** "Aren't there any Jews left?"
> Volunteer Grandmother says: Times have changed. Some have come back. You will find them if you go to the village at the foot of the mountain.
> Volunteer dreidel says: "Thank you for telling me."

She wound herself up again and spun all the way down to the village marketplace, chanting at the top of her voice, "If ever you heard the story of Judah Maccabee, drop what you are doing and come along with me."

As the song drifted through the air, doors opened. A handful of children with their mothers and fathers came out. All together they said, standing, "We are Jews. We know the story of the Maccabees."

> Have volunteer participants stand up and say: We are Jews. We know the story of the Maccabees.
> **Volunteer dreidel says:** Come with me then and celebrate Hanukkah with Reisele and Asik. They haven't seen a Jewish face for a long time.

The people started to embrace each other for joy and cried, "We would love to come!"

Everybody followed the shimmering, glimmering dreidel to the mountain cabin. When Asik and Reisele saw all the people coming, they rushed outside and welcomed them with open arms. Many stories were told, while helping hands ground up potatoes and made them into delicious latkes. Everybody praised the wonderful berry sauce, but the best thing was being together again, worshiping their God without fear.

When the sun went down in the West, Asik lit the first Hanukkah candle. Both he and Reisele began to chant, and all the people repeated after them. Asik would say one line and Reisele would follow with another.

"There once was a wicked king named Antiochus. He came to Jerusalem.

> **Audience replies:** "There once was a wicked king named Antiochus. He came to Jerusalem."

"His sword was sharp and bright. He told the Jews they must give up their God or else he will spill their blood."

> **Audience replies:** "His sword was sharp and bright. He told the Jews they must give up their God or else he will spill their blood."

"Who was he, who was he?"

> **Audience replies:** "Who was he, who was he?"

"Antiochus was his name."

> **Audience replies:** "Antiochus was his name."

"Shame, shame, shame."

> **Audience replies:** "Shame, shame, shame."

"He tore up the holy Torah."

> **Audience replies:** "He tore up the holy Torah."

"He broke the holy menorah."

> **Audience replies:** "He broke the holy menorah."

"Who was he?"

> **Audience replies:** "Who was he?"

"Antiochus was his name."

> **Audience replies:** "Antiochus was his name."

"Shame, shame, shame."

> **Audience replies:** "Shame, shame, shame."

"There came a hero named Judah."

> **Audience replies:** "There came a hero named Judah."

"Who was he, who was he?"

> **Audience replies:** "Who was he, who was he?"

"Judah, Judah Maccabee, was his name."

> **Audience replies:** "Judah, Judah Macabee, was his name."

"Judah set us free."

> **Audience replies:** "Judah set us free."

They all chanted together and celebrated together. Afterward, the children spun the dreidel.

And so it came to be, that Reisele's Hanukkah dream came true after all.

ABOUT THE STORY

At Hanukkah, Jewish people light candles in a menorah. On the first day, they light just one candle. Then on each of the next seven days, they light one more candle until all eight are burning. Lighting one more candle each day of Hanukkah helps Jewish people remember an eight-day battle that happened thousands of years ago. Often given to children, dreidels are sometimes kept for years. Dreidels might be found in a science museum. It's called "optictop" and is manufactured by Brimms Inc., Tonawanda, NY 14150. Another source is online at http://www.dreidelsandmore.com.

RELATED STORIES AND BOOKS

1. "The Parakeet Named Dreidel," from *THE POWER OF LIGHT* by Isaac Bashevis Singer (Farrar, Straus & Giroux, 1980).

2. *THE WISEST MAN IN THE WORLD* by Benjamin Elkin, illustrated by Anita Lobel (Parents Magazine Press, 1968).

3. "The Shipwrecked Merchant," from *A PIECE OF THE WIND,* retold by Ruthilde Kronberg (Harper & Row, 1990).

4. *EIGHT TALES FOR EIGHT NIGHTS: Stories for Chanukah* by Penninah Schram (Aronson, 1990).

5. *THE POWER OF LIGHT: Eight Stories for Hanukkah* by Issac Bashevis Singer (Farrar, Straus & Giroux, 1980).

ACTIVITIES

For children, there is the *HANUKKAH FUN BOOK*: *Puzzles, Riddles, Magic & More* by David A. Adler (Bonim Books, A division of Hebrew Publishing Company, 1976).

HOLIDAY BACKGROUND INFORMATION

Every year, Jewish people all over the world gather to celebrate Hanukkah. They light and bless special Hanukkah candles, exchange gifts, and tell the story of how a small courageous band of people fought for the right to practice their own religion, and how, after the Jews had cleaned up the temple, they searched for a special pure oil to light their menorah. They found only one jug, barely enough to burn for one day. Miraculously, the oil lasted for eight days.

The children play various games with the dreidel, receive Hanukkah gifts, listen to Hanukkah stories, and sing Hanukkah songs.

For more details, visit Fact Monster: http://www.factmonster.com/spot/hanukkah.html. For "Happy Hanukkah Holiday Ideas," visit www.lafamily.com/display_article.php?id=958.

Search the Internet for other Web sites related to *Hanukkah.*

BIOGRAPHY

Ruthilde Kronberg has been telling stories in the St. Louis and County school districts since 1971. She has been a guest lecturer in several universities and a feature teller at the St. Louis Storytelling Festival, Missouri River Story Festivals, Shakespeare Festivals, and Fourth of July Festivals. Ruthilde has also told stories in various parks and in St. Louis County churches and temples. She is the author of *A Piece of the Wind* (Harper & Row, 1990) and *Clever Folk: Tales of Wisdom, Wit and Wonder* (Libraries Unlimited, 1993). Ruthilde was also one of the contributors to *Joining In* (Yellow Moon Press, 1988) and is coauthor of *The Bible Tells Me So* (Concordia, 1979).

CONTACT

Ruthilde Kronberg
608 Bacon Avenue
St. Louis, MO 63119
E-mail: peterakronberg@aol.com

December

This story may be told anytime during the holiday season.

Silent Night, 1914 or "The Peace Message for Christmas"

INTRODUCTION

Storyteller or friend passes out German and English versions of the song *Silent Night*. The storyteller asks the audience to be prepared to sing or hum when prompted. Instruments may be used.

STORY SCRIPT

It was 1914. World War I had just begun. I was a stretcher-bearer with the Welsh Regiment of Fusileers.

Oh it was dreadful. Cold, wet, brutal. Moreover, no one on the front line really knew what he was fighting for. Or against. Nations were generally ignorant of one another. Radio and the airplane were new inventions. If you traveled at all, it was by horse or ship or steam locomotive. Not very fast and rarely very far. Even the city dwellers were provincial. And there we were, all of us green young fellows, shivering in desolate trenches way over on the European Continent.

The shaking was only partly due to the cold. Smoking bombs fell near us. Friends were torn limb from limb. And you see, we couldn't really say what for. After all, as the officers told us, we weren't there to think but to fight. So the soldiers fought, primarily to stay alive, and we stretcher-bearers carried their broken bodies back to the hospital tents. It was that simple, that terribly simple.

December came. I longed for that miserable war to be over so that I could go back to my home in Wales. Little did I know what awaited us! Such is life. I remember feeling hollow and bewildered. I was so young! As long as I live, I'll never forget that first Christmas at the front. There were few of us who didn't want to be home, safe and sound, roasting chestnuts on the hearth, eating meat pies, and spiriting a piece of plum pudding off to bed on Christmas Night.

The morning of the 24th, we walked about with grim looks on our faces. Christmas Eve, and we at war! We may not have been very worldly, but we knew a bit about life . . . and now about death. We weren't boys, after all, but men: blacksmiths and shepherds, waggoners and farmhands, masons and clerks. War was no lark for us, and we clearly saw the irony in shooting and being shot at on the anniversary of Christ's birth. We still had our humanity, you know. We were no Christmas bombers.

In any case, evening inevitably came. After a special ration of dried meat and cornbread, I went out with B Company to help keep a few fires going while they manned the trenches. The night sky was like obsidian, glistening from countless points of starlight. As we talked, we could see one another's words billow out in small clouds of breath that faded into the night along with the sound.

I stared deep into the night toward the German lines. There was little detectable movement there. I felt uneasy, as always. Who could feel at peace with this world at such a moment?

Down in a trench, I huddled my arms and legs together, trying to feel as much as possible like a small group of friends, and I blew warm breath into my hands. Then something caught my eye and I looked up. Off to my right a man stood, his helmeted head facing the heavens, his thin body silhouetted against the stars.

Then, this heedless figure began to sing! As the first heartbreakingly beautiful notes reached me, I recognized the fine tenor voice of Wells, the cooper's helper. He sang as he had never sung before.

Teller sings these lines softly, alone.

SILENT NIGHT . . . HOLY NIGHT . . . ALL IS CALM . . . ALL IS BRIGHT . . .

Each note of each phrase struck deep into me, into the farthest reaches of my troubled soul.

Transported, I felt a strong breath rush into me and the words soar back out in accompaniment.

Teller should continue singing alone.

'ROUND YON VIRGIN . . . MOTHER AND CHILD . . . HOLY INFANT . . . SO TENDER AND MILD . . .

Some members of the audience almost imperceptibly pick up the refrain.

Tears welled in my eyes when voice after voice joined in, sending the song out into the cavernous night.

Teller and audience sing together.

SLEEP IN HEAVENLY PEACE . . . SLEEP IN HEAVENLY PEACE . . .

We all began again to sing this familiar first verse. After the second round, something happened that was even more extraordinary. Floating back through the cold night air came the sound of the German troops answering us.

Since the audience has both English and German lyrics to "Silent Night," the teller suggests that the audience choose just one language to sing, whichever they feel comfortable with. Pronunciation follows each word in the German handout.

STILLE NACHT . . . HEILIGE NACHT . . . . . . ALLES SCHLAFT . . . EINSAM WACHT

Imagine! Our "enemies" had joined us! The longings of brothers had locked arms. We sang with new joy—and new sorrow:

 Teller announces that they will sing one entire stanza in the English version, then one with the German version, they will all hum together to a soft fade-out.

(English)	(German—as pronounced)
Silent night, holy night	Shteal-lay nahcht, hi-lee-gay nahcht
All is calm, all is bright	Ah-lays shlaft; ine-sahm vahcht
Round yon virgin	Noor dahs trou-tay,
Mother and child	Hoke-hi-lee-gay paar
Holy infant	Hole-dare knahb'
So tender and mild	Eem low-kig-en haar
Sleep in heavenly peace	Shlahf in him-lish-air roo
Sleep in heavenly peace	Shlahf in him-lish-air roo

The song rolled back and forth across no man's land. The distant voices gathered into one rising surge of wishful lament:

Sleep in heavenly peace . . . Schlaf im him-lish-air-roo.

Sleep in heavenly peace . . . Schlaf im him-lish-air-roo.

Over and over we sang these resonant and simple lyrics until we were hoarse and emotionally spent. Then we went further. We climbed out of the trenches to do what one does with brothers—fraternize. All that night we sang and laughed and traded rations and gifts from home. German beer flowed as freely as British ale. Chocolate bars were pressed into our hands and we reciprocated with sticks of cinnamon and peppermint. Those of us from each side who knew a few words of the other language acted as stumbling interpreters, causing great hilarity. The dawning of Christmas Day found some of us dancing to a mouth organ, others smiling broadly as they pulled out tattered pictures of family members and girlfriends to pass around in the pale rays of morning light.

When we arrived back at camp, our rising officers were furious. They threatened to throw us in the nearest stockade and to have us court-martialed. Only the fact that it was Christmas saved us . . . and rightly so. We were ordered to maintain total silence about the incident. Similar occurrences were not subsequently heard of (though I later learned, of course, that this was neither the first nor last such event in human history!). You know, it must have been the same on the German side. And what's more, in our case, the press back home never printed our story. Thus, most of our people heard nothing of what had happened faraway on the battlefront, one silent night in nineteen hundred and fourteen.

No. 1. Silent Night! Holy Night!

1. Si - lent night! Ho - ly night! All is calm, all is bright

Round yon Vir - gin Mother and Child! Ho - ly In - fant, so ten-der and mild,

Sleep in heav - en - ly peace, Sleep in heav - en - ly peace.

Stille Nacht, heilige Nacht

ABOUT THE STORY

This is a true story. It was told to me by a small white-haired Quaker as the two of us waited in line at the United Nations in New York City. My newfound friend spoke of his frequent trips to the UN and of his efforts over the years to halt or prevent violent discord between groups of human beings. Then he told the story I just told you, which appeared in 1981 in *Quaker Life* (a monthly magazine that has given us permission to reprint).

RELATED RESOURCES

1. *SILENT NIGHT, HOLY NIGHT: The Story of the Christmas Truce* (Book and CD, VHS, or DVD) by David Warner and Stephen Wunderli, illustrated by Robert T. Barrett; narrated by Walter Cronkite (Deseret Book Company, includes CD, VHS, or DVD, 2003; see http://www.alibris.com/booksearch?qsort=&page=1&matches= 12&browse=1&qwork=10301113&full=1).

2. *CHRISTMAS IN THE TRENCHES* by John McCutcheon, illustrated by Henri Sorensen. (Peachtree Publishers, Book & CD edition, 2006). For children.

3. *WAR GAME: Village Green to No-Man's-Land* by Michael Foreman (Anova Books, 2006). For children.

4. *JOYEUX NOELLE* (Movie; Sony Pictures Classics; in English, French, and German, with subtitles; 2006).

5. Translations: There are 193 versions of "Silent Night" in 130 languages (and reportedly more than 300 existing translations). See http://silentnight.web.za/.

RELATED STORIES

1. *SILENT NIGHT: The Story of the World War I Christmas Truce* by Stanley Weintraub (Plume, 2002).

3. *CHRISTMAS TRUCE: The Western Front December 1914* by Malcolm Brown and Shirley Seaton (Pan Grand Strategy Series, 1999).

3. *CHRISTMAS EVERYWHERE: A Book of Christmas Customs of Many Lands* by Elizabeth Sechrist (Omnigraphics, 1997).

4. *TALL BOOK OF CHRISTMAS* by Dorothy Hall Smith (Harper Brothers, 1954).

5. *CHRISTMAS BOOK OF STORIES OLD AND NEW* by Alice Dalgliesh (Charles Scribner's Sons, 1961).

CLASSIC CHRISTMAS STORIES

1. *BABOUSKHKA AND THE THREE KINGS* by Ruth Robbins (Houghton Mifflin, 1960). This book received the Caldecott Award for Nicolas Sidjakov's illustrations.

2. *THE CAT ON THE DOVREFELL,* collected by Asbjornsen & Moe, illustrated by Tomie dePaola (G.P. Putnam's Sons, 1979).

3. *THE TAILOR OF GLOUCESTER* by Beatrix Potter (Frederick Warne & Co., copyright renewed 1931).

4. *CHRISTMAS EVERYWHERE: A Book of Christmas Customs of Many Lands* by Elizabeth Sechrist (Macrae-Smith Company, 1936).

5. *LEGEND OF OLD BEFAZNA: An Italian Christmas Story* by Tomie dePaola (Harcourt Brace & Company, 1989). For young audiences.

6. *CHRISTMAS: A Book of Stories Old and New* by Alice Dalgliesh (C. Scribner's Sons, 1954).

7. *JOY TO THE WORLD:* Christmas ledgends by Ruth Sawyer (Little Brown, 1966).

8. *THE REMARKABLE CHRISTMAS OF THE COBBLER'S SON* by Ruth Sawyer (Viking, 1994).

9. *THE WEE CHRISTMAS CABIN OF CARN-NA-WEEN* by Ruth Sawyer (Candlewick, 2005).

OTHER INFORMATION

In the United States, many Americans celebrate December 6, December 25, and January 6.

December 6: *Legend of St. Nicholas, St. Nicholas, The Real Santa Claus,* **and** *The Real St. Nicholas* are a few of the veritable plethora of books about St. Nick. Christmas became more of a universal celebration in the Middle Ages. Gradually, St. Nick became an ingrained part of the Christmas holiday festivities. You will find decorations, parties, and the exchange of gifts in many churches and private schools striving to keep the spirit of St. Nicholas alive. Consult: www.stnicholascenter.org.

St. Nicholas was a real person who lived in Asia Minor during the fourth century. While a bishop, he performed many good deeds. He became the patron saint of Greece, Sicily, and Norway, as well as Russia, where czars were named after him. In many parts of Europe, the holiday is celebrated on December 5, the anniversary of the bishop's death in A.D. 343.

Recommended Books

1. *THE LEGEND OF ST. NICHOLAS* by Verena Morgenthaler (Henry Z. Walk, 1970). The author herself must have done each of the illustrations—magnificent pictures in full fascinating detail and rich in color. For juveniles.

2. *ST. NICHOLAS* by Ann Tompert, illustrated by Michael Garland (Boyds Mills Press, 2000). As early as the twelfth century, St. Nicholas was credited with giving gifts to good children on the eve of his feast day, December 6. He left gifts in their shoes, in stockings, and in paper boats that were set out for that purpose.

3. *THE REAL SANTA CLAUS* by Marianna Mayer (Penguin Putnam Books for Young Readers, Phyllis Fogelman Books, 2001). This begins with a poem. You may know it. *A Visit from St. Nicholas* was first published anonymously in 1823, but in 1844 Dr. Clement C. Moore took credit for penning it, explaining that he had originally written the poem for his family. (Today, scholarly debate casts some doubt as to his authorship.)

4. *THE REAL ST. NICHOLAS: Tales of Generosity and Hope from Around the World*, Louise Carus editor and translator (Theosophical Publishing House, First Quest Edition 2002). Complete with two St. Nicholas Maps that detail St. Nick's geographic wanderings from Turkey, Romania, Ukraine, Russia, Finland, Estonia, Sweden, the Netherlands, Germany, Bari (Italy), France, Spain, and Ireland. Every stop along his itinerary resulted in a story or legend. Every one of his stories or legends is printed in this beautiful 214-page book.

December 25: For answers about Christmas history, the origins of Christmas, Christmas traditions, and even Christmas recipes, consult: http://www.religion-cults.com/saints/december25.htm and www.allthingschristmas.com.

Classic Christmas Stories

1. *THE CAT ON THE DOVREFELL,* collected by Asbjornsen & Moe, illustrated by Tomie dePaola (G.P. Putnam's Sons, 1979).

2. *THE TAILOR OF GLOUCESTER* by Beatrix Potter (Frederick Warne & Co., copyright renewed 1931).

3. *CHRISTMAS EVERYWHERE: A Book of Christmas Customs of Many Lands,* by Elizabeth Sechrist (Macrae-Smith, 1936).

4. *LEGEND OF OLD BEFAZNA: An Italian Christmas Story* by Tomie dePaola (Harcourt Brace, 1989). For young audiences.

5. *CHRISTMAS: A Book of Stories Old and New* by Alice Dalgliesh (C. Scribner's Sons, 1954).

6. *TALL BOOK OF CHRISTMAS* by Dorothy Hall Smith (Harper Brothers, 1954).

7. *JOY TO THE WORLD: Christmas Legends* by Ruth Sawyer (Little Brown, 1966). Look for other Christmas books by Ruth Sawyer as well.

January 6: Epiphany—Three Kings: In Puerto Rico, Mexico, Cuba, Spain, and other Latin American countries, Epiphany is called El Dia de los Reyes, or the Day of the Kings. This is the day when a group of kings or magi arrived to worship and bring three gifts to the baby Jesus after following a star in the heavens. In Spanish tradition, on the day of January 6, three of the kings—Melchor, Caspar, and Balthazar, representing Europe, Arabia, and Africa—arrived on horse, camel, and elephant, bringing, respectively, gold, frankincense, and myrrh to the baby Jesus. One of many sites about this holiday include: www.inside-mexico.com/ReyesMagos.htm.

Recommended Books

1. *BABOUSKHKA AND THE THREE KINGS* by Ruth Robbins (Houghton Mifflin, 1960). This book received the Caldecott Award for Nicolas Sidjakov's illustrations.

2. *FEDERICO AND THE MAGI'S GIFT* by Beatriz Vidal (Knopf Books for Young Readers, 2004).

3. *HURRAY FOR THE THREE KINGS' DAY!* by Lori Marie Carlson. (HarperCollins, 1999). The text is in English, with a smattering of Spanish words that flow smoothly and naturally throughout.

4. *THREE KINGS DAY: A Celebration at Christmastime* by Diane Hoyt-Goldsmith (Holiday House, 2004).

5. *THREE KINGS' DAY* by Beatriz McConnie Zapater (Modern Curriculum Press, 1992). Includes a glossary of Spanish words used.

HOLIDAY BACKGROUND INFORMATION

Christmas is a well-known holiday throughout many regions of the world. It is celebrated on December 25 and commemorates the birth of a child, named Yehoshua (Jesus), to a poor carpenter and his wife. The couple were able to find lodging only in a stable in Bethlehem, Judea, now Palestine, where the child was born.

Consult the following Web sites: http://neris.mii.lt/CHRISTMAS/christmas.html; also http://www.religion-cults.com/saints/december25.htm.

BIOGRAPHY

Charles David Kleymeyer, born in 1944 in Indiana, holds a bachelor's degree in creative writing from Stanford University and a doctorate in socioeconomic development from the University of Wisconsin. He has worked for four decades in the Andean nations, supporting the efforts of indigenous and African-descendent peoples to carry out self-help projects. Charles is a writer and performing storyteller, and he chairs the board of a wilderness retreat center that enables people to connect nature with the spirit.

CONTACT

E-mail: ckleymeyer@yahoo.com

Retold by

LAURA SIMMS

The Christmas season is always a time for sharing gifts and new beginnings. We are reminded to enjoy whatever we can offer and whatever we receive, big or small. What matters is that it is done with an open heart. With the rebirth of the sun comes our own potential to start fresh and cross over any obstacles or hesitations!

How the Squirrel Got Its Stripes

INTRODUCTION

The tale of the Squirrel is a story that can be enacted by children in two ways during or after a storytelling. During the telling, all the children can repeat the words of the storyteller and become each of the characters. Or, if you have the time, you can tell the story and then let groups of children act out the story.

STORY SCRIPT

Long ago a ten-headed demon called Ravana (a Rakshasa) kidnapped a king's beloved wife. The king was named Rama and his queen was named Sita.

Everyone loved the king and the queen because their hearts were pure, their intentions were generous, and they were the perfect examples of great leaders.

When King Rama set off to find his wife Sita and battle the monster, the king of Monkeys named Hanuman, he led an army of monkeys to help him.

> 🖑 Audiences of children can clap their hands and screech a monkey's war cry loudly: *KI KI KI KI!*

The king and his retinue of monkeys traveled until they came to a vast sea that they had to cross to reach Ravana's Kingdom.

Rama attempted to calm a raging ocean by shooting magic arrows into the waves. But the king of the Sea, named Viruna, rose up and said, "The seas cannot be overcome by force, but only by building a strong bridge."

> 🖑 I suggest the storyteller let the child audience repeat Viruna's words. Audience repeats: "The seas cannot be overcome by force, but only by building a strong bridge."

Rama ordered his monkey soldiers to construct a bridge made of stones that could hold his entire army: a bridge that would connect King Rama's land with the island of Lanka ruled by Ravana (the Rakshasa).

Monkey after monkey set to work carrying huge stones and enormous boulders to the seaside. Thousands of monkeys worked ceaselessly.

Rama was pleased.

> Again, the cry of the monkeys, combined with clapping and hopping up and down, can be choreographed as children pretend to carry huge stones to make the bridge.

Then the king noticed a small brown squirrel, who rushed up and down from the hills to the shore carrying tiny pebbles in her mouth.

"What is that little creature doing?" he wondered.

> Instruct the children to each become a tiny humble squirrel, with a little pebble in their mouths or in their hands.

The monkeys also saw the squirrel. They grew angry. "Get out of my way," they screeched. "You are too small. You are not needed."

> Let children pump up their chests with pride and anger and repeat the words of the monkey army:
> "You are too small. You are not needed."

The little squirrel looked up shyly and said, "I am helping to build the bridge to save Queen Sita."

> Once again, children can relax and call out the words of the squirrel, using high-pitched tiny little voices.
> "I am helping to build the bridge to save Queen Sita."

All the monkeys began to laugh. They held their sides screeching as they hopped and mocked the little squirrel, saying, "I have never heard anything so foolish in my entire life!"

> The children can pretend to be arrogant and proud monkeys, repeating:
> "I have never heard anything so foolish in my entire life!"

The squirrel said, "I cannot carry rocks or stones. I can only lift small pebbles. But that is what I can do to help. My heart weeps for Sita and I want to be of assistance."

> This is a chance for children to enact the generosity and simplicity of the honest squirrel who is trying her best. They say:
> "My heart weeps for Sita and I want to be of assistance."

The monkeys pushed her away. However the squirrel continued to carry small pebbles and pile them up nearby.

Finally, one monkey grew so irritated that he lifted the little animal and threw her into the air. The squirrel cried out for help, "RAMA!"

King Rama lifted his hand and caught the squirrel safely on his palm.

It was just at that moment that the monkeys realized they *needed* the little pebbles to place between the large stones to keep the bridge from falling into the sea.

Rama said to them, "Monkeys, never despise the weak or the small. The deeds of those that are not as strong as you are equally important. Each serves according to their strength and capacities. Each is needed to make this bridge."

With three fingers, Rama drew three lines down the squirrel's back, "What truly matters is not the strength one has, but how great one's love and devotion is."

From that day forth, squirrels have had three pale stripes on their rich brown furry backs. These are the marks made by the Great beloved King Rama.

And that is how the strongest bridge across any sea was built. It supported the King, his retinue, and the monkey army in the quest to save the great Queen Sita.

Because of this remarkable feat and the monkey's increased appreciation for all beings, in time Queen Sita was brought back home. The monster Ravana was defeated by the power of sharing and love.

ABOUT THE STORY

This story was adapted from a tale from the Ramayana of Malaysia. Throughout all of Southeast Asia, a great epic called *The Ramayana* (the story of Rama) is told. Within its vast journey of adventure, an ideal king of immense goodness and generosity sets out and succeeds in retrieving his devoted and beautiful queen who has been kidnapped by a demon named Ravana. The demon was greedy and jealous. One of the most famous characters in this epic is Hanuman, a devoted monkey general of a monkey army. As we soon will read, even the greatest hero must learn the lessons of tolerance and humility.

Smaller tales, often based on known folklore, are woven within the fabric of the epic. They offer examples of how to manifest wisdom, increase one's generosity, and know joy. Sometimes a sorrowful tale exemplifies the consequences of being selfish. It is often these tiny episodes that move the great story forward. They remind us of important inherent qualities of our own capacities for happiness generated by generosity. This tale is about how enormous endeavors succeed when we each share our greatest gift, whether it is big or small in scope. Most cultures in the world remind us that sharing is the essential quality that creates happiness and completion. "One hand no fit tie bundle" is a West African Proverb, that means: "One hand cannot tie a bundle alone."

ACTIVITIES

I have divided groups of children into small teams. One team enacted the great monkey army carrying huge stones, being very proud and arrogant. Another group has chosen to be the tiny squirrel ceaselessly carrying small pebbles. One child has been the Great King Rama. Three children became the waves and the God Viruna, and ten children became the ten-headed monster Ravana. Lastly, one child became the beautiful Queen Sita.

First, they showed their acts to each other. Then, with myself as narrator—repeating the story slowly—they enacted the tale.

Afterward, we drew the bridge and made a great mural of celebration with drawings and best wishes for peace and sharing in the world.

How you choose to tell the story and how you engage the children is up to you. But in this tale, there is great joy, and no one is hurt!

One last activity could be to decide on the ten terrible aspects of the monster that are destructive. Each aspect could have a weapon (for example: jealousy, pride, greed, anger, bad wishes, etc.). Then you can decide on how that terrible aspect could be transformed into a very powerful positive energy used to save the world. (For example, inner confidence and appreciation, humility, generosity, calm, good wishes.)

These so-called destructive characteristics can be drawn on one side of a panel, and the opposite on the other. So much of this tale is about transformation. The secret to all great stories lies not in the lesson learned but the experience felt during the telling and enactment. The monkeys learn to appreciate what they have made fun of. The monster learns how powerful love and selflessness is. The little squirrel learns to appreciate herself. You can make a list of what the children listening have learned as well.

At the end of every performance or storytelling, you can have a celebration. The reunited king and queen can have a procession and a great feast or party.

BACKGROUND INFORMATION

1. *THE RAMAYANA* by R. K. Narayan (Penguin Books, 1972).
2. *THE MAGNIFICENT RETELLING OF THE RAMAYANA* by William Buck (New American Library, 1978). Introduction by Ram Dass.
3. *THE MONKEY KING AND OTHER STORIES* by Griffin Ondaatje (Harper Perennial, 1995).

BIOGRAPHY

Laura Simms is a professional storyteller who tours the world performing, teaching, and creating humanitarian projects that aid through the use of storytelling and meditation. Laura is an author and a recording artist. She teaches at the University of Manitoba's Arthur Mauro Peace and Justice Center, is an Associate of Columbia University's International School of Conflict Resolution, and is co-director of Life Force Project, which works to move youth affected by war from trauma to resilience. See www.laurasimms.com.

CONTACT

Laura Simms
814 Broadway
New York, NY 10003
storydevi@earthlink.net

KATHY CULMER

Kwanzaa (pronounced: kwahn-ZAH) is a seven-day African American celebration that lasts from December 26 to January 1. KWANZAA is the first African American holiday to come into existence and has been practiced since 1965. It is a warm, social holiday where people gather to reinforce each other's spirit and friendship, and was founded by Professor Maulana Karenga.

Feasts-a-Plenty

INTRODUCTION

The name Kwanzaa means "first" and comes from the saying *mantunda yo kwanzaa,* which means "first fruits." The extra "a" represents the African American values. Kwanzaa is a holiday when Blacks acknowledge their African roots while reminding themselves of their goals as people.

1. The Kinara (candleholder), a traditional candleholder symbolic of African American roots, holds seven candles to reflect the seven principles of *Kwanzaa.* It is placed atop the Mkeka (mat, usually straw). The Mishumaa Saba (seven candles) refer to the Nguzo Saba (seven principles). Each candle represents a distinct principle beginning with Umoja, which means unity represented by the black center candle, and ending with Imani, which means faith. The black candle is lit on the first night of *Kwanzaa,* December 26, to represent the principle of unity (*umoia*). Three red candles should be placed on the left; three green candles should be placed on the right. These are lit each day, alternately, from left to right.

2. *Zawadi* are gifts that are given during *Kwanzaa* and are often of an educational or artistic nature. Although they may be exchanged at any time, gifts are traditionally given on January 1, the last day of *Kwanzaa. Karamu* is the feast held on the sixth night of the festival, or December 31.

STORY SCRIPT

Let me explain that we will be repeating certain refrains that you will follow as I say them. For example:

Ananse the Spider

Ananse the Spider

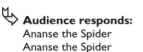 **Audience responds:**
Ananse the Spider
Ananse the Spider

Sometimes he's a spider;

Sometimes he's a man

Whichever of the two best suits his plan

Ananse the Spider

Ananse the Spider

Say it with me.

↳ **Audience responds:**
Ananse the Spider
Ananse the Spider

Every now and then, he causes harm—but much of what he does, he just does for fun. Some of that fun is, of course, for you. Let's see what Ananse's up to now.

All the people of the village were busy gathering in the harvest, busy separating the wheat from the chaff and the riff from the raff. Everyone was getting ready for the Festival of the First Fruits of the Harvest Celebration, called Kwanzaa.

For seven days, there would be celebration and remembrance of family and history, the creativity and hope of the people.

In every home, they were decorating their houses with red, green, and black streamers and balloons. The *kinara* was placed in the center of the table, with special red, green, and black candles for the daily lighting of the candles.

The children were making *zawadi*, special gifts, to be shared with their parents and friends. Cooks were cooking all sorts of good things to eat throughout the week but especially for the *Karamu* feast that would be held on the sixth night of the festival.

Everyone looked forward to the game-playing, the singing, dancing, family sharing, and, of course, the eating that would soon take place in all the homes in the village, along with the giving of thanks for the year's blessings.

This was an especially favorite time of year for friend Ananse. Can you guess why?

↳ Look to audience for guesses.

Well, did you mention *singing*? Ananse thought he had a fine voice and loved to show it off. Actually, what he really loved about this time of the year, more than anything else, was the EATING. You got that right!

Oh, he liked the decorating all right. And he surely liked the gift giving, especially receiving gifts, but there was no question that he liked the *eating* part best.

Next to playing tricks on people, *eating* was absolutely, positively Ananse's favorite thing to do. He could EAT and EAT and EAT and then EAT some more!

↳ Let the audience show you how he eats.

As time grew near for the *Karamu* Feast, Ananse began to imagine all the wonderful foods that would soon fill his relatives' tables. His itsy-bitsy spider jaws began to grow tighter, his teensy weensy spider lips pressed harder, and his mouth drooled at the thought of all that would soon delight his palate and fill his belly.

Foods like yams, corn, salt fish, sweet breads, plantains, pineapple, and on and on. YUM! He could hardly wait. GRRRWLLLLLLLL went his hungry belly.

 Ask the audience: "What foods do you like?" Let them share answers.

Now, do you think Ananse did anything to help in any of the preparations for the feast? Did he grind wheat for fresh bread? Did he stir a pot of fine broth? Did he baste a bird for the big spread? Are you kidding? No No No!

You see, Ananse did love to eat, but he did *not* like to cook or help his wife cook, or do any other work, for that matter. So, instead of his joining any of that business, he was busy scheming. This scheming, you might say, is what Ananse is best known for. C'mon say after me—

Click – Clack – Click

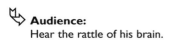 **Audience:**
Click – Clack – Click

Hear the rattle of his brain.

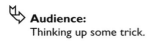 **Audience:**
Hear the rattle of his brain.

Thinking up some trick.

 **Audience:**
Thinking up some trick.

Click – Clack – Click.

 **Audience:**
Click – Clack – Click

Why must we use *our* time and money

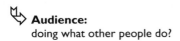 **Audience:**
Why must we use *our* time and money

doing what other people do?

 **Audience:**
doing what other people do?

Rack – Brain – Rack

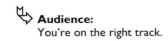 **Audience:**
Rack – Brain – Rack

You're on the right track.

Audience:
You're on the right track.

"Aso," said Ananse to his wife on the eve of *Karamu*, "This year we shall eat from my cousin's table." Aso answered, "From what cousin's table shall we eat?"

"Everybody is your cousin!" Ananse replied. "We shall see in the morning. I have a plan."

Spider set his plan in motion by getting an early start the next day. He popped into the houses of a few of his cousins to see what was cookin'.

Ananse arrived at his first cousin's house. He went inside and said to his cousin, "*Habari gani*, what's the news?"

The cousin answered, "*Kuumba*," which means "creativity," and is the principle celebrated on the sixth day of *KWANZAA*. Once they had greeted each other, the others joined in saying,

C'mon, say it with me—

Come in, come in, Cousin

Audience:
Come in, come in, Cousin

Come in and rest your feet.

Audience:
Come in and rest your feet.

But, if it's the meal you've come for,

it's much too early to eat.

Audience:
But, if it's the meal you've come for,
it's much too early to eat.

Ananse could hardly contain himself when his nose got wind of the delicious aroma of turkey roasting, nuts toasting, and sweet bread rising.

"Cousin," he answered, "I have not come to stay, but to wish you a Happy Kwanzaa day. I have many friends and family to visit, though, and many wishes to make, so I must be on my way. But, if you would like my wife and me to share *Karamu* with you, perhaps I can leave you a strand of my web, and you can give it a tug to call me when the meal is ready.

"Oh, Cousin, of course we will! Kwanzaa is a time for families to share."

Ananse quickly unraveled one long strand of a brightly colored web he had wound around his waist. He handed one end to his cousin, leaving the other in place around his belly.

"Here, Cousin, take this," Ananse said.

"When the turkey is done baking and the food is all spread, just give my web a tug, and I'll be back before you bow your head—for giving thanks, that is."

"*Tutaonana*" (which means see you later), they said to one another, and off Ananse went.

Soon Ananse arrived at his next cousin's door. "*Habari gani*?" Ananse called as he was greeted at the door.

"*Kuumba*," was the answer as they welcomed him inside. Then they greeted him by saying—C'mon, say it with me—

Come in, come in, Cousin

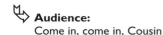
Audience:
Come in, come in, Cousin

Come in and rest your feet.

Audience:
Come in and rest your feet.

But, if it's the meal you've come for, it's much too early to eat.

Audience:
But, if it's the meal you've come for, it's much too early to eat.

The aroma of the food cooking at this cousin's house was no less enticing than at the other cousin's house. Here, he smelled fish stewing, yams cooking, and pies baking. How would he ever decide which feast to feast upon?

"Which feast will we go to?" Ananse thought. Then he thought, which was really what he'd thought all along, "maybe we will go to both. We can eat from my cousin's table where the food is ready first, and when the food is settled, we can eat at my other cousin's table."

Ananse said, "Oh no, Cousin, I have not come to stay, I'm just here to wish you and your family a Happy Kwanzaa day.

"I have many friends and family to visit, though, and many wishes to make, so I must be on my way. But . . . if you would like my wife and me to come back and share *Karamu* with you, perhaps I can leave you a strand of my web, and you can give it a tug to call me when the meal is ready."

"Oh, Cousin, of course! *KWANZAA* is a time for families to share."

Ananse quickly unraveled another strand of the brightly colored web from around his waist. He handed one end to his cousin, and left the other in place around his belly as he had done with the other cousin.

"Here, Cousin, take this," Ananse said. "When the fish is done stewing and the food is all spread, just give my web a tug, and I'll be back before you bow your head—for giving thanks, that is."

"*Tutaonana*," they said to one another, and off Ananse went to go home and get his wife so they'd be ready when the first cousin's meal was ready.

Ananse had almost reached home when he felt a pull on the strand of web he had given to his first cousin.

"Aso," he called out to his wife inside, "hurry, the feast is ready. We must go before it's all gone."

But before he reached his house or before his wife could hear, there came a pull on the other strand of web. It seems that both feasts were ready at the same time. I will need your help with the pulling.

Have one side of the audience pull to the left and the other side pull to the right.

Ananse pulled this way and that way. Then, he was pulled this way and that way at the same time.

231

"Please let go," Ananse cried out in pain. But no one seemed to hear.

He struggled and struggled to get free, but his cousins just pulled harder and harder. They did not stop pulling until the meal was all finished and the food was all gone.

After a long while, Aso found her husband not far from home.

"What's the matter with you, Ananse, sitting here on the ground? I thought we were going to eat at your cousin's house. Get up, let's go."

But when Ananse was finally able to struggle to his feet, Aso saw that her husband had changed in appearance. He did not look the same. He was now very small in the middle, between his top and bottom, right where the web had been pulled so tightly around his waist.

Spider never recovered. He passed his new shape on to his descendants, and to this day, spiders are small in the middle because Ananse was pulled two ways between his cousins. Harambee!

Harambee! (pronounced *Ha-ram-bay). Harambee* is a Swahili word that means "pull together." It is sometimes said by all at the close of the *Karamu. Harambee* is a sign of unity or working together.

Let us say it all together *seven* times.

> **Teller:** Harambee!

> **Audience:** Harambee!

> **Teller:** Harambee!

> **Audience:** Harambee!

> **Teller:** Harambee!

> **Audience:** Harambee!

> **Teller:** Harambee!

> **Audience:** Harambee!

Kwanzaa yenu iwe na heri! (kwahn-ZAH YEH-noo EE-weh nah heh-REE)

> **Audience:** *Kwanzaa yenu iwe na heri!*

HAPPY KWANZAA!

ABOUT THE STORY

About Ananse: This is a variation of the traditional African folktale of "How Spider Got a Thin Waist," sometimes called "Two Feasts for Ananse." Ananse the Spider is always full of tricks and schemes, especially when it comes to getting out of work. In the book *Joining In*, you will find some fantastic research on Ananse stories and related books provided by Barbara Reed (pages 87–88).

HOLIDAY BACKGROUND INFORMATION

Founded in 1966 by Dr. Maulana (Ron) Karenga, Kwanzaa is a unique African American celebration that focuses on the traditional African values of family, community responsibility, commerce, and self-improvement. Each day of the seven-day celebration, a different principle is celebrated that highlights one of these values. On the sixth night of the celebration, family and friends gather for the Kwanzaa Feast of *Karamu*. *Karamu* is a communal and cooperative effort, where all join in and bring food to share together. On the evening of the sixth day on which *Karamu* is celebrated, the principle of *Kuumba*, a Swahili word that means *creativity,* is observed.

Additional information may be found at the official Kwanzaa Web site (www.officialkwanzaawebsite. org/index.shtml) and at the international Kwanzaa Exchange (T.I.K.E.) Web site (www.tike.com/welcome.htm), as well as at a host of other sites.

BIOGRAPHY

Kathy Culmer is a storyteller, teacher, and writer. A graduate of Spelman College and the University of South Florida, Kathy has taught on the secondary and college levels in a variety of subject areas, including English, speech communications, broadcast journalism, and religious education. While living in Evansville, Indiana, Kathy cofounded with Teresa Miller The River Town Storytellers (www.rivertownstorytellers.com). Her storytelling work includes performances at the Children's Museum of Indianapolis, the Hoosier Storytelling Festival, the Texas Storytelling Festival, and the National Storytelling Festival Exchange Place. She is the featured storyteller for the 2008 Network of Biblical Storytellers Festival Gathering. Kathy has also been a workshop presenter at the National Storytelling Conference and the National Christian Education Conference for the Episcopal Church. Kathy is the author of "Big Wheel Cookies: Two for a Penny," published in *The Rolling Stone and Other Read Aloud Stories*. She edited a collection of personal narratives called *Yes Jesus Loves Me: 31 Love Stories*. For more information, consult: http://www.kathyculmer.com.

CONTACT

E-mail: khculmer@aol.com

Partial Glossary

Folklore: Cultural traditions transmitted by example and oral retellings. Folklore includes traditional narratives such as myths, legends, folk and fairytales, as well as jokes, proverbs, folk music, folk dance, folk medicine, rituals and games. One way of identifying folklore is that there are a variety of variants, for example, recognizing that although we have a traditional Thanksgiving meal, there is great variety in each families' recipes and the specific dishes served.

Folktale: Traditional stories from a specific country or culture that are used to entertain, educate, or pass on cultural insights. Folktales are stories of everyday people, animals, or plants or forces of nature that talk and behave as people. When folktales cross geographic and political boundaries, they may become retellings that adapt and reflect that culture's worldview—an adopted and adapted traditional tale.

Participation Story: A story in which the audience participates. This may be by joining in on a chorus or refrain, providing sound effects, suggesting plot elements, using a physical response, putting shapes on a felt board, having a discussion as in the dilemma tale, and so on.

Tale Type: Folklorists use assigned numbers to identify basic plot patterns in folk and fairytales that are used in the identification and analysis of these tales. This system was published in 1910 by Finnish scholar Antti Aarne and in 1961 enlarged and translated into English by Stith Thompson.

Trickster Tales: Popular usage applies the term "trickster tale" to any story in which the plot entails a clever protagonist outwitting the enemy with a humorous or deceptive hoax. Often the protagonist is a creator who is funny and even vexing, often a renegade breaking rules.

Bibliography of Holiday Books

There are many excellent books on holidays—books that encourage and teach the art of storytelling. In addition, there are numerous story anthologies with tales appropriate for holiday use. In this bibliography, we have listed some of our favorites.

NOTE: For Christmas, Halloween, Hanukkah, and Peace stories, see the chapters related to each holiday.

See your local library or bookstore and online sources for materials that explain holiday customs for both adults and children. Following are a few sources that might help in program planning and discovering useful stories to tell.

Barchers, Suzanne I. *HOLIDAY STORYBOOK STEW: Cooking Through the Year with Books Kids Love* (Fulcrum Resources, 1998).

Casey, Dawn. *THE GREAT RACE: The Story of the Chinese Zodiac* (Barefoot Books, 2006).

Cohen, Hennig, and Tristram Potter Coffin. *FOLKLORE OF AMERICAN HOLIDAYS* (Gale Research, 1991).

Conover, Sarah, and Freda Crane. *AYAT JAMILAH: Beautiful Sign* (Eastern Washington University, 2004). A Treasury of Islamic Wisdom for Children and Parents.

Goldin, Barbara Diamond. *TEN HOLIDAY JEWISH STORIES*. Illustrated by Jeffrey Allon (Pitspopany, 2000).

Hayden, Carla D. *VENTURE INTO CULTURES: A Resource Book of Multicultural Materials & Programs* (American Library Association, 1992).

Jaffe, Nina. *THE UNINVITED GUEST and Other Jewish Tales*. Illustrated by Elivia Savadier (Scholastic, 1993).

Kimmel, Eric A. *DAYS OF AWE: Stories for Rosh Hashanah and Yom Kippur*. Illustrated by Erika Weihs (Puffin Books, 1993).

Lima, Carolyn W., and John A. Lima. *A TO ZOO: Subject Access to Children's Picture Books,* 7th ed. (Libraries Unlimited, 2006). Lists picture books for various holidays.

MacDonald, Margaret Read. *BOOKPLAY: 101 Creative Themes to Share with Young Children* (Library Professional Publications, 1995). Holiday programs with picture books.

MacDonald, Margaret Read. *BOOKSHARING* (Library Professional Publications, 1988). Holiday programs with picture books.

MacDonald, Margaret Read. *CELEBRATE THE WORLD: Twenty Tellable Folktales for Multicultural Festivals* (H.W. Wilson Company, 1994).

MacDonald, Margaret Read. *THE FOLKLORE OF WORLD HOLIDAYS* (Gale Research, 1992). Information on hundreds of holidays.

MacDonald, Margaret Read. *THE STORYTELLER'S SOURCEBOOK: A Subject, Title and Motif-Index to Folklore Collections for Children* (Gale Research, 1982). See subject index for story sources.

MacDonald, Margaret Read, and Brian Sturm. *THE STORYTELLER'S SOURCEBOOK: A Subject, Title, and Motif-Index to Folklore Collections for Children 1993–1999* (Gale Research, 2000). See subject index for story sources.

Olcott, Frances Jenkins. *GOOD STORIES FOR GREAT HOLIDAYS* (Biblio Bazaar, 2006). Paperback reprint of 330-page collection.

Orozco, José-Luis. *FIESTAS: A Year of Latin American Songs of Celebration*. Illustrated by Elisa Kleven (Dutton Children's Books, 2002).

Pearl, Sydelle. *ELIJAH'S TEARS: Stories for the Jewish Holidays.* Illustrated by Rossitza Skortcheva Penny (Pelican, 2004).

Pellowski, Anne. *STORYTELLING HANDBOOK* (Simon & Schuster, 1995).

Renfro, Nancy, and Tamara Hunt. *CELEBRATE!* (Nancy Renfro Studios, 1987).

Simonds, Nina, Leslie Swartz, & the Children's Museum of Boston. *MOONBEAMS, DUMPLINGS & DRAGON BOATS: A Treasury of Chinese Holiday Tales, Activities and Recipes.* Illustrated by Meilo So (Harcourt, 2002). Activities and recipes.

Whitfield, Susan. *THE ANIMALS OF THE CHINESE ZODIAC.* Illustrated by Philippa-Alys Browne (Crocodile Books, 1998).

Yolen, Jane. *MILK AND HONEY: A Year of Jewish Holidays.* Illustrated by Louise August (G.P. Putnam's Sons, 1996). Musical arrangements by Adam Stemple.

Zeitlin, Steven, with Amy J. Kotkin and Holly Cutting Baker. *A CELEBRATION OF AMERICAN FAMILY FOLKLORE* (Pantheon, 1982). Mother's Day, Father's Day, and Grandparent's Day.

FOR IMMIGRANTS TO THE UNITED STATES

What better way to celebrate a festival than to share stories from that ethnic group's heritage? These collections provide excellent sources, compiled by authors from the many cultures represented.

Almeida, Livia de, and Ana Portella, edited by Margaret Read MacDonald. *BRAZILIAN FOLKTALES* (Libraries Unlimited, 2006).

Altmann, Anna E. *THE SEVEN SWABIANS and Other German Folktales* (Libraries Unlimited, 2005).

Bunanta, Murti, edited by Margaret Read MacDonald. *INDONESIAN FOLKTALES* (Libraries Unlimited, 2003).

Curry, Linda Soon, and Chan-eung Park. *A TIGER BY THE TAIL and Other Stories from the Heart of Thailand* (Libraries Unlimited, 1999).

Davison, Gary Marvin. *TALES FROM TAIWANESE* (Libraries Unlimited, 2004).

Edgecomb, Diane, Mohammed Ahmed M. A., and Ceto Ozel. *A FIRE IN MY HEART: Kurdish Tales* (Libraries Unlimited, 2007).

Fujita, Hiroko, and Fran Stallings. *FOLKTALES FROM THE JAPANESE COUNTRYSIDE* (Libraries Unlimited, 2007).

Keding, Dan, and Amy Douglas. *ENGLISH FOLKTALES* (Libraries Unlimited, 2005).

Lewis, I. Murphy, and Izak Barnard. *WHY OSTRICHES DON'T FLY and Other Tales from the African Bush* (Libraries Unlimited, 1997).

Livo, Norma J., and Dia Cha. *FOLK STORIES OF THE HMONG: Peoples of Laos, Thailand, and Vietnam* (Libraries Unlimited, 1991).

Livo, Norma J., and George O. Livo. *THE ENCHANTED WOOD and Other Stories From Finland* (Libraries Unlimited, 1999).

Louis, Liliane Nerette, and Fred J. Hay. *WHEN NIGHT FALLS: KRIC! KRAC! Haitian Folktales* (Libraries Unlimited, 1999).

Marshall, Bonnie C., and Alla V. Kulagina. *THE SNOW MAIDEN and Other Russian Tales* (Libraries Unlimited, 2004).

Marshall, Bonnie C., and Vasa D. Mihailovich. *TALES FROM THE HEART OF THE BALKANS* (Libraries Unlimited, 2001).

Marshall, Bonnie C., and Virginia Tashjian. *THE FLOWER OF PARADISE and Other Armenian Tales* (Libraries Unlimited, 2007).

McLeod, Pauline E., Francis Firebrace Jones, June E. Barker, and Helen F. McKay. *GADI MIRRABOKA: Australian Aboriginal Tales from the Dreaming* (Libraries Unlimited, 2001).

McNeil, Heather, and Nancy Chien-Eriksen. *THE CELTIC BREEZE: Stories of the Otherworld from Scotland, Ireland, and Wales* (Libraries Unlimited, 2001).

McNeil, Heather. *HYENA AND THE MOON: Stories to Tell from Kenya* (Libraries Unlimited, 1994).

Meder, Theo. *THE FLYING DUTCHMAN and Other Folktales from the Netherlands* (Libraries Unlimited, 2007).

Mitakidou, Soula, Anthony L. Manna, and Melpomeni Kanatsouli. *FOLKTALES FROM GREECE: A Treasury of Delights* (Libraries Unlimited, 2002).

Pelton, Mary Helen, Jacqueline DiGennaro, and Jennifer Brady-Moral (Ts'anak). *IMAGES OF A PEOPLE: Tlingit Myths and Legends* (Libraries Unlimited, 1992).

Peréz, Elvia, translated by Paula Martín, edited by Margaret Read MacDonald. *FROM THE WINDS OF MANGUITO: Desde los vientos de Manguito* (Libraries Unlimited, 2004).

Spagnoli, Cathy, and Paramasivam Samanna. *JASMINE AND COCONUTS: South Indian Tales* (Libraries Unlimited, 1999).

Thompson, Susan, Keith Thompson, and Lidia Lopez de L'opez. *MAYAN FOLKTALES: Cuentos folkloricos Mayas* (Libraries Unlimited, 2007).

Tossa, Wajuppa, with Kongdeuane Nettavong, edited by Margaret Read MacDonald. *LAO FOLKTALES* (Libraries Unlimited, 2008).

Vathanaprida, Supaporn, edited by Margaret Read MacDonald. *FOLKTALES OF THAILAND* (Libraries Unlimited, 1994).

Vigil, Angel. *THE CORN WOMAN: Stories and Legends of the Hispanic Southwest* (Libraries Unlimited, 1994).

Vigil, Angel. *THE EAGLES AND THE CACTUS: Traditional Stories from Mexico* (Libraries Unlimited, 2000).

Yuan, Haiwang. *THE MAGIC LOTUS LANTERN and Other Tales from the Han Chinese* (Libraries Unlimited, 2006).

RELIGION

As for religion, there are many books at libraries, at bookstores, and on the Internet that describe the major religions of the world. Search Buddhism, Christianity, Confucianism, Taoism, Hinduism, Islam, Judaism, Kabbalah, Scientology, Shinto, Zorastrianism, and so on. These beliefs have their own stories.

For example, if you are looking for a professional Christian storyteller, contact the Network of Biblical Storytellers (NOBS). Kathy Culmer (see her story about Kwanzaa in this book) serves on the board and is a dynamic storytelling thespian. More than five hundred laypeople, ministers, and Bible scholars share tales from Scripture. Contact: nobsint@nobs.org or call 1 (800) 355-NOBS.

Boomershine, Thomas E. *STORY JOURNEY: An Invitation to the Gospel Storytelling* (Abingdon Press, 1981). Biblical stories to be learned and explored in various ways.

Kurtz, Ernest, and Ketcham, Katherine. *THE SPIRITUALITY OF IMPERFECTION: Storytelling and the Journey to Wholeness* (Bantam Books, 1992). Steeped in the rich traditions of the Hebrew prophets and Greek thinkers, Buddhist sages, and Christian disciples.

Shaw, Susan M. *STORYTELLING IN RELIGIOUS EDUCATION* (Religious Education Press, 1999). Covers virtually all phases of religious storytelling.

Stone, Richard. *THE HEALING ART OF STORYTELLING: A Sacred Journey of Personal Discovery* (Hyperion, 1996). A fresh approach to issues such as coping with death and grieving, building esteem in ourselves and our children, finding courage in the face of uncertainty, and discovering the miraculous in the everyday.

OTHER NOTABLE SOURCES

Dresser, Norine. *MULTICULTURAL MANNERS: New Rules of Etiquette for a Changing Society* (John Wiley & Sons, 1996). Includes a chapter, "At Places of Worship," with important rules in various churches and synagogues—Buddhist and Hindu temples and more.

Williams, Ray, and Louise Kessel. *THE FIVE FAITH PROJECT* (University of North Carolina at Chapel Hill, 1998). Hinduism, Buddhism, Islam, Judaism, and Christianity for K–12 teachers.

Wolkstein, Diane. *ESTHER'S STORY.* Illustrated by Juan Wijngaard (Morrow Junior Books, 1996). This story reveals the transformation of a shy, orphan girl into a compassionate queen who risks the wrath of a king to save her people.

Wolkstein, Diane. *TREASURES OF THE HEART: Holiday Stories That Reveal the Soul of Judaism* (Schocken Books, 2003). Retellings of classic biblical and traditional stories associated with each Jewish holiday. The ancient Near East is shown on maps inside the jacket. The author has woven biblical, rabbinic, Hasidic, and feminist Jewish stories into the cycle of Jewish festivals.

MAY YOU GO IN PEACE TO LOVE AND SERVE HUMANITY.

Permissions Acknowledgments

Grateful acknowledgment is made to the following for permission to reprint, adapt, or publish their material.

JANUARY

"Horace the Horrible" (New Year's Day)—original story by Arlean Hale Lambert

"A Different Kind of New Year's Celebration: Hogmanay" (New Year's Day)—original story by Norma McKissick Livo

"The Caterpillar's Blues" (Martin Luther King, Jr. Day)—original story by Linda Goss, with activity designs by Gretchen Shannon and an original biographical story by Kathy Culmer

FEBRUARY

"The Great Groundhog-Day Get Together" (Groundhog Day)—original story by Larry Johnson and Elaine Wynne

"Oni Wa Soto" (Setsubon, Japanese New Year)—an original retelling by Cathy Spagnoli

"White Wave" (Valentine's Day)—original story by Diane Wolkstein

"The Little Loyalist"—retold by Teresa Miller

MARCH

"St. Patrick and the Musical Leprechaun" (St. Patrick's Day)—original story by Gail N. Herman

APRIL

"The Legend of Songkran, the Thai New Year" (Thai New Year)—an original retelling by Supaporn Vathanaprida and Margaret Read MacDonald

"A Blessing in Disguise" (Passover)—retold by Peninnah Schram from *Tales of Elijah the Prophet,* published by Jason Aronson, Inc. (An imprint of Rowman and Littlefield Publishers, Inc). Copyright 1991. Adapted with permission of the publisher.

"Esta Noche Es Alvada," a Sephardic folk melody in Ladino, the Judeo-Spanish language of the Sephardic Jews, from *The Gerard Edery Sephardic Song Book,* reprinted with permission of the publisher, Sefarad Publishing, New York, 2003.

"The Earth Dreamers" (Earth Day)—original story by Regina Ress

"Why the Evergreens Keep Their Leaves in the Winter" (Arbor Day)—retold by Ruth Stotter

MAY

"The Garden Rainbow" (May Day)—original story by Linda Marchisio

"Kelly's Memorial Day Parade" (Memorial Day)—original story by V. J. Richey

"The Buddha's Birthday in Thailand" (Buddha's Birthday)—an original retelling by Wajuppa Tossa

JUNE

"The Freedom Flag" (Flag Day)—original story by Gay Merrill Gross

JULY

Fourth of July Holiday (Fourth of July)—an original retelling by Teresa Miller and Andrea Bielecki

SEPTEMBER

"Charity" (Ramadan)—an original retelling by Cathy Spagnoli

"El Grito de Dolores (Cry of the City of Dolores)" (Mexican Independence Day)—an original retelling by Norma Cantú

"The Constitution Jive" (National Constitution Day)—original story by Linda Marchisio

"The Boy Who Called the King a Fool" (International Peace Day)—original story by Ruthilde Kronberg

OCTOBER

"The Magic Paint Box" (United Nations Day)—original story by Gerald Fierst

"The Halloween Pumpkin" (Halloween)—original story by Stephanie Mita

NOVEMBER

"Gluskonba and the Maple Trees" (American Indian Heritage Month)—an original retelling by Joseph Bruchac

"Eleven Bells" (Veterans Day)—original story by Larry Johnson

"Rabbit, Bobcat, and the Wild Turkeys" (Thanksgiving Day)—an original retelling by Fran Stallings, with holiday background information by Teresa Miller

DECEMBER

"Reisele's Hanukkah Dream" (Hannukah)—original story by Ruthilde Kronberg

"Silent Night, 1914 or 'The Peace Message for Christmas' " (Christmas Eve)—by Charles David Kleymeyer from his story, "Silent Night, 1914," which first appeared in *Quaker Life* magazine (December 1981)

"How the Squirrel Got Its Stripes" (Christmas Day)—an original retelling by Laura Simms

"Feasts-a-Plenty" (Kwanzaa)—an original retelling by Kathy Culmer

Partial Glossary created by Ruth Stotter

About the Editor

VIOLET TERESA deBARBA MILLER tells stories as "Teresa Miller." She compiled *Joining In: An Anthology of Audience Participation Stories and How to Tell Them*, with assistance from Anne Pellowski, edited by Norma Livo, Introduction by Laura Simms.